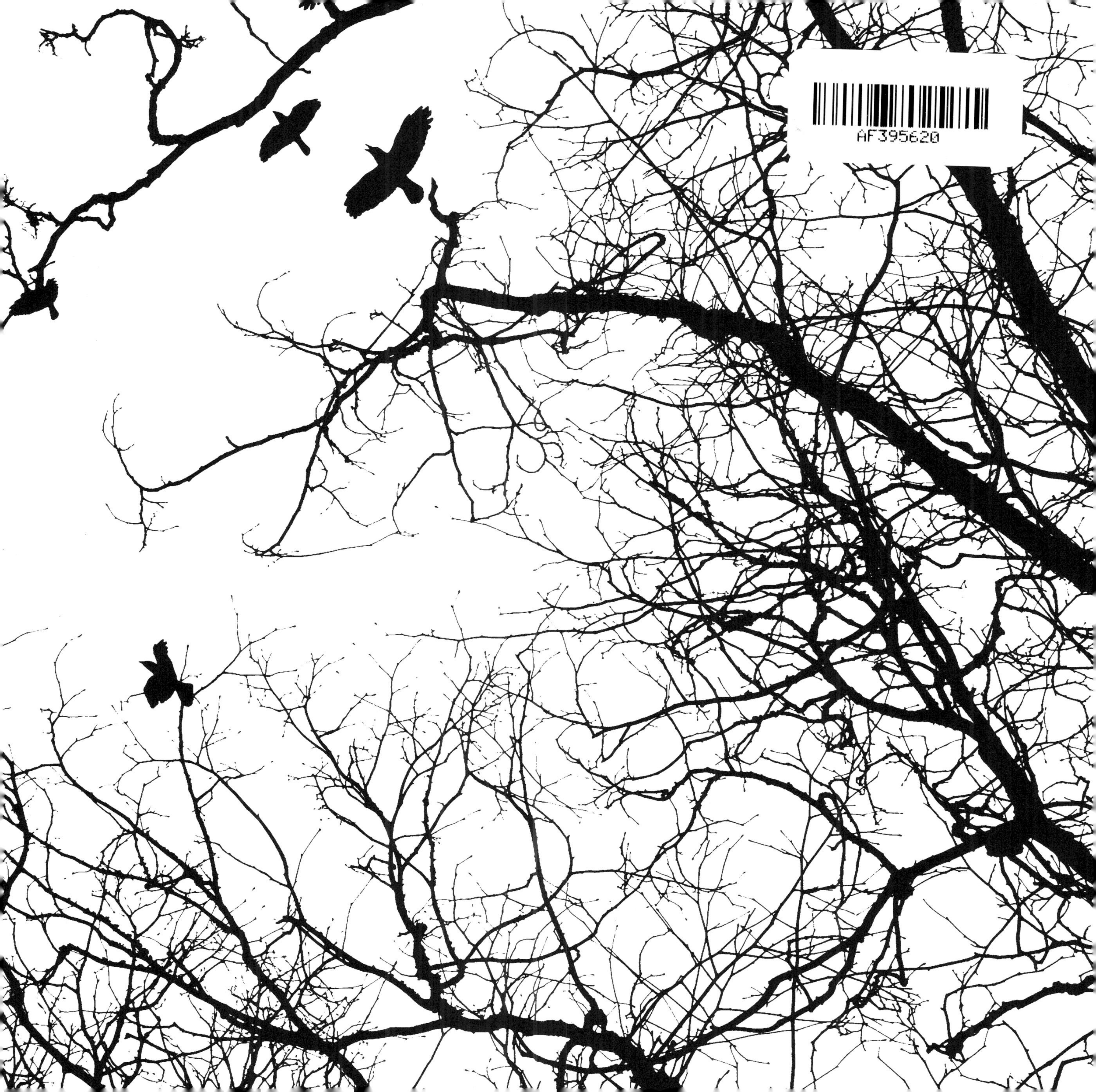
AF395620

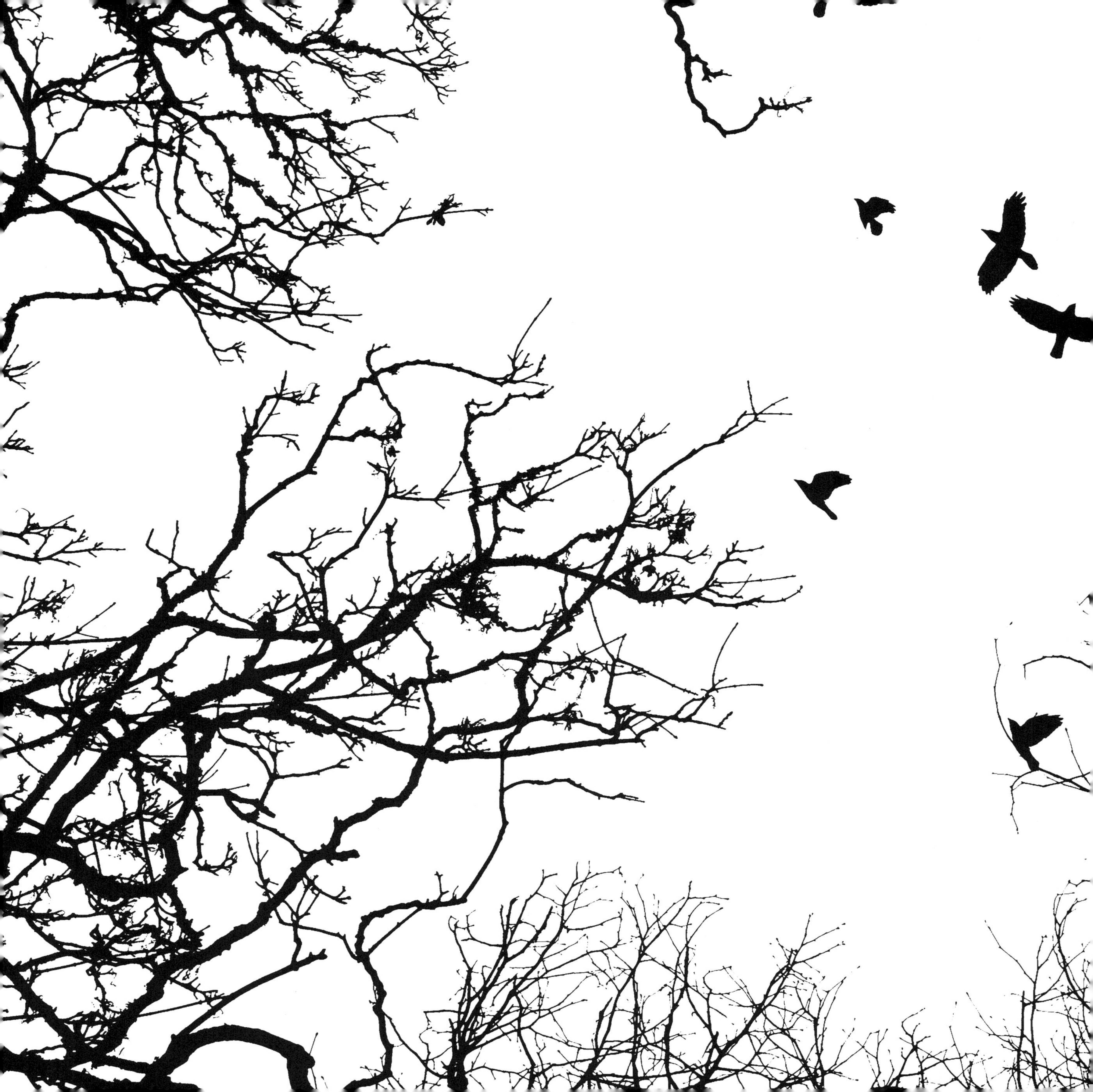

PEMBROKESHIRE

DAVID WILSON

BIRD EYE BOOKS

A GRAFFEG IMPRINT

For Anna, Charlie and Harry

Pembrokeshire
Text and photographs © David Wilson.
Jamie Owen image © Martin Cavaney.
David Wilson image © Anna Wilson.
www.davidwilsonphotography.co.uk.
Designed and produced by Graffeg. www.graffeg.com.

This third edition published by Bird Eye Books,
an imprint of Graffeg Limited in 2021.
ISBN 9781802580051

Compact edition published by Graffeg in 2013.
ISBN 9781905582938
Second edition published by Graffeg in 2013.
ISBN 9781905582921
First edition published by Graffeg in 2009.
ISBN 9781905582358

Graffeg Limited, 24 Stradey Park Business
Centre, Mwrwg Road, Llangennech, Llanelli,
Carmarthenshire, SA14 8YP, Wales, UK.
www.graffeg.com.

Graffeg are hereby identified as the authors of this
work in accordance with section 77 of the Copyrights,
Designs and Patents Act 1988.

A CIP Catalogue record for this book is available from
the British Library.

All rights reserved. No part of this publication
may be reproduced, stored in a retrieval system or
transmitted, in any form or by any means, electronic,
mechanical, photocopying, recording or otherwise,
without the prior permission of the publishers
Graffeg.

CONTENTS

JAMIE OWEN

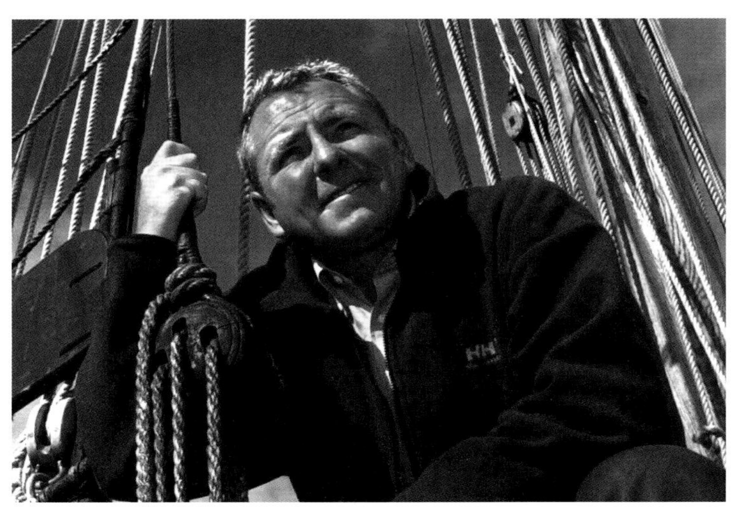

It is not often that you walk down a street and are stopped in your footsteps by a photograph, but that is what happened to me when I saw one of David Wilson's photographs in a gallery window. The work seemed to reach out and touch me in the way that hearing music can transport you to another place. The stark black and white study of The Preseli Hills reeled me in to look a little closer. It takes a particular talent to capture the landscape; this study of those familiar hills sent a bolt down my spine, transporting me back to my childhood and picnics in North Pembrokeshire. But there is more to David's work than a romantic snap of beautiful countryside. In this one image he rolled back thirty years and made me shiver in the memory of summer days that were never warm enough to take off your jumper and remember too that for every sunny field the shadows were walking over neighbouring paddocks. This is landscape photography at its most powerful – he has the ability to delight and unnerve simultaneously.

FOREWORD

I stand in front of the Abandoned Farm and it makes me feel bereft at the sadness of its emptiness. I wonder what became of the family who once worked there, then I feel a sense of yearning to live in the house and enjoy the simplicity it offers. I begin to impose my memories of farming, walking, family and my hopes and dreams on the building. When I am away from Pembrokeshire this is one of those images that makes me want to get in the car and drive to West Wales. Is this David's memorial to a chapter in Welsh farming or perhaps it is the promise of a tired old house that might be restored to its former glory?

Has the tide gone out at Porthgain Harbour or is it coming in – and what weather awaits outside the harbour wall? The isolated chapel in its resplendent white paintwork is without a congregation, or perhaps they are inside and singing on a Sunday, though I think their numbers will be in decline, and the pews mostly empty. Just by looking at the outside I can smell the wax from timber and candles. We see Tenby Harbour in its wintry slumber awaiting the onslaught of summer and the hordes of tourists.

Having travelled all over the world I believe Pembrokeshire to be the most beautiful place on earth, but it is a complicated land full of contradictions and contrasts. It takes great talent to interpret those degrees of light and shade and to encapsulate them in a photograph, but David Wilson has done it. He follows in the great tradition of painters and writers, poets and priests who have wandered the lanes of West Wales in search of that elusive essence of this magical landscape. It is our great good fortune that we can all share in his acts of homage to a place that he so clearly loves.

DAVID WILSON

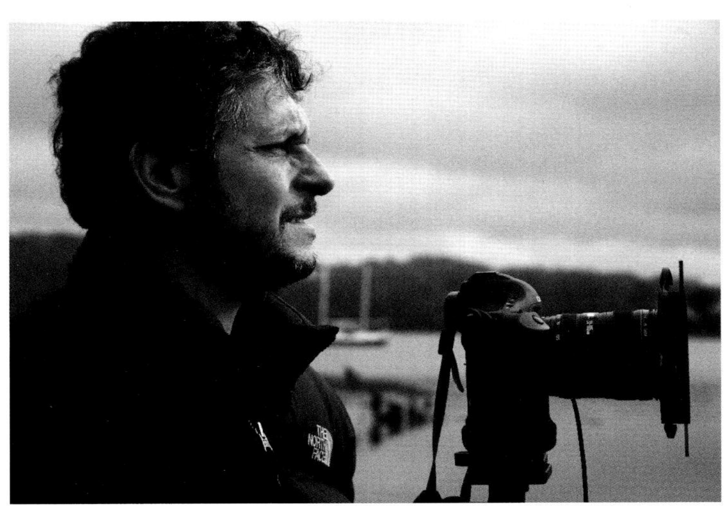

I discovered my passion for landscape photography at the age of seventeen. Being born and brought up in Pembrokeshire it seemed like the most natural thing in the world to buy a camera and get out snapping the coast and countryside. Back then I had a motorbike and I spent many carefree days riding aimlessly round the county taking frame upon frame of, if the truth be told, pretty uninspiring photographs. But as with any amateur landscaper there was always that deeply cherished dream, or maybe delusion, that one day it could provide a living. Anyway, due to my uncanny knack of colliding with obstacles – hedges, cars, and inexplicably the back of a stationery milk tanker on one occasion – the bike soon became history but my love of photographing the landscape survived. It was to be many years though before I finally dredged up the courage to turn my hobby into that dream vocation.

INTRODUCTION

For me, there is one thing I love doing above all else – photographing the Pembrokeshire landscape in black and white. It might seem like a narrow aspiration to some people, but clichéd as it may sound, this county is in my blood. I live and breathe this landscape of ours. To interpret Pembrokeshire using the tonal building blocks of monochrome is certainly a challenge. But once you become attuned to the subtleties and vagaries of this enchanted land, photographing it in black and white is the most rewarding experience any landscape photographer could possibly imagine.

I see the landscape as an ever-changing canvas with an intriguing story to tell. It's about the run-down farmhouses, ramshackle cottages, derelict outbuildings, isolated chapels; it is about the people who have lived, loved and dared to dream within a diverse landscape that envelopes us all. With each image I strive to take the viewer on a journey, causing them to contemplate what the landscape means to us here and now, and perhaps what it meant to our ancestors.

Each generation utilises and appreciates the landscape in a different way. I am fortunate to be able to record this landscape while it still retains all of these visual clues to our recent past, as with each passing year we lose ever more of those tangible bridges to that precious heritage.

To conclude, we have a stunning coastal National Park in Pembrokeshire which is loved by all who experience it and which I adore photographing. Beaches such as Barafundle, Whitesands, Freshwater East and a host of others are true gems. And the coastline linking all of these beaches is breathtaking. But we also have a captivating, almost secret Pembrokeshire away from the coast – the meandering wood-fringed Cleddau estuary, the rolling Preseli Hills, the fields, the farms, the chapels and lanes. Pembrokeshire is a mesmerising mix and recording it for posterity is my enduring passion.

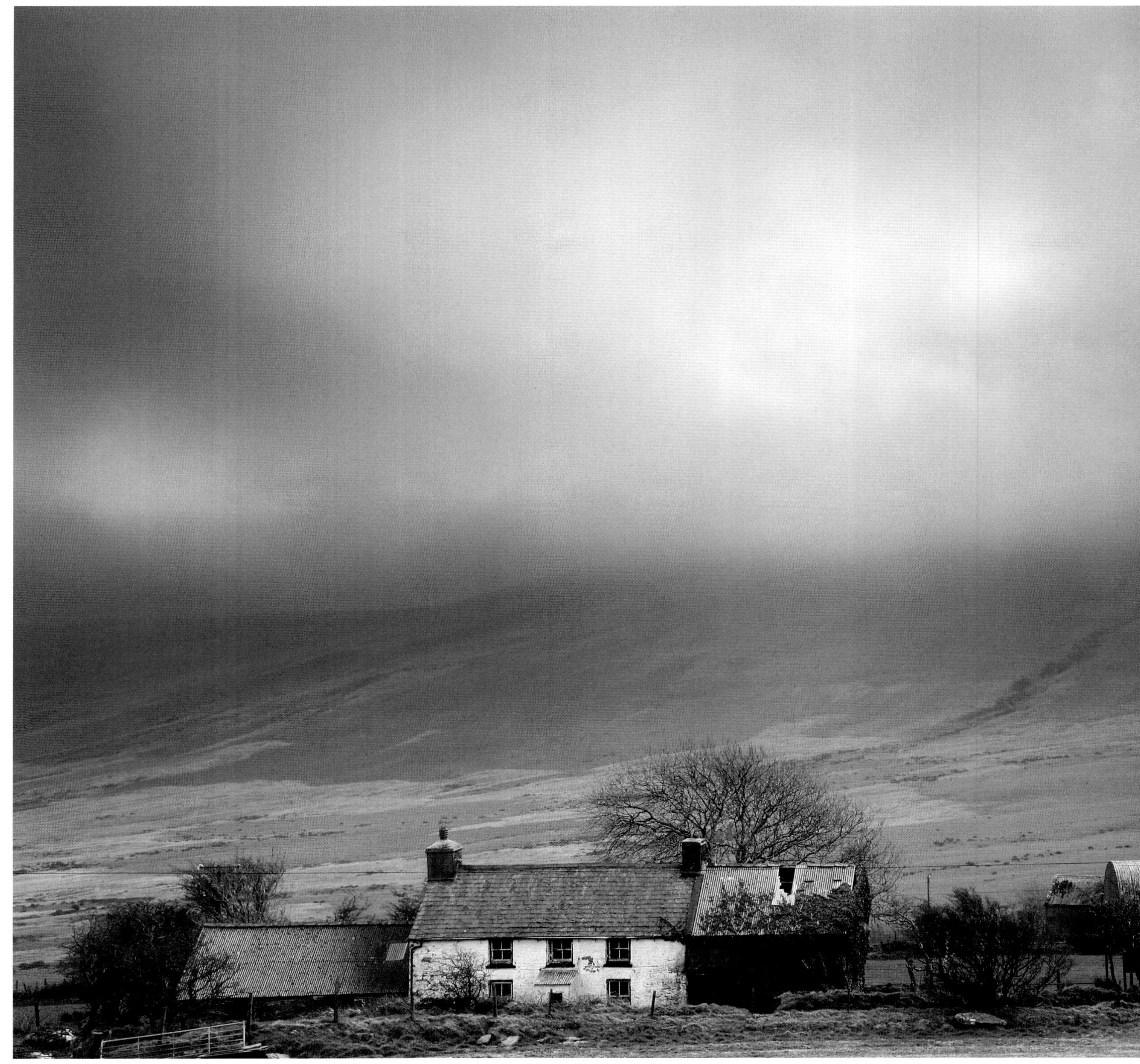

ABANDONED FARM, THE PRESELI HILLS

Capturing images like this is what makes photographing landscapes such an immense and rewarding experience. When this composition fell into place right in front of my eyes the sense of excitement and anticipation was enormous. I'd spotted the farmhouse before, but the sight of the thick blanket of mist pouring down the hill behind it suddenly created what I hoped was a potentially classic photograph. I recall a nervous fumbling as I grabbed the camera and fixed it on the tripod, anxious not to lose 'the moment'. I was on top of a gently sloping hill in front of the farmhouse, which helped me achieve the necessary elevation, and I decided to place the buildings at the bottom of the photograph. The brooding mist and the Preseli hills looming threateningly above inject a sense of eerie foreboding.

Plate 01

BARAFUNDLE

Pembrokeshire has a treasure trove of beautiful beaches and Barafundle has to figure in the top three. Anyone who visits it for the first time is simply awestruck by its innate beauty and magnificent natural features. To photograph it and include all the elements which people associate with the beach is a challenge. For starters you have to include the stone arch which is synonymous with Barafundle. Then there is that majestic sweep of almost-white sand and the distinctive headland. Finally, you need to get there at dawn in the winter months. Why? Well, you want the sun behind you, illuminating the composition, and also, if you are lucky, as I was, the beach will be deserted.

Plate 02

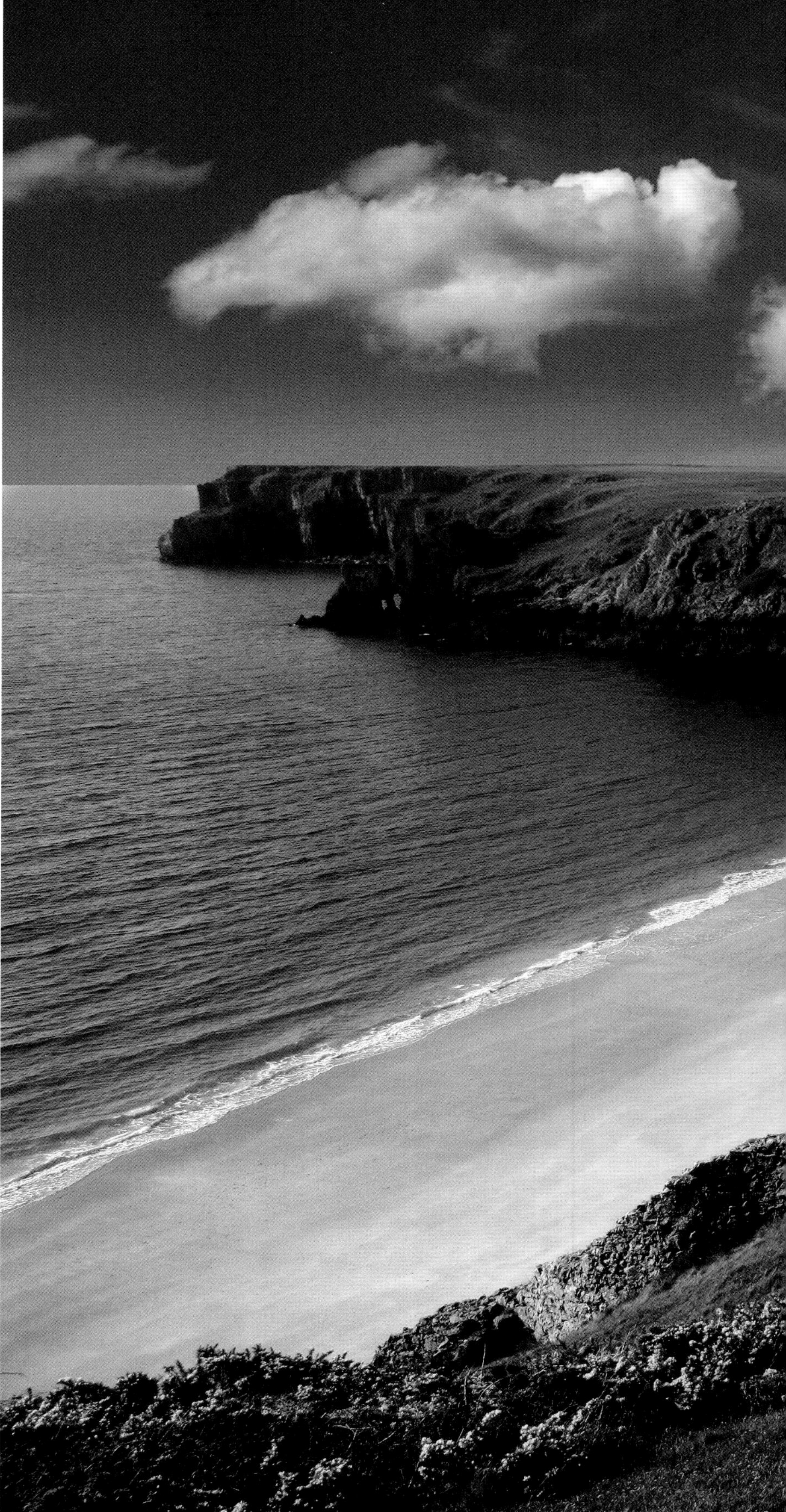

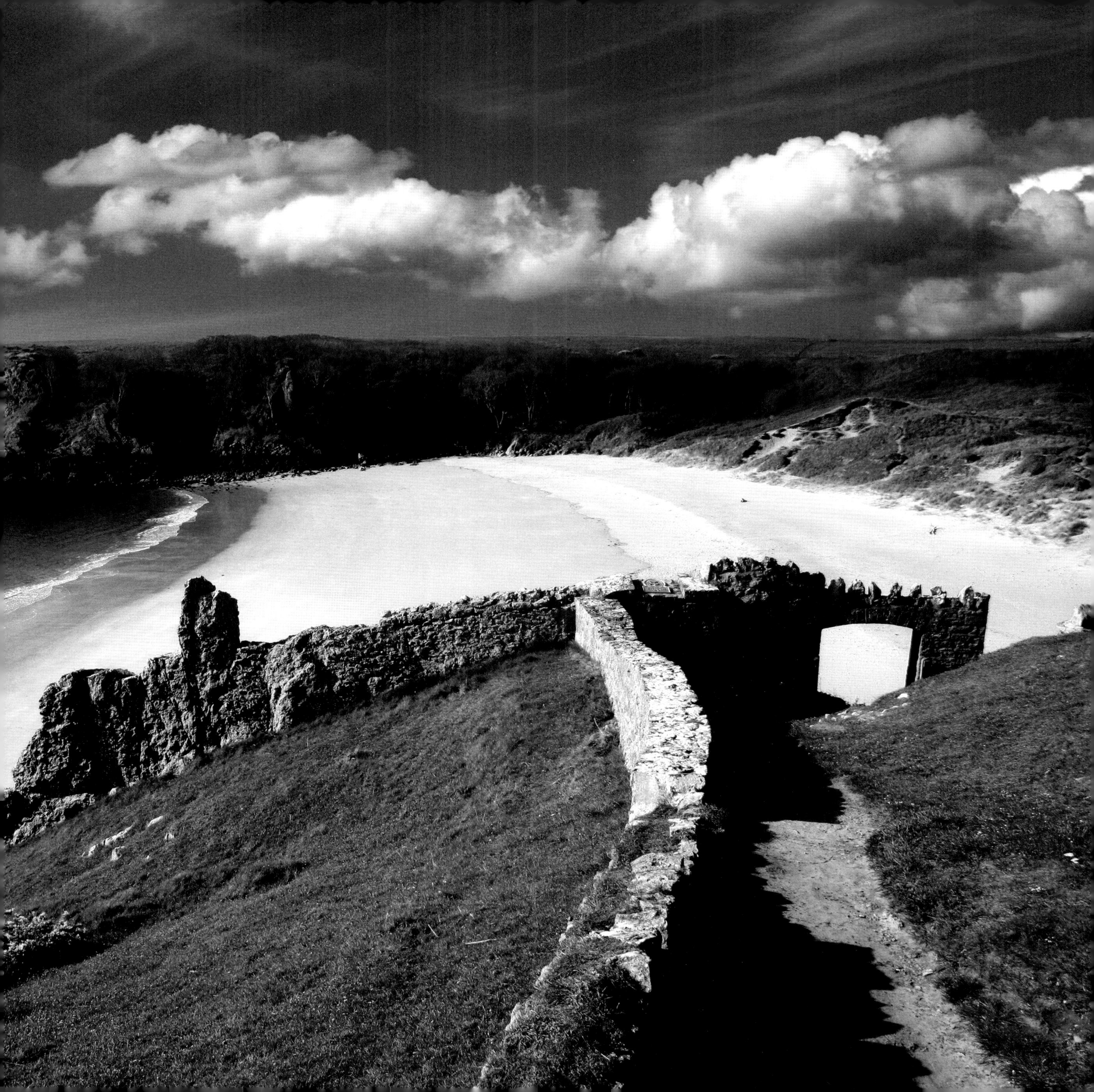

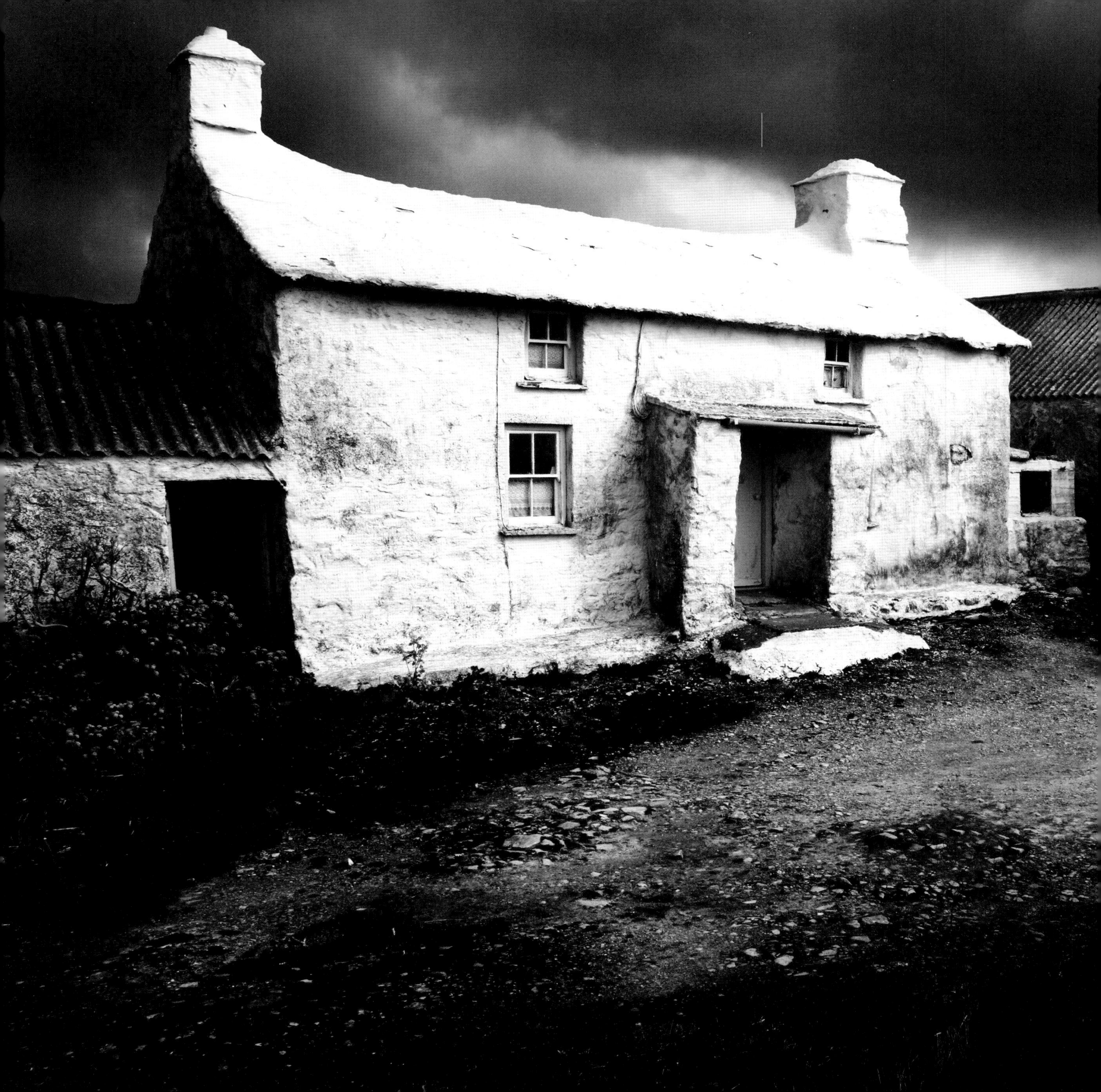

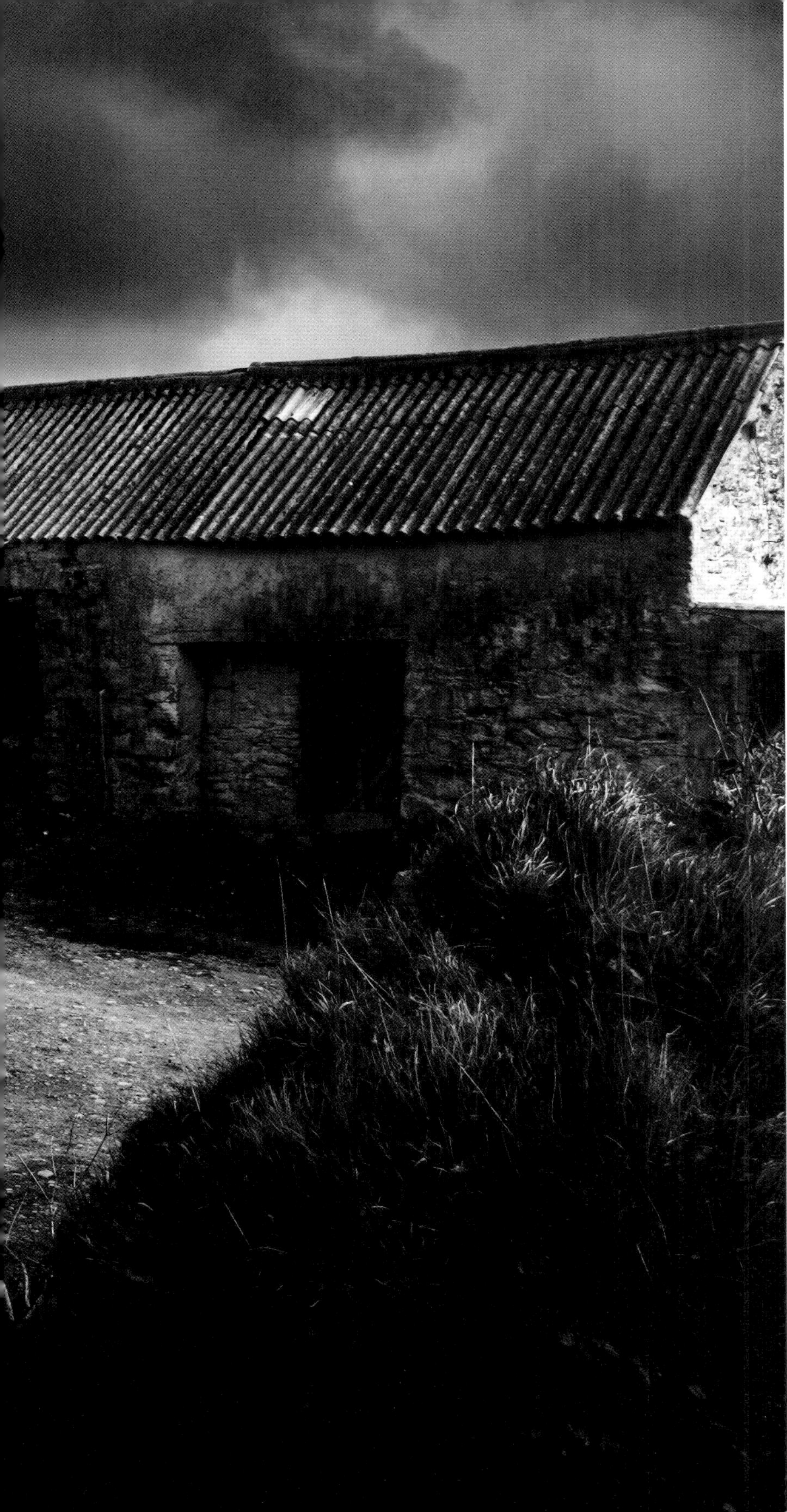

TRELEDDYD FAWR, NEAR ST DAVIDS

This is a stunningly well-preserved cottage in the Pembrokeshire vernacular style. At one time and within living memory, the Pembrokeshire landscape would have been dotted with similar buildings, some of which have been unsympathetically restored or modernised in recent times. There are now very few – if any – remaining in the county which retain as many original features as Treleddyd Fawr. Probably built in the early nineteenth century, its only major concession to the modern world is that it has electricity. To enter this cottage is to literally step into a bygone age. As a self-confessed architectural history junkie, discovering places like this is manna from heaven.

Plate 03

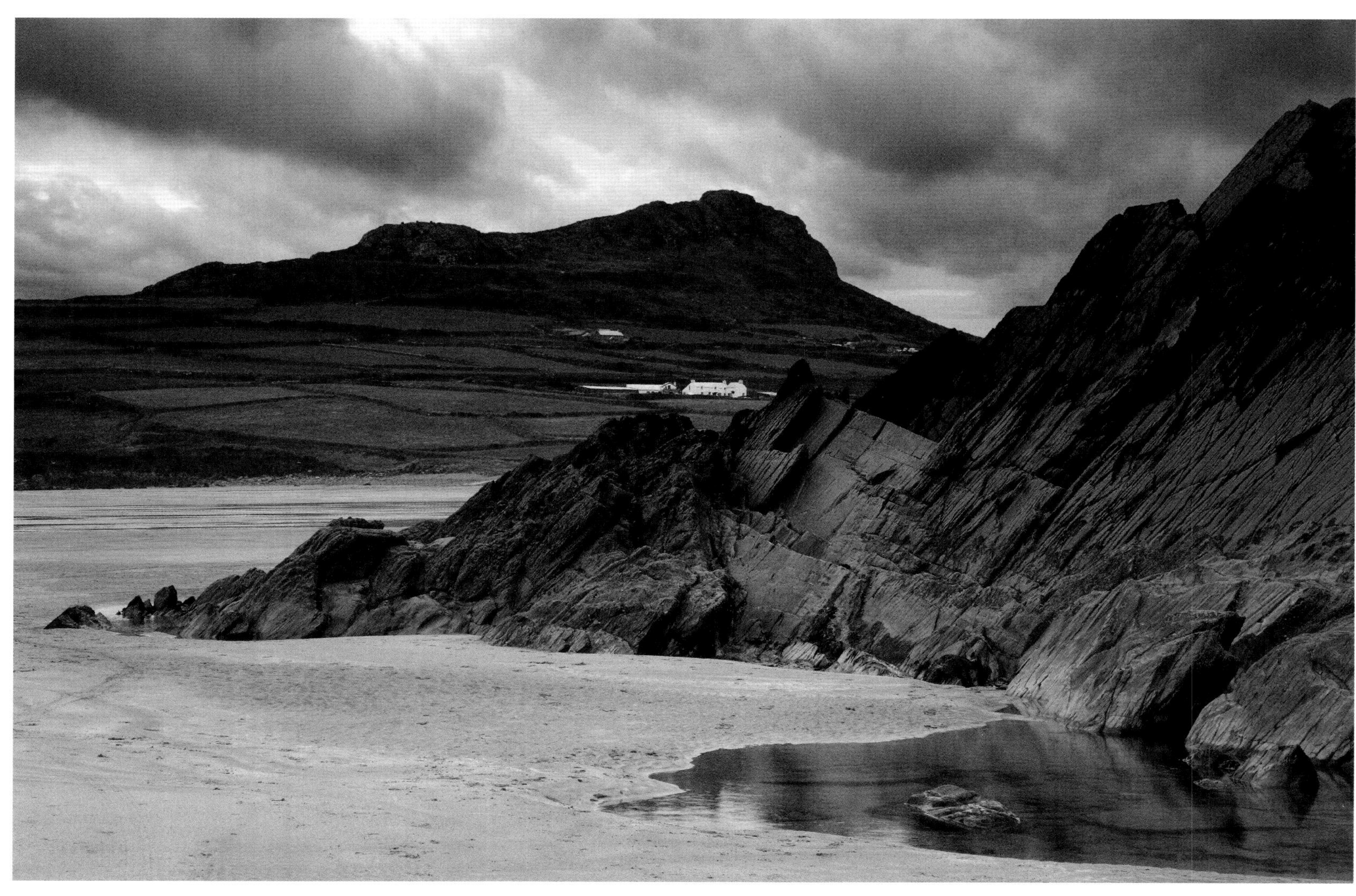

WHITESANDS

I spoke to an elderly lady from the
north of the county a while ago
who said she had never been to
Barafundle beach in the south.
She had heard on many occasions
how beautiful Barafundle is
but it may as well have been in
another country as far as she was
concerned. Hers and indeed her
family's 'local beach' had always
been Whitesands. They might,
if the fancy took them, venture
down as far as Newgale, but no
further. Whitesands is one of
the more distinctive beaches in
Pembrokeshire, with the towering
rocky outcrop of Carn Llidi
standing menacingly over it.

Plate 04

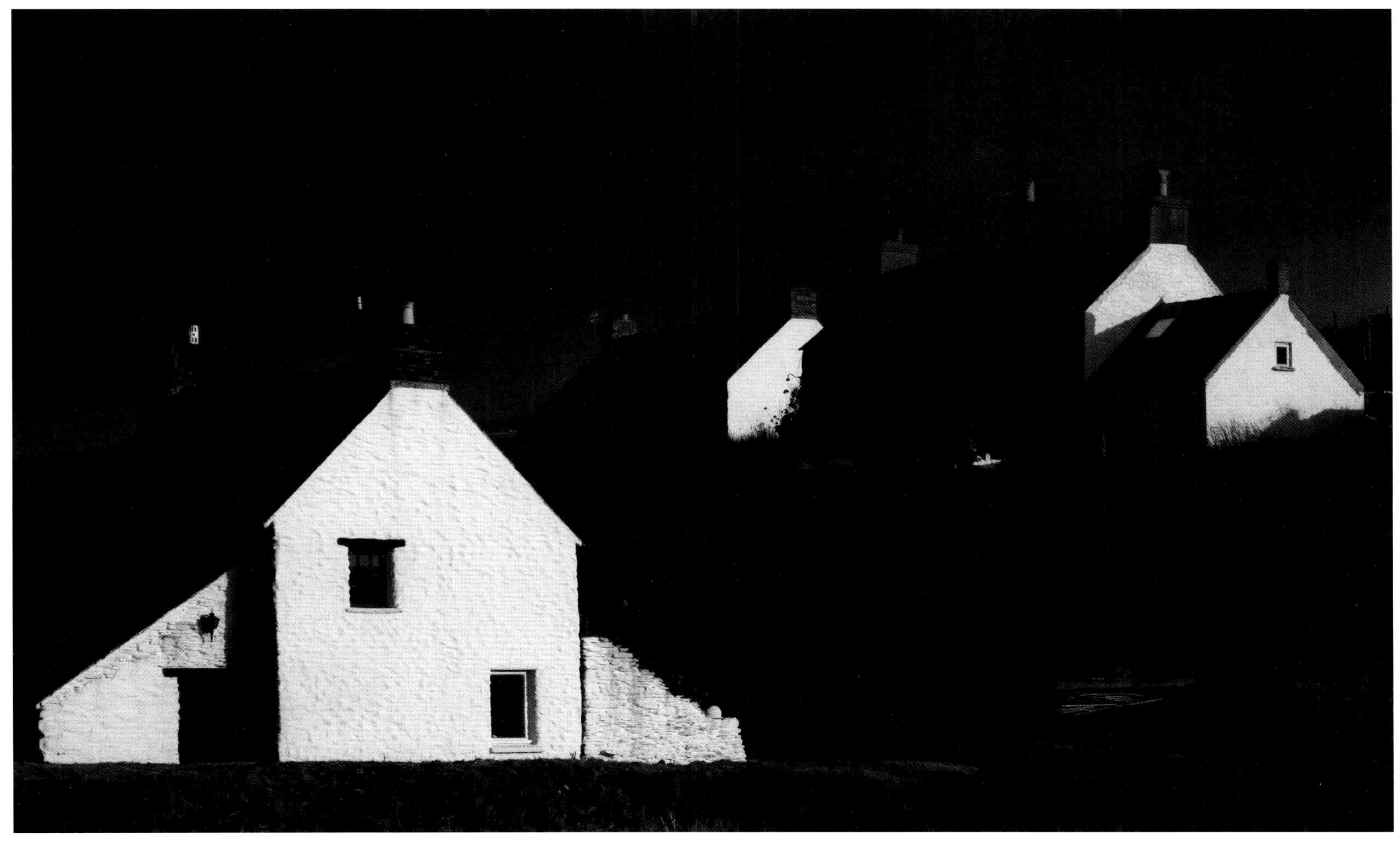

ABEREIDDI

As a landscape photographer I am drawn to buildings that provide a striking contrast within a composition. By spot metering the white pine-ends of the cottages, the remainder of the image has been heavily under-exposed, resulting in a truly 'black and white' photograph with a strong abstract feel.

Taken on a late winter's afternoon with the sun glancing off the cottages at an acute angle, it is all about geometric shapes and patterns in the landscape. It encapsulates to me the foundation of monochrome landscape – light and shade, shape and form.

Plate 05

TENBY HARBOUR

Tenby Harbour is perhaps the iconic image of Pembrokeshire. I wanted to photograph it from a different perspective and breathe new life into a recognisable subject. I got there early one morning when I knew the tide would be out and walked around the harbour floor looking for inspiration. After strolling around for ages, this composition suddenly jumped out at me. I was drawn to the reflection of St Mary's Church spire and the surrounding Georgian townhouses in the water and also the texture of the sand in the foreground.

Plate 06

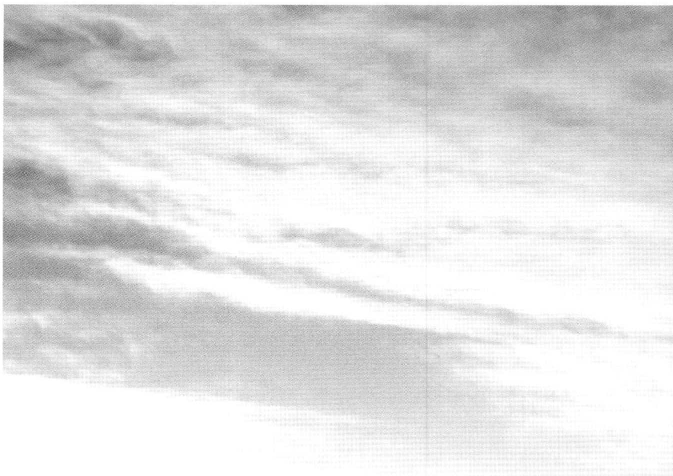

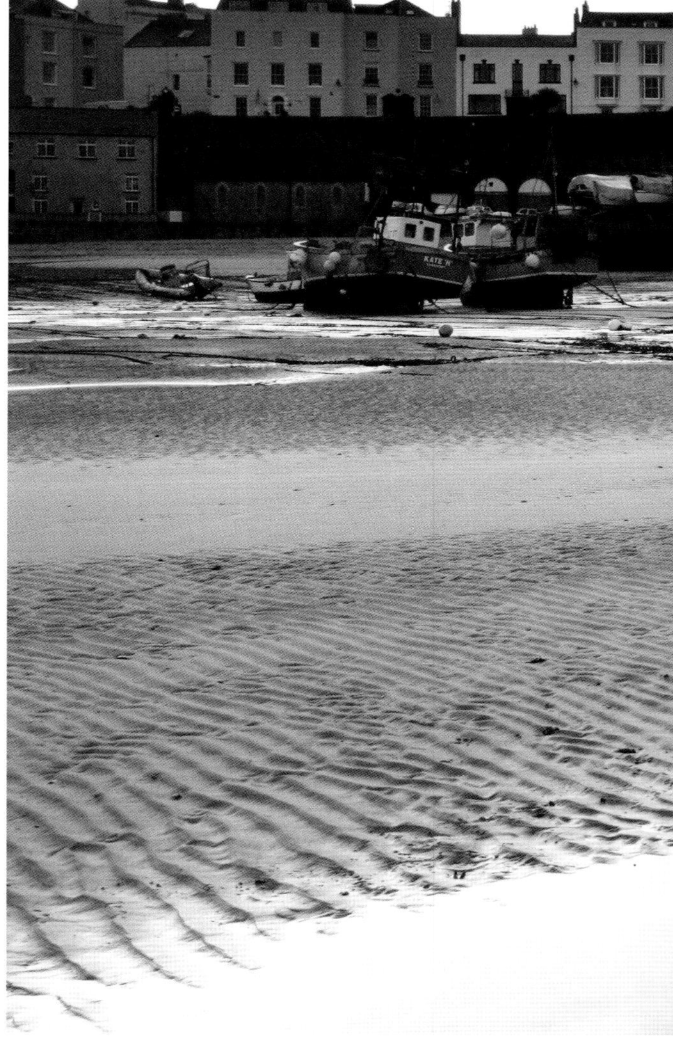

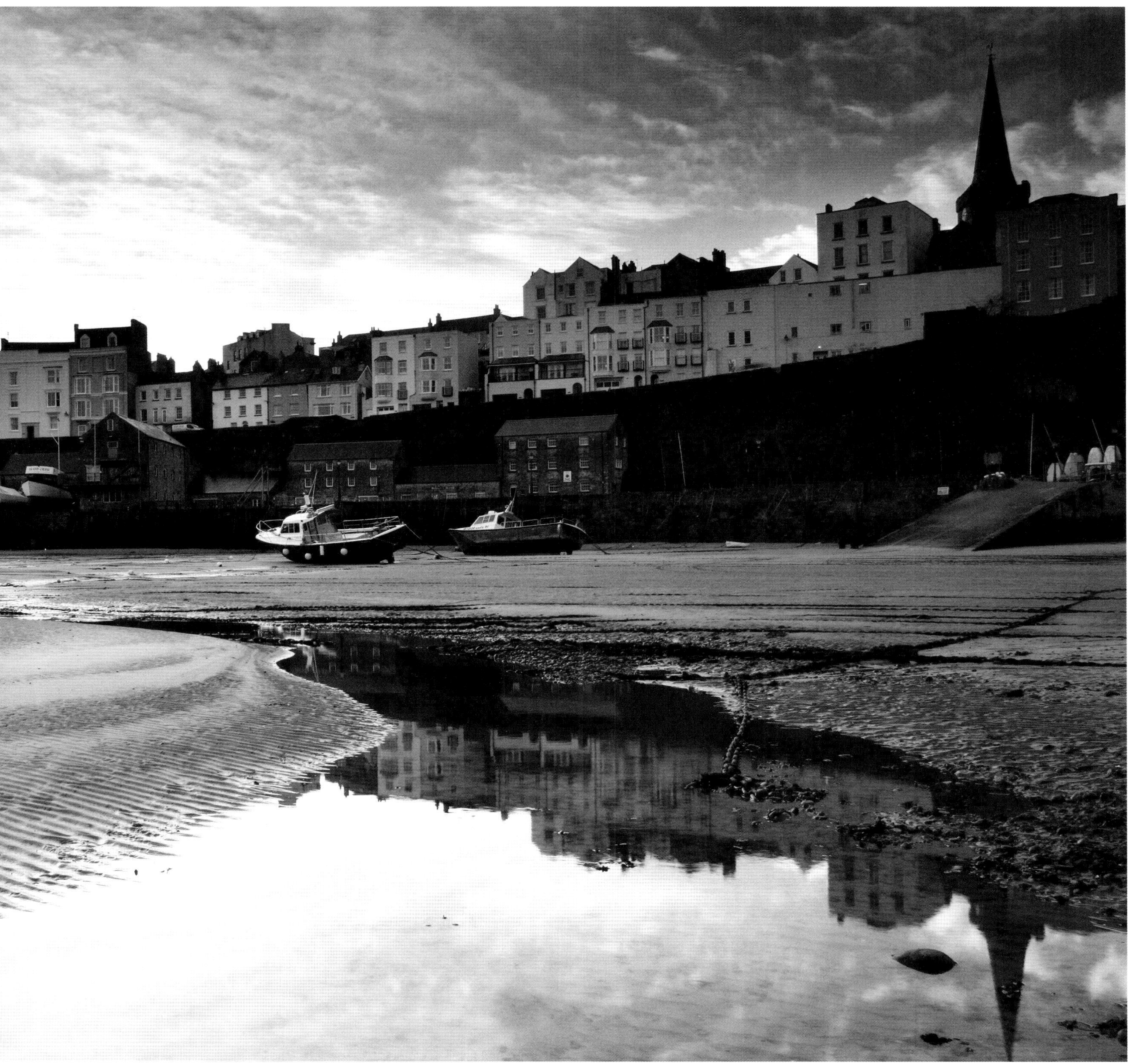

STARLINGS

Patience is a virtue, apparently, and sometimes you most definitely need it to bag the image you are after. This was one of those occasions. There were two elements that drew me to this composition – firstly, the symmetry of the mud track leading to the horizon, and secondly the starlings. When I set up my gear they were flitting from one spot to another at the bottom end of the field. I thought, 'Wait a little while and they'll soon head up my way'. Nearly an hour later they finally did the decent thing and swept up the field, performing a quite spectacular flypast right in front of me. Well worth the wait.

Plate 07

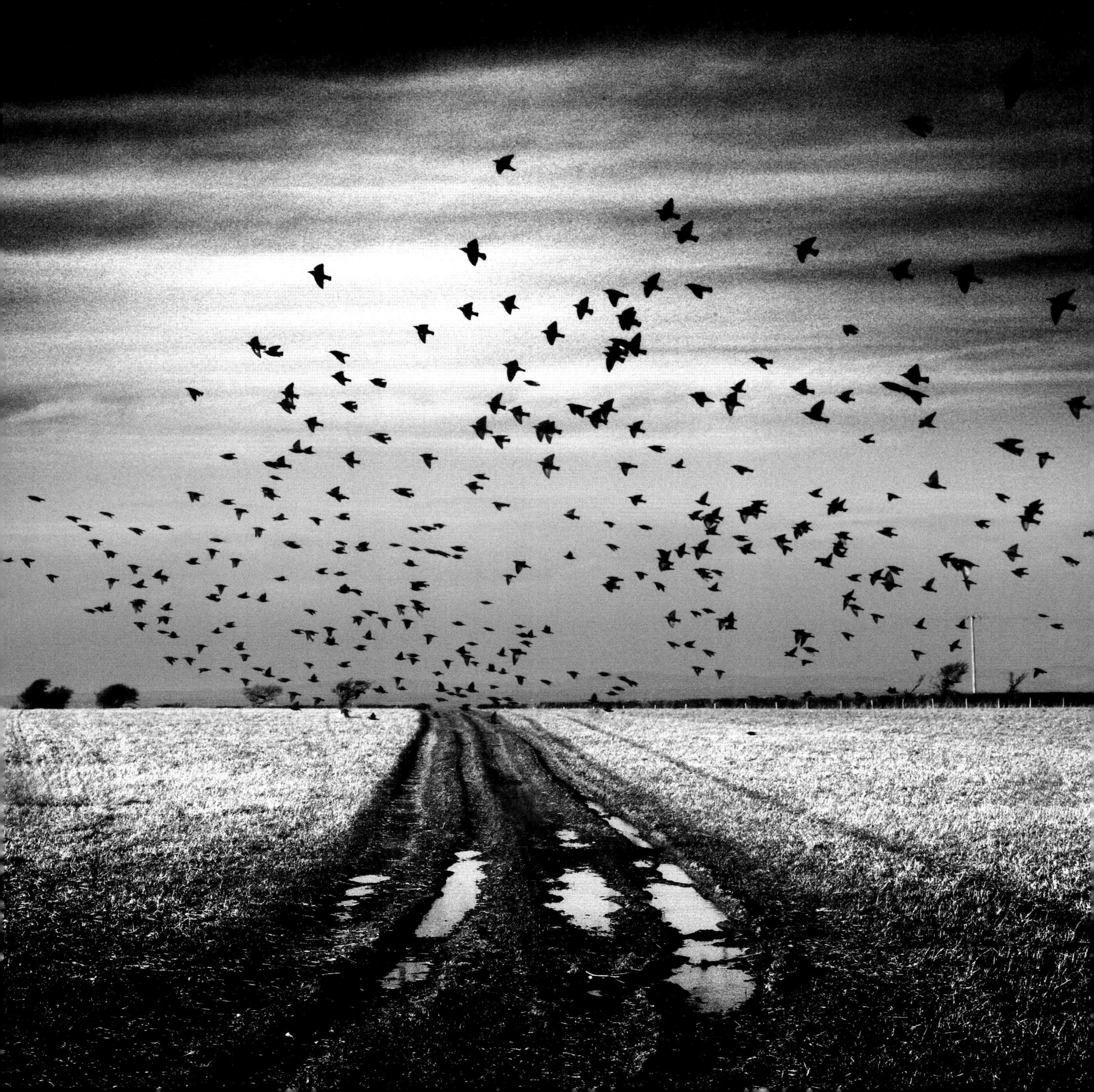

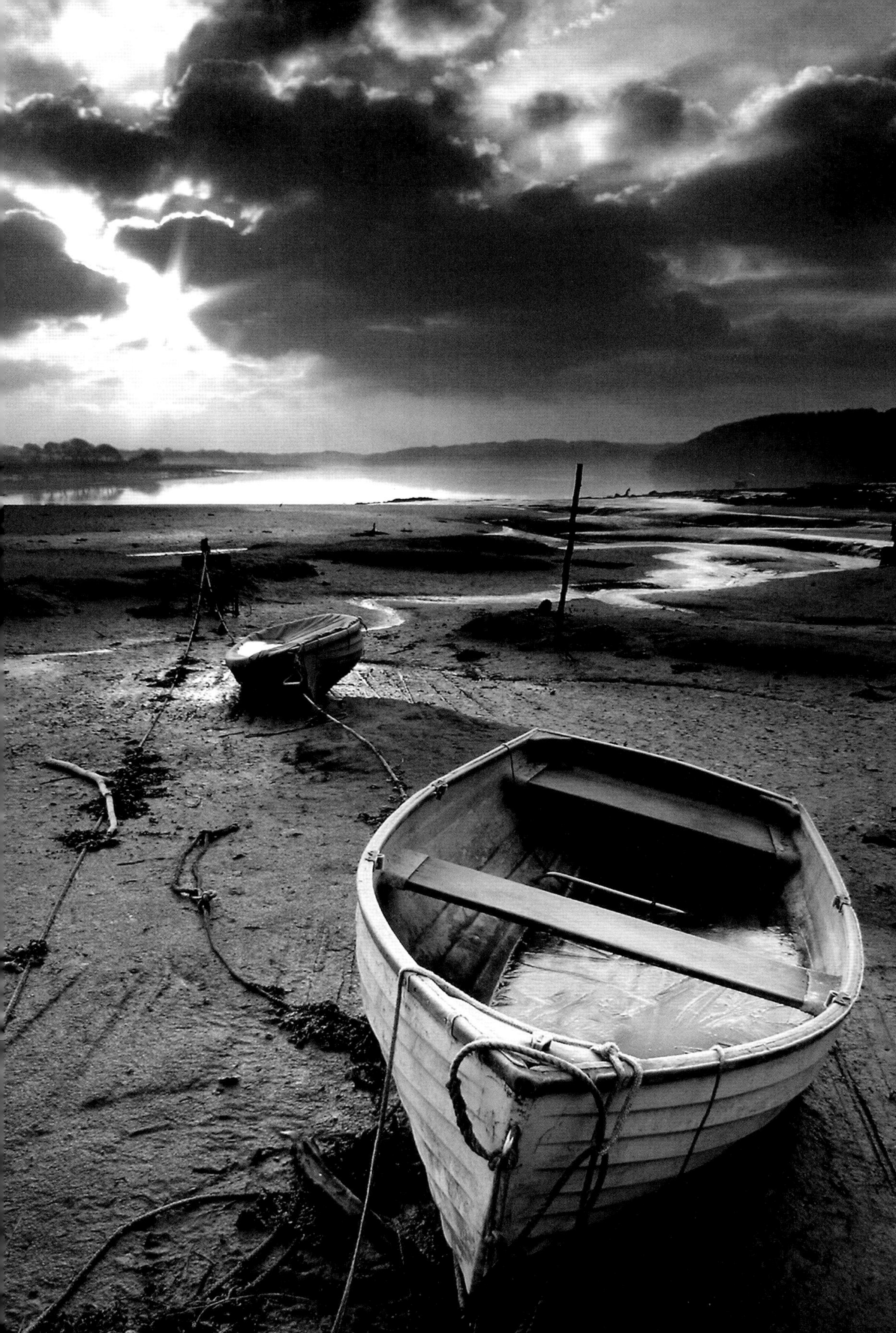

PORT LION

When I first allowed the dream of becoming a professional landscape photographer to take a hold in my imagination, this was one of the first photographs I took. Because of that special association it remains one of my favourites, even though it has been superseded by many dozens of images since. It was a bitterly cold morning on the river just around the corner from where I live and all the elements for a successful image were there – the stranded ice-filled boat, a desolate stretch of foreshore leading to the water and a beautiful winter's sun rising over distant woods. What more could I ask for?

Plate 08

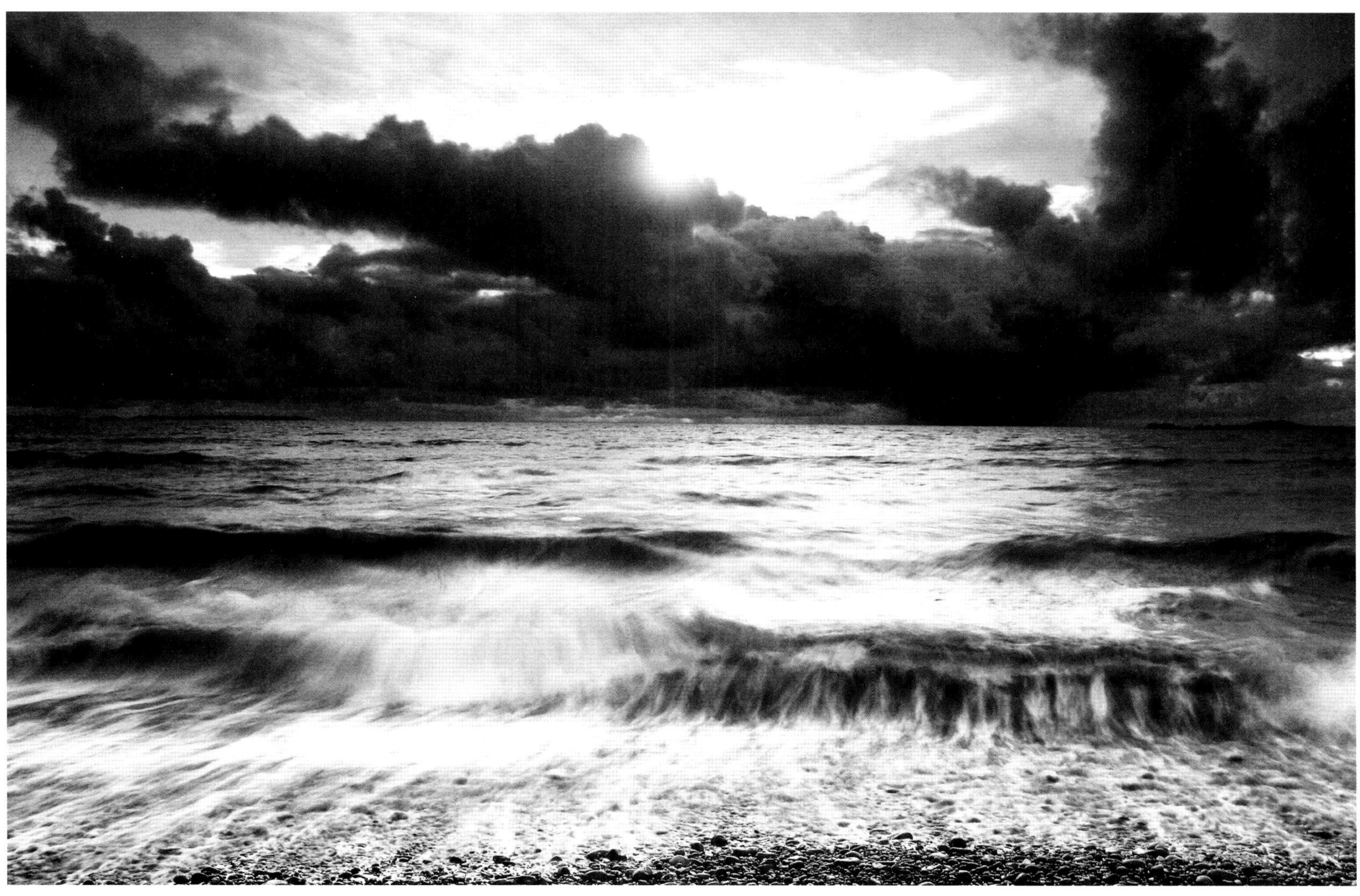

NEWGALE

Occasionally, the elements combine to produce what I would call 'perfect weather'. By that I mean awe-inspiring cloud formations. A sky can dominate more than half of a landscape image so the more engrossing it is the better. And this sky was pretty extraordinary, with the sun just dropping behind the blackest of storm clouds and rain falling as a dark sheet to the right on the horizon. I used a slow shutter speed to capture the roll and motion of the wave as it crashed onto the pebbles. Not long after taking this that ominous rain cloud was overhead and I was packing up frantically to head back to the sanctuary of the car.

Plate 09

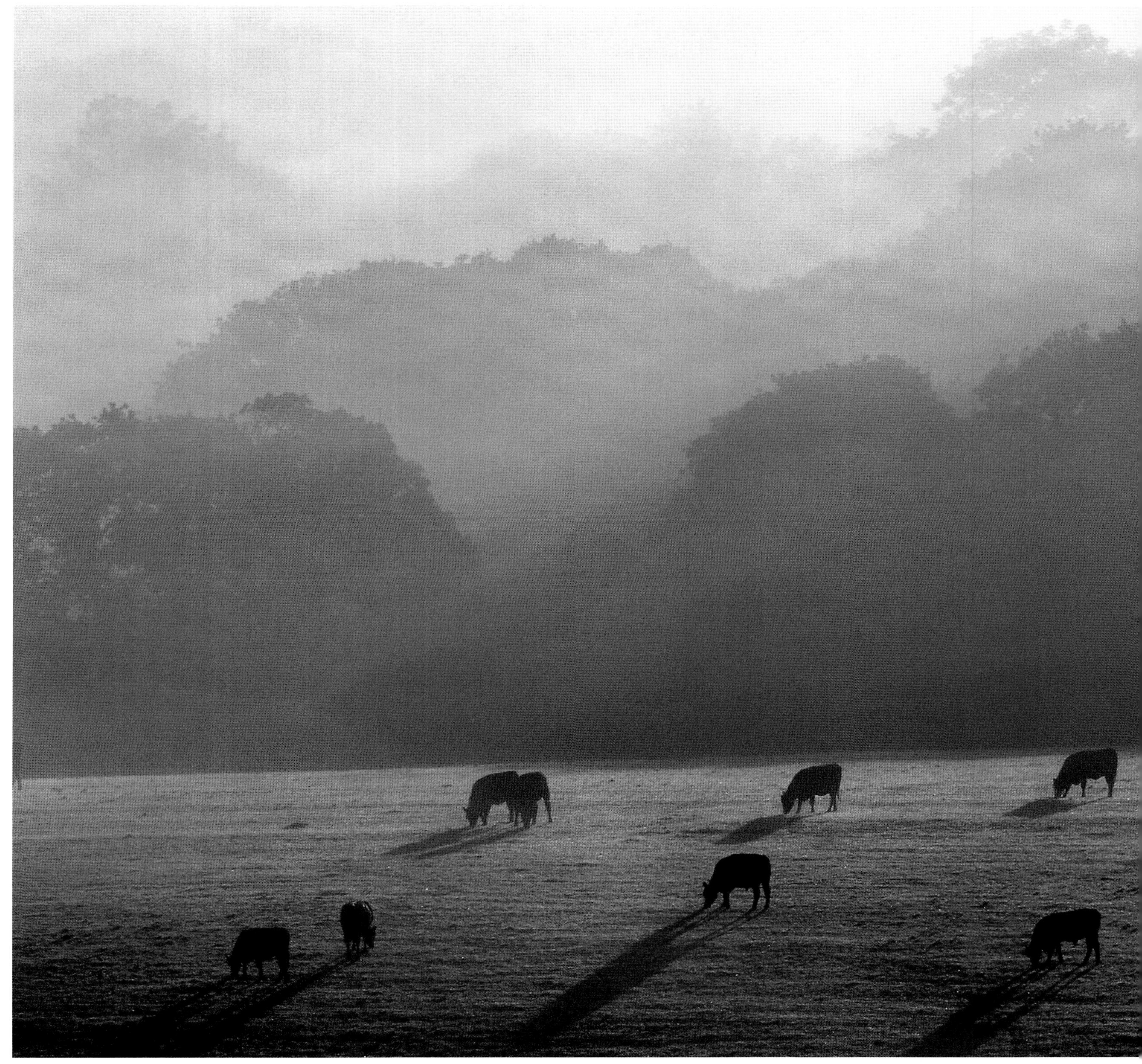

LLAWHADEN

A little after dawn on a wonderful May morning, this image whispers calm and tranquillity. It was taken with a very long lens to compress the scene and flatten perspective, thereby bringing the mist-shrouded trees right into the heart of the image. The cows were enjoying a leisurely breakfast, all moving in unison away from the rising sun. Like us, why would they want to eat with the sun in their eyes? But what really makes this image is that all-enveloping mist. Just one of those lucky bonuses which add the magic ingredient to the resultant photograph.

Plate 10

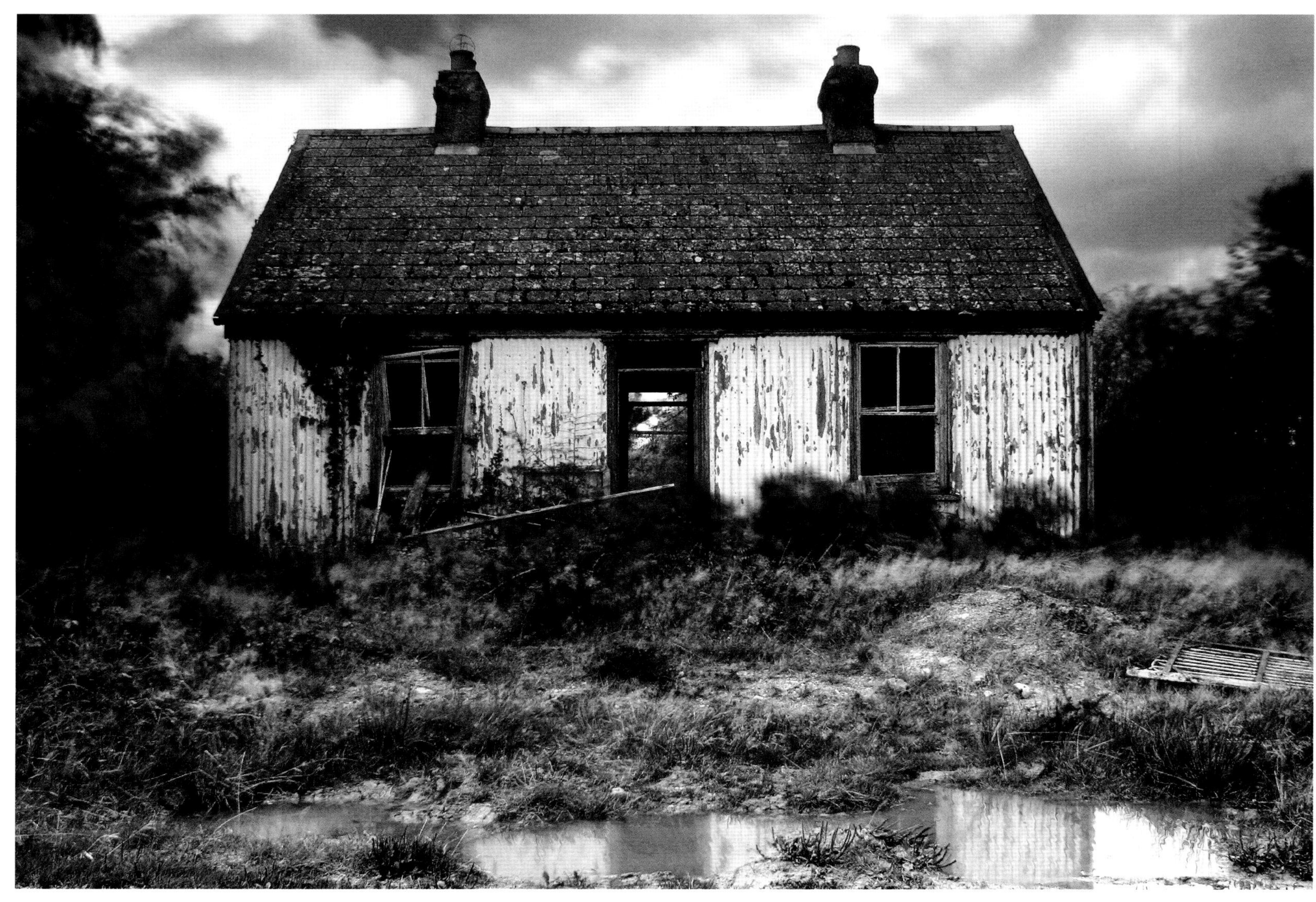

CAMROSE

A good proportion of my work, I hope, is characterised by a certain atmospheric drama – some would call it bleakness! Guilty as charged. But it is that sense of bleakness, the drama and feeling of tempest that can give an image depth and soul.

When people view this image I want them to feel that cold gale-force wind rattling through them as I did. I want them to absorb the utter dereliction and sense of pathos. Holding on desperately to my tripod for support, I shot this at a slow shutter speed so that everything except the building became a windswept blur of movement. The gate lying on the floor adds a certain poignancy – one day not so long ago it would have provided the entrance into someone's garden.

Plate 11

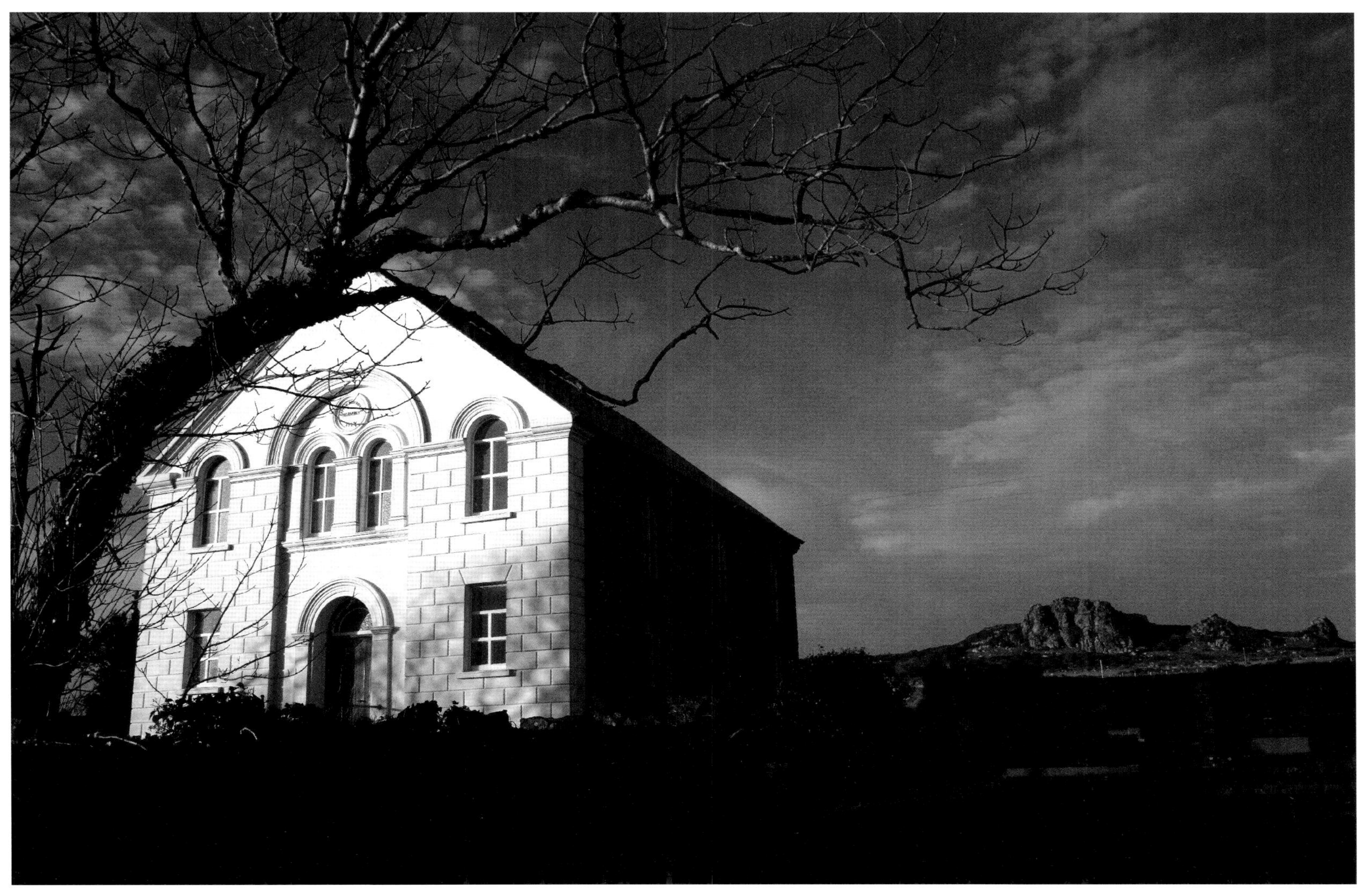

CAPEL HARMONI, NEAR STRUMBLE HEAD

Over the years I had seen this chapel many times without ever having paid much attention to it. On this particular day, I was passing late in the afternoon and noticed how the winter sun had lit up the front of the chapel while the rest of the immediate surroundings were in shadow. I knew that if I exposed the area of white correctly the remainder of the image would be under-exposed, thereby creating a very powerful angular white shape in the landscape. The arching tree provided the perfect framing device and the composition is enhanced by the distant rocky outcrop of Garn Fechan illuminated by the sun.

Plate 12

CEIBWR BAY

The stretch of coastline running
from near Moylegrove and up
towards Cardigan is one of
the most spectacular in
Pembrokeshire, and even in
Wales and beyond. This was a
particularly blustery day, a heavy
swell causing huge wave surges
against the cliffs. I stood on an
exposed headland buffeted by high
winds and showers of sea-foam
floating on the air, blown up from
the bottom of the cliffs and carried
up onto the road above and behind
me. Fortunately, the wind was
coming in off the sea so there was
little chance of me going over the
edge – always a plus!

Plate 13

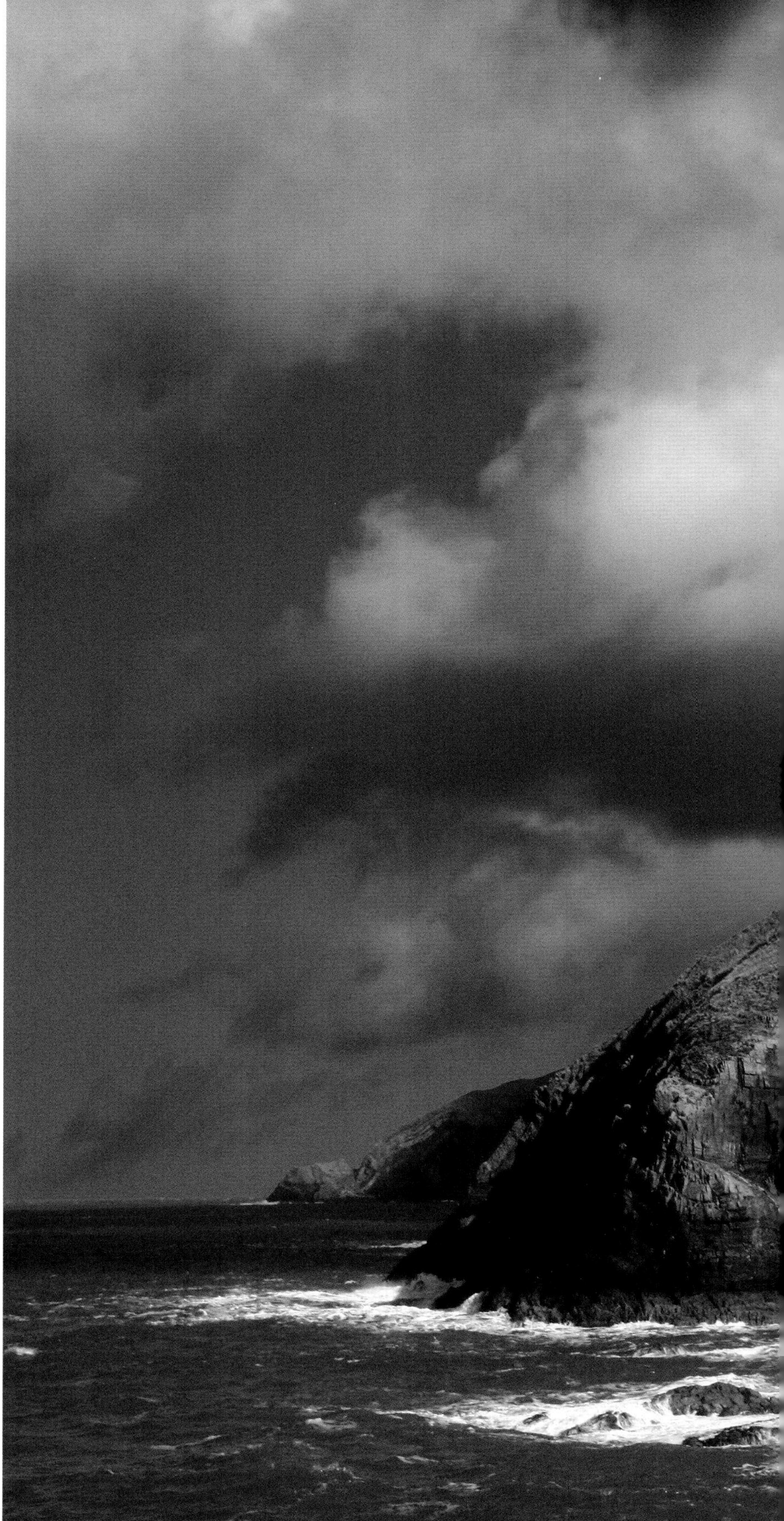

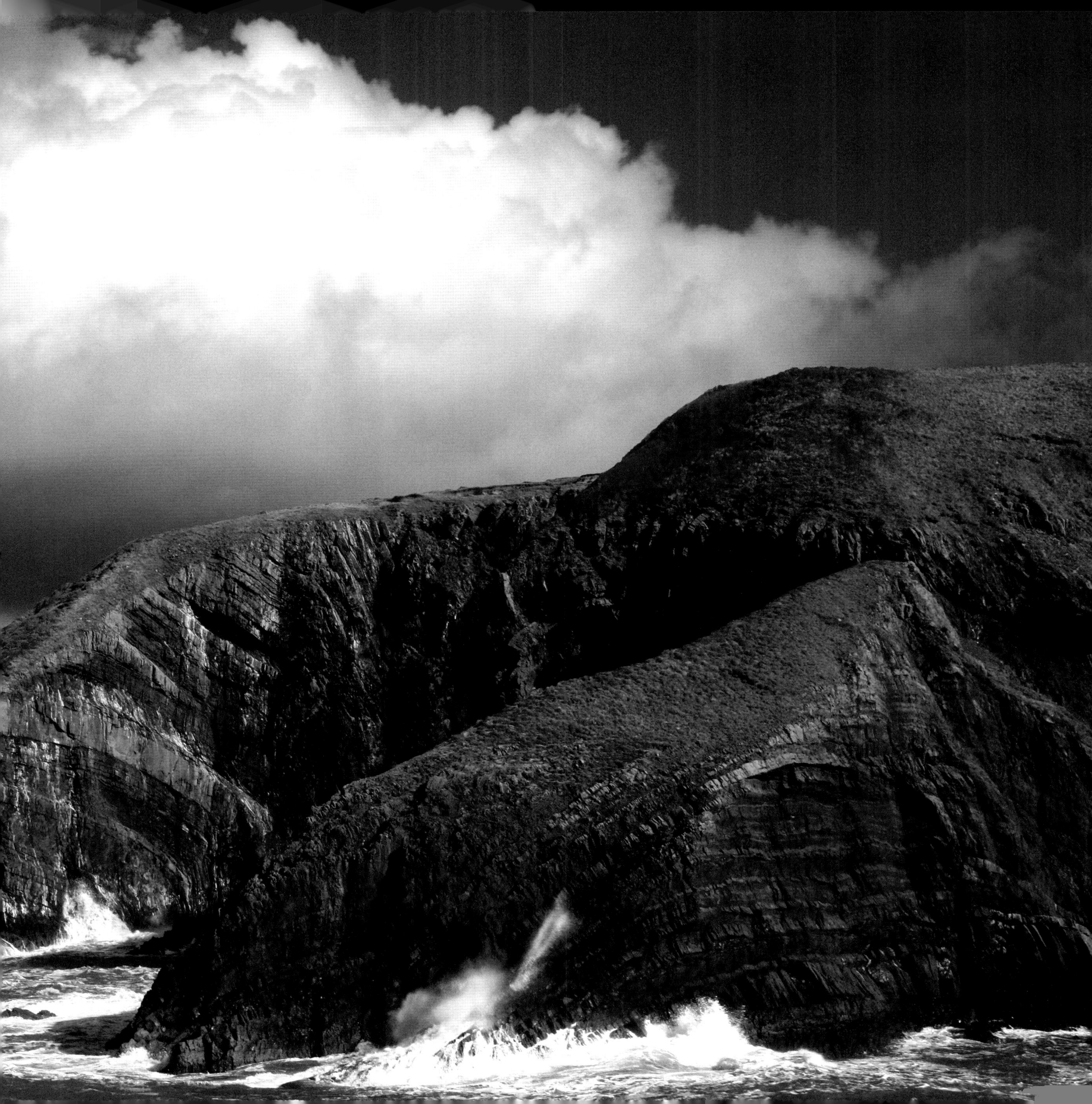

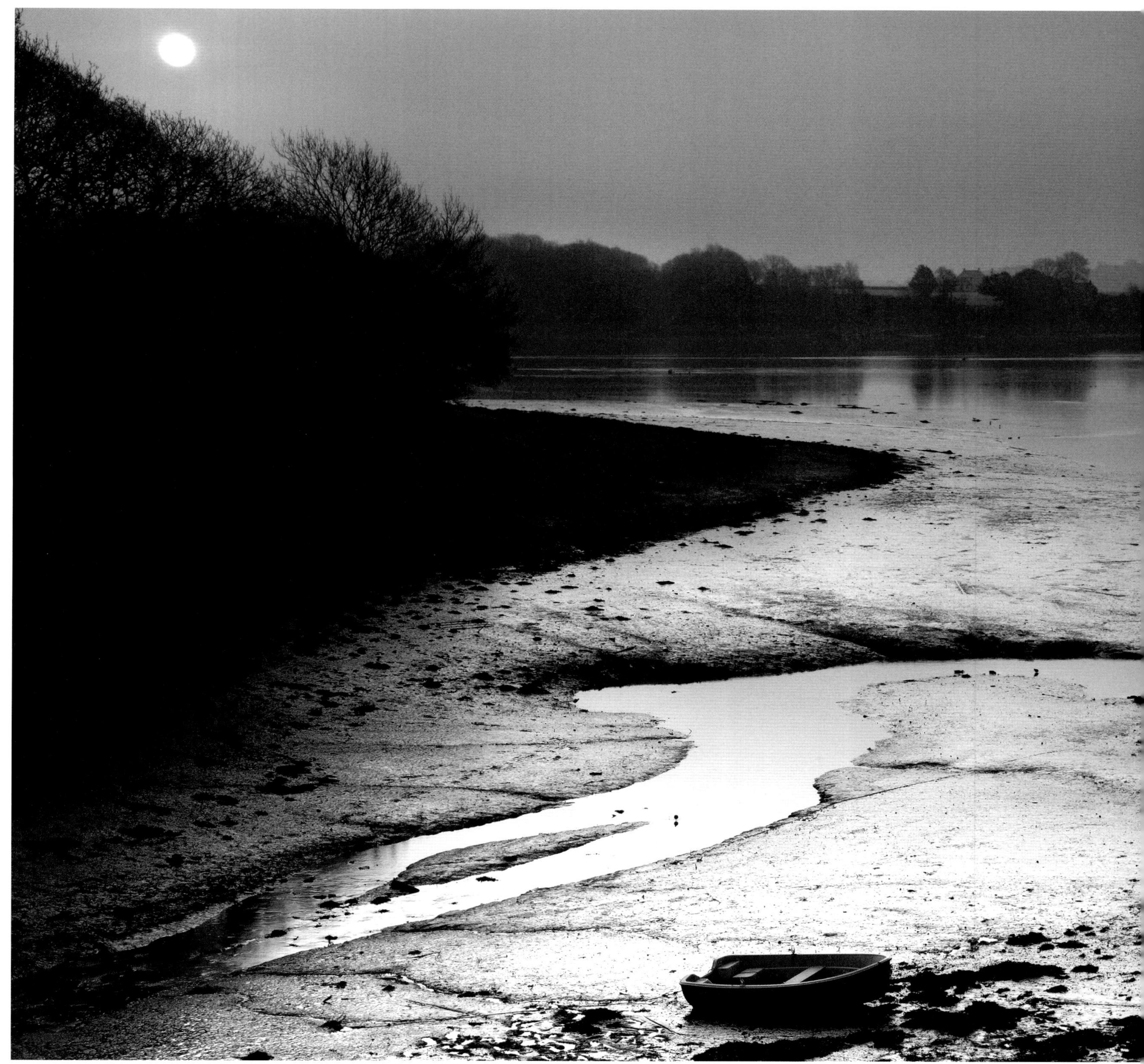

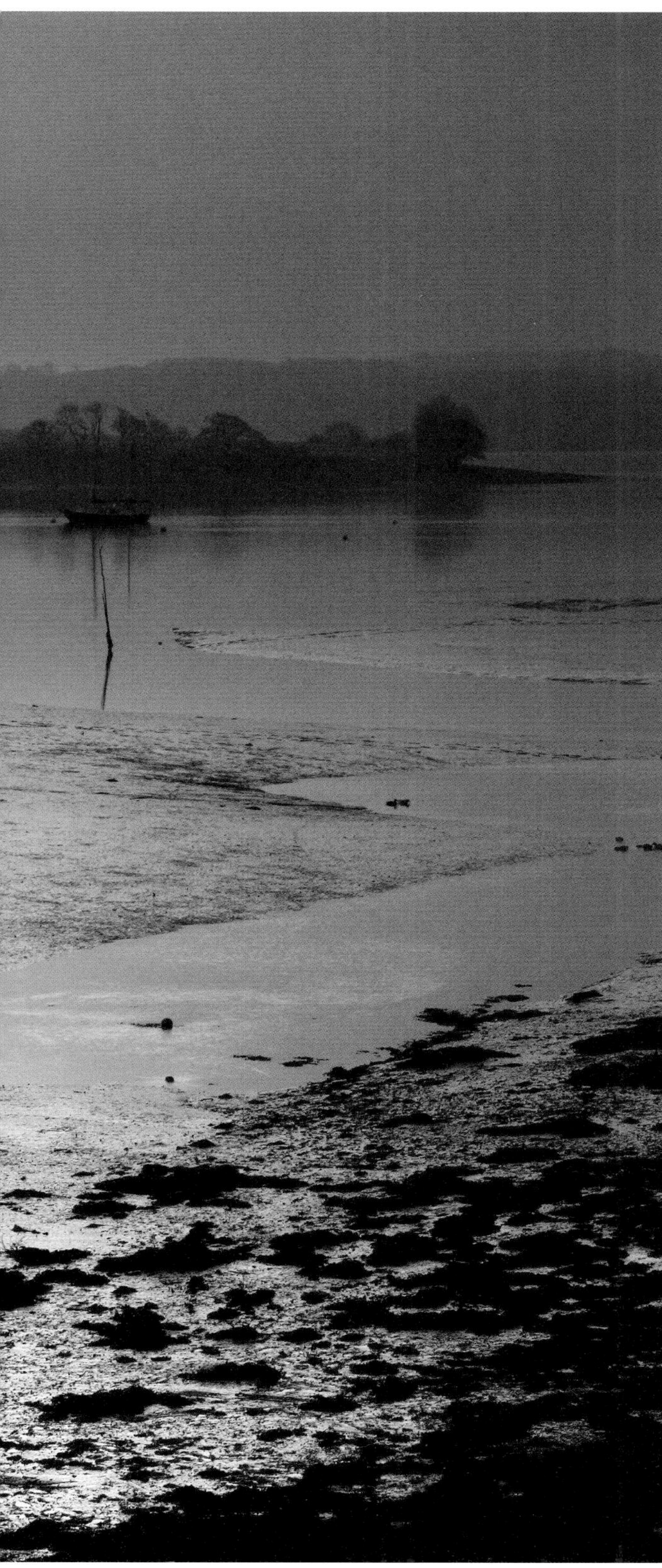

EDWARD'S PILL

The river is an eternal source of inspiration to me. For those of us who live near its timeless ebb and flow, the consensus is that we are a very fortunate bunch. The solitude and tranquillity as you wander its banks at the crack of dawn cannot be beaten. The mudflats which are exposed at low tide are a great ingredient for black and white landscape as they add essential contours and texture, helping to build the composition. A hazy sky has diffused the strength of the rising sun, giving the image an almost moonlit feel.

Plate 14

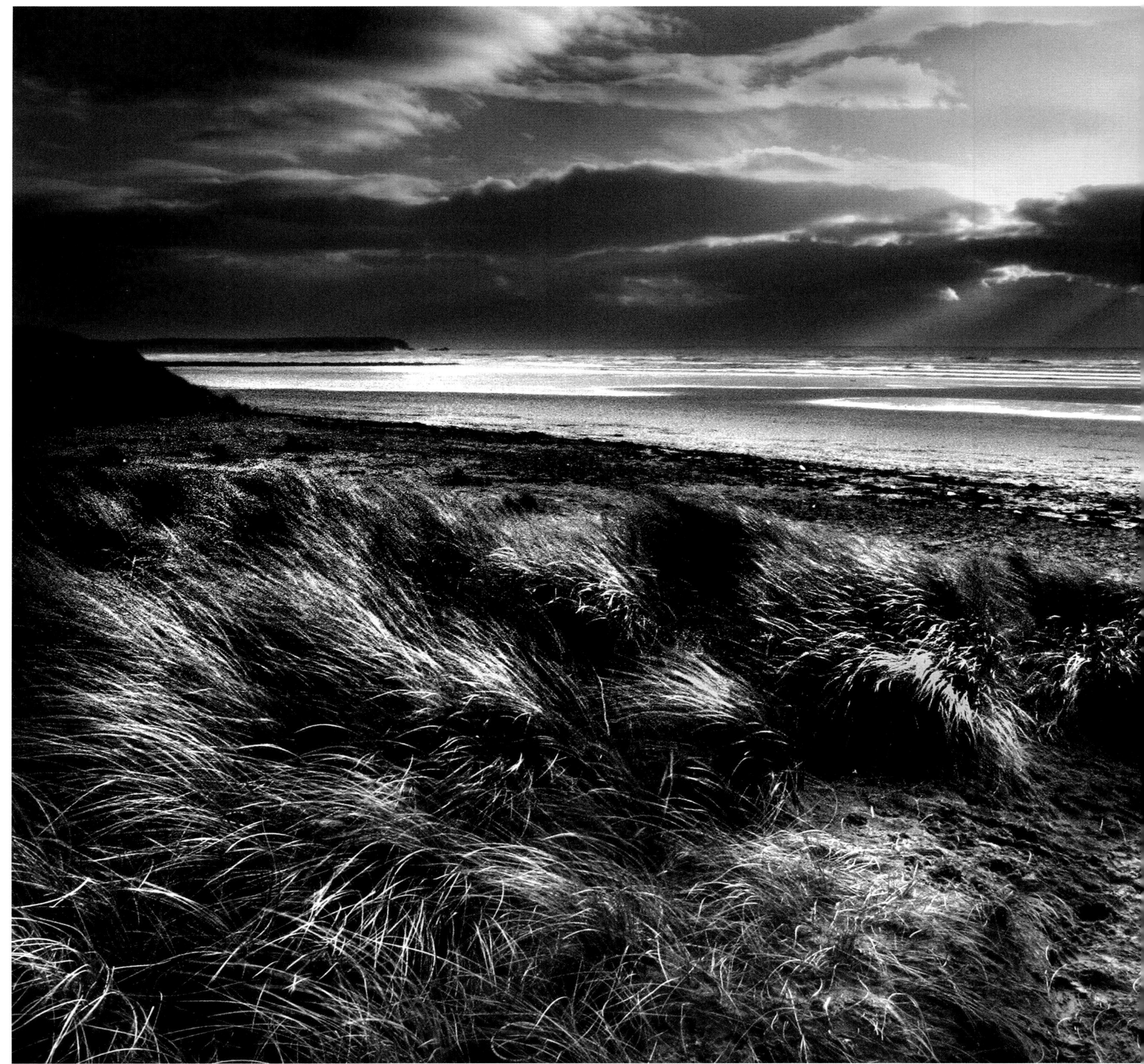

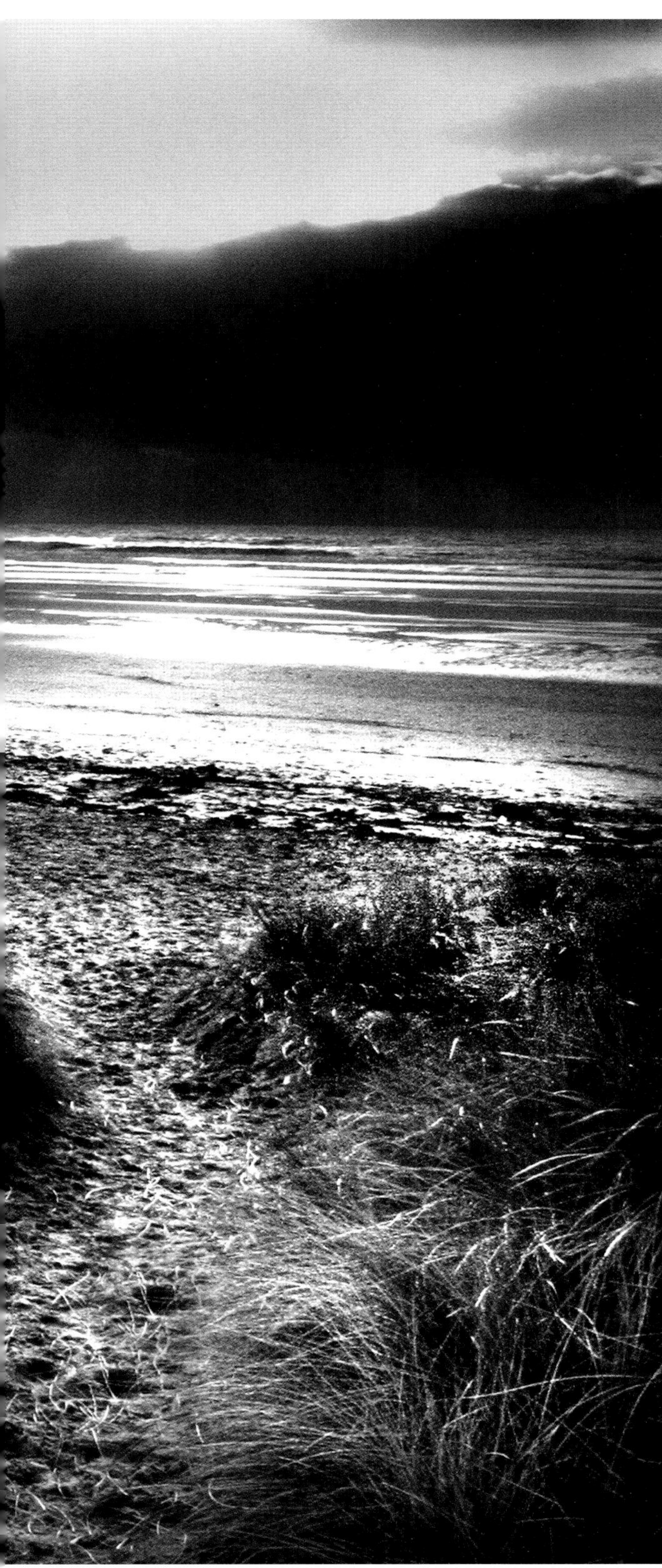

FRESHWATER WEST

All of my photographs are taken in the late autumn, winter and spring. There are certain reasons for this: firstly, the light is so much crisper and cleaner than the summer months when the air gets suffocated with ozone, dust and dirt, making long-distance visibility poor. Also, the sun follows a lower arc in the sky resulting in longer periods of the day where you have consistent areas of light and shade, which are crucial for black and white landscape as it is the interplay of these tones that build the composition. And best of all with beach shots, there are no crowds cluttering up the image.

Plate 15

DRUIDSTON HAVEN

Druidston beach is wonderfully
isolated, hemmed in by sheer
cliffs and with just a steep narrow
track allowing access.
A fortuitous lack of a car park
makes it a sparsely populated
stretch of sand even in the height
of summer. It also means there's
no commercial presence at all –
no ice-cream parlours, no bucket-
and-spade shops, not even a loo! I
love the idea that this view has not
changed in hundreds of years.

Plate 16

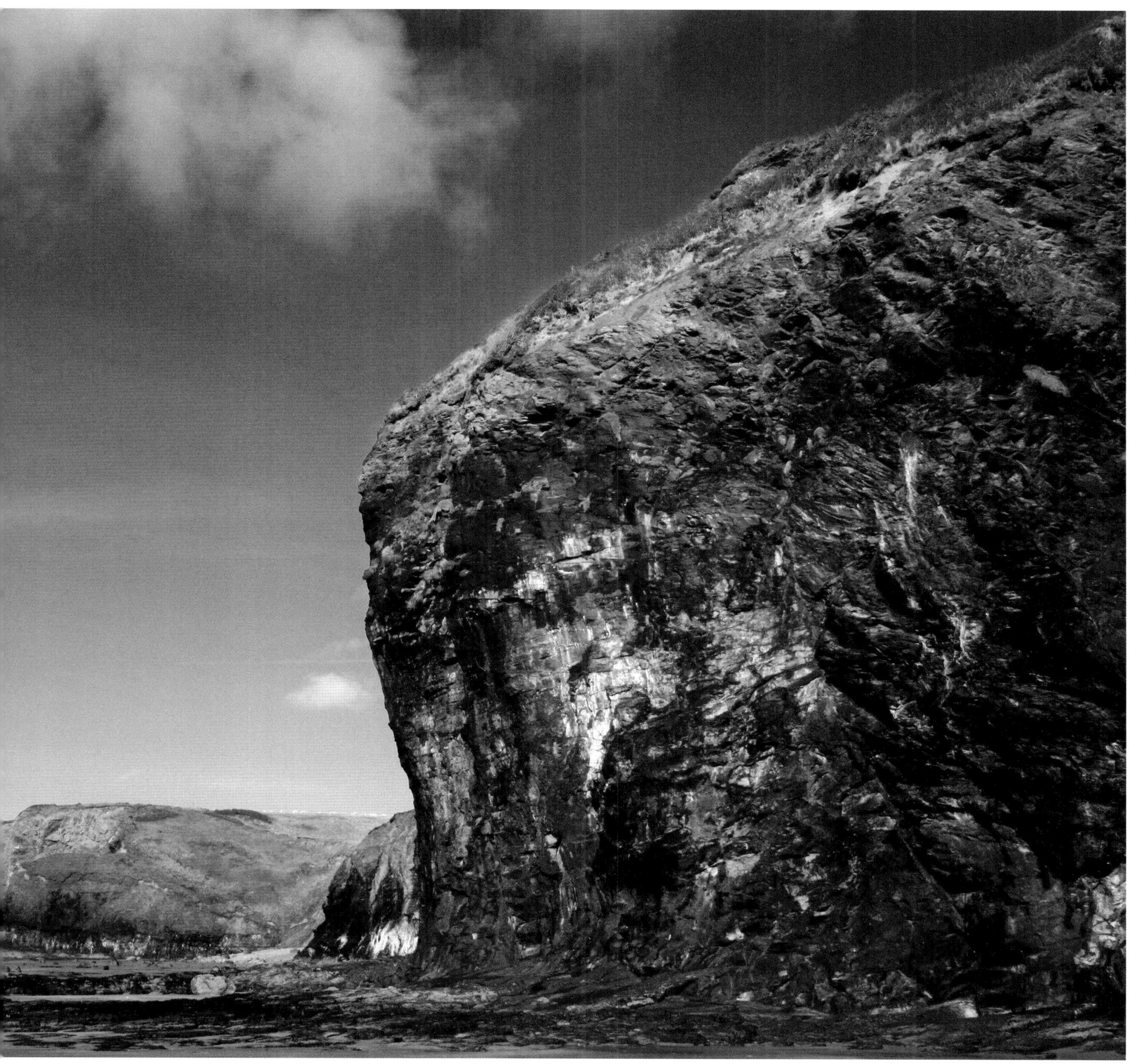

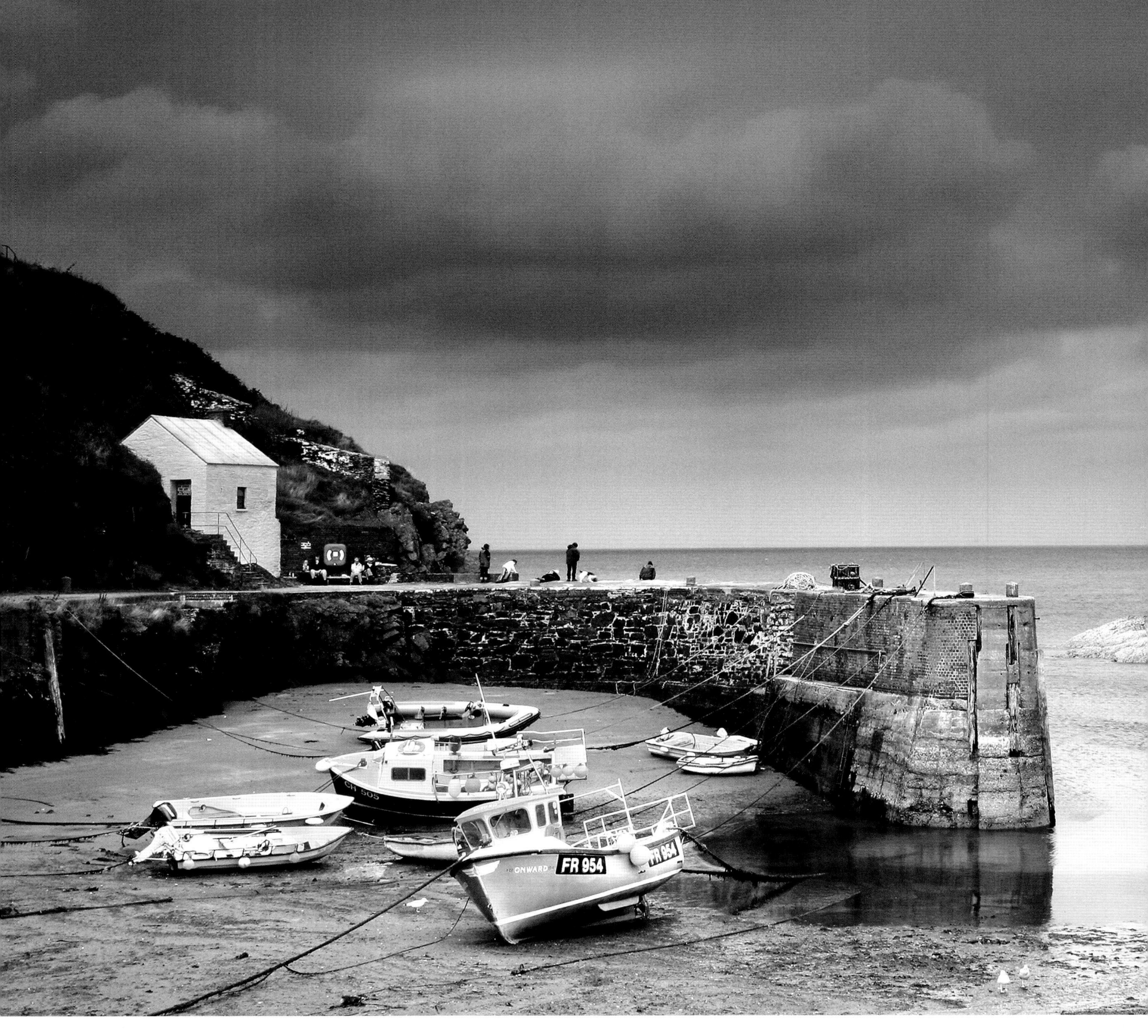

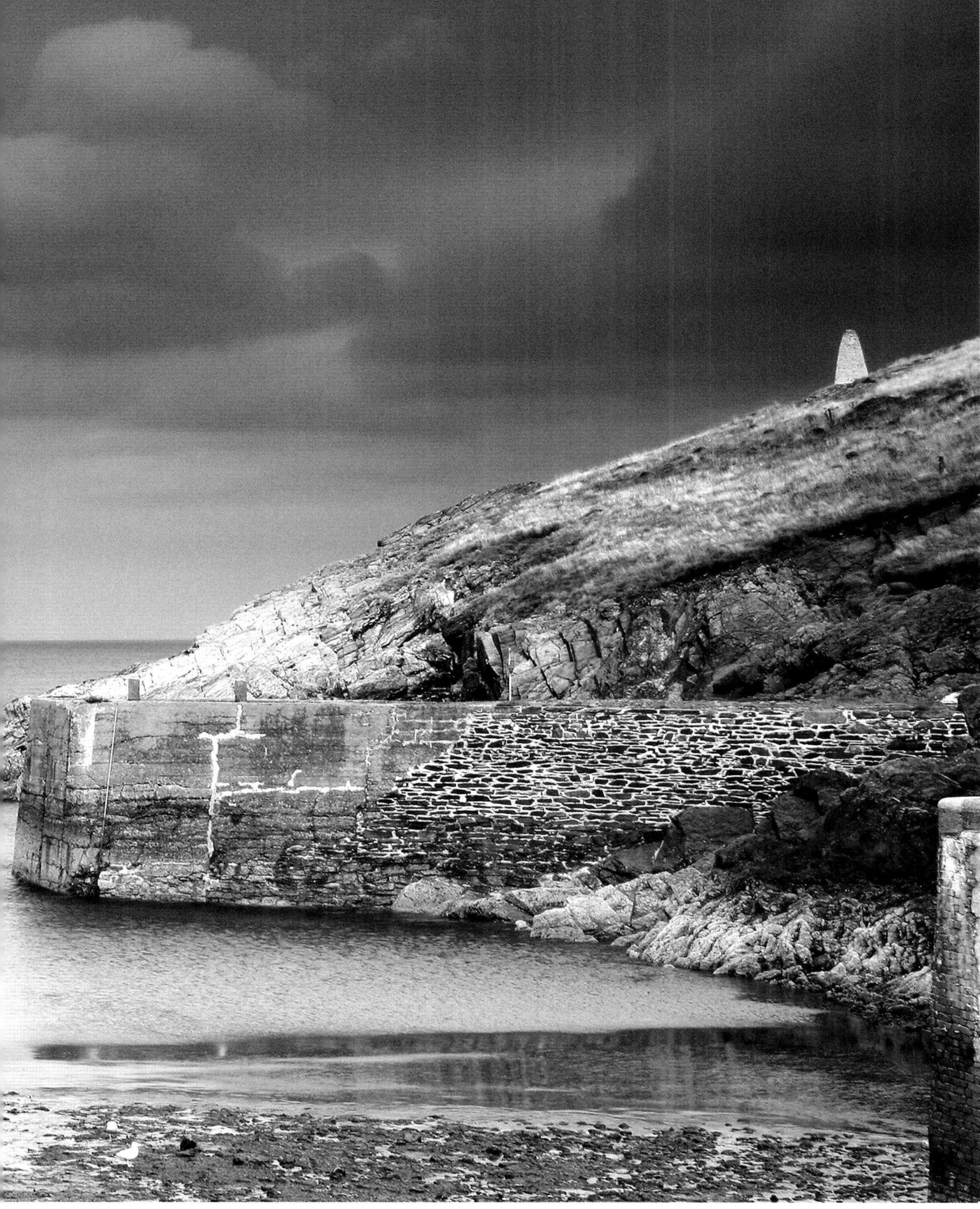

PORTHGAIN

Once a thriving harbour exporting roofing slate and hardcore, Porthgain is now a busy, picturesque tourist destination and home to a small fleet of fishing vessels. In its industrial heyday, the slate and granite were mined from quarries up on the headland, the granite being crushed and transported by tramway to specially built hoppers at Porthgain, where the hardcore was graded and loaded onto ships or taken away by road. The venture was never very profitable and eventually ceased operating in the 1930s.

Plate 17

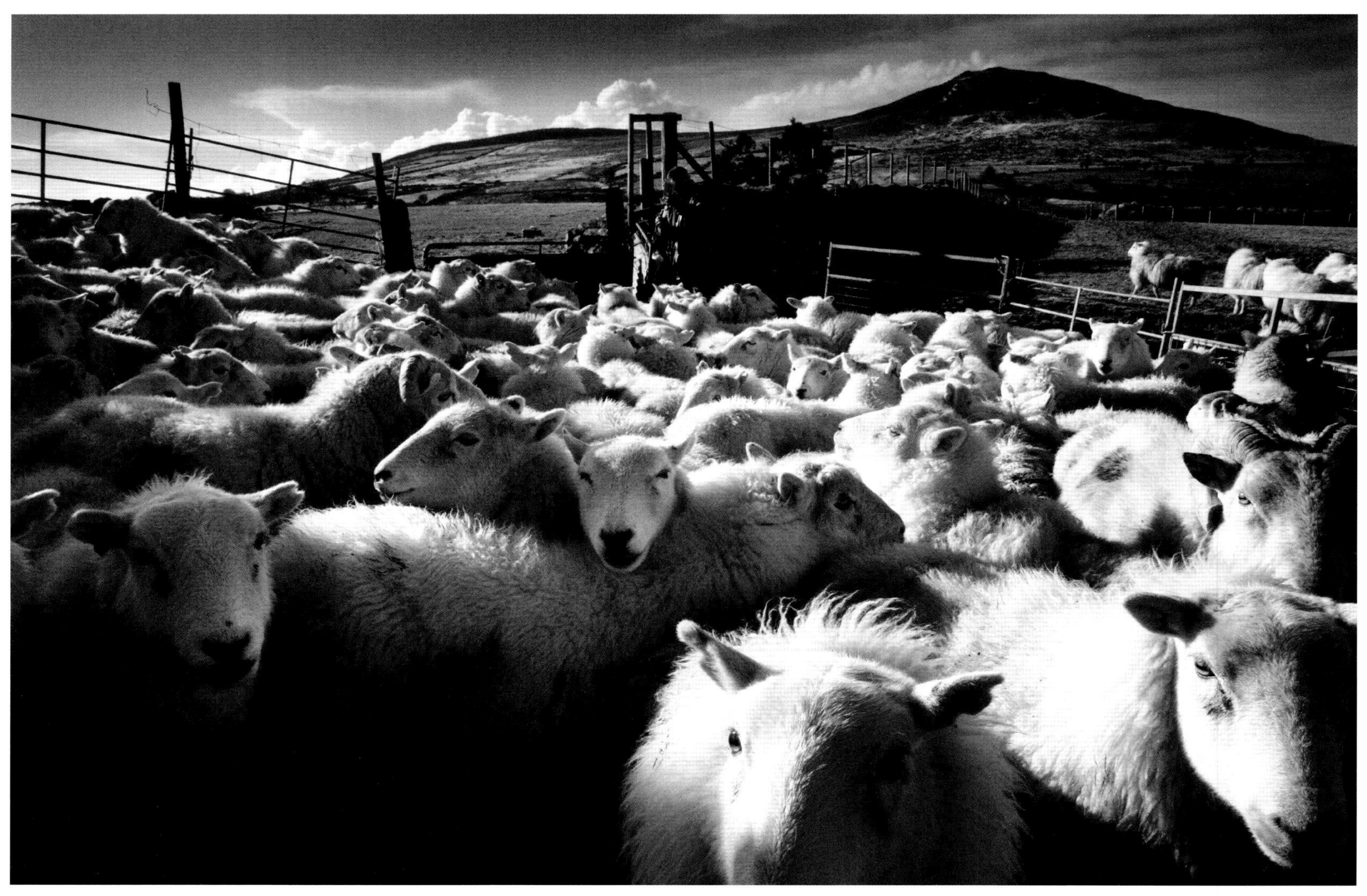

SHEEP AT THE FOOT OF FOEL DRYGARN

I came across these sheep penned in at the foot of Foel Drygarn, waiting for inoculation. This image encapsulates perfectly life on and around the fringes of the Preseli Hills. It is a farming community where generations of the same families have made a living from the hills; hardy individuals whose working lives are spent predominantly outdoors doing a physically demanding job. More than any of us they live and breathe the seasons: the biting winds of winter, the gentle warmth of spring sunshine punctuated by short, sharp showers, the heat of summer, and the cooling rains of autumn.

Plate 18

THE BULL

I could spin you some yarn of
how I trekked intrepidly across a
field to square up to this brute,
staring him straight in the eye
before snapping his portrait, but,
of course, I would be lying. He
was actually in a pen with very
substantial metal bars between
us. I love the texture of those tight
curls which make you want to run
your hands through them. There
is a faintly welcoming look in his
eyes but needless to say I resisted
the temptation to step inside the
pen with him.

Plate 19

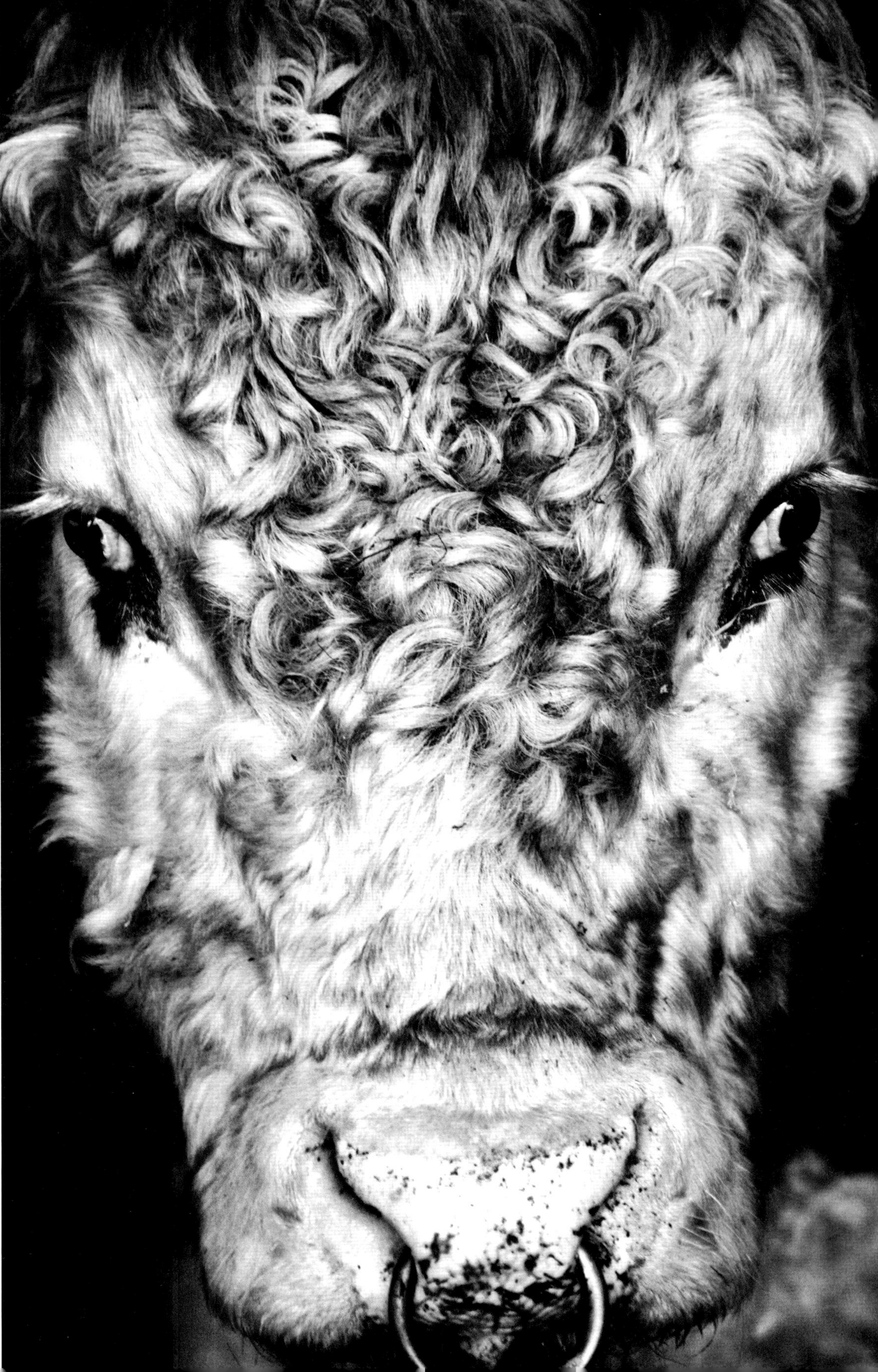

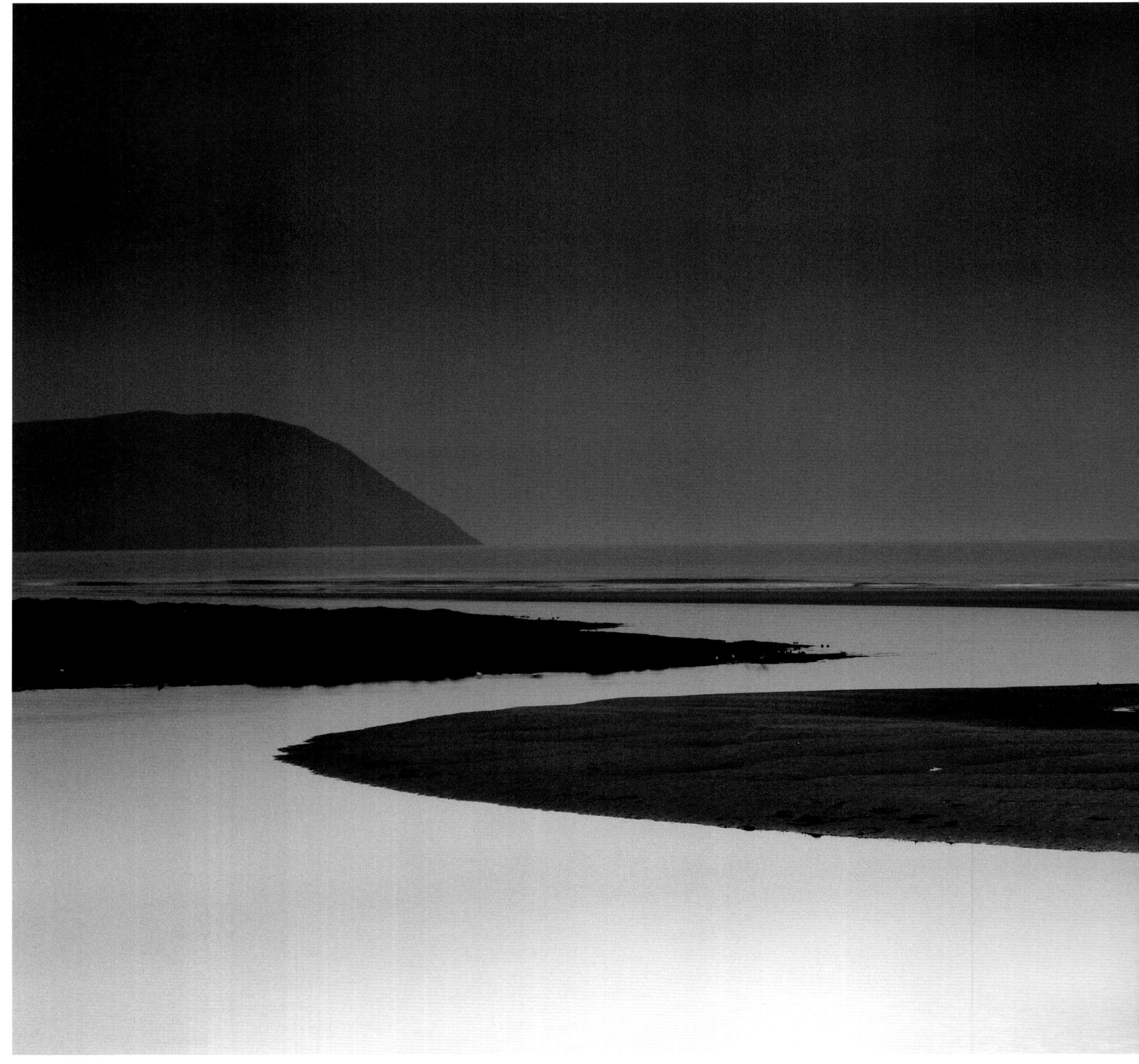

THE PARROG, NEWPORT

Occasionally, as the old adage goes, less is more. That was certainly the case with this image. The silvery 'S' shape of the River Nevern meandering down the beach is quite mesmerising. It draws you on an inexorable journey to the foreshore and out to sea. Dinas Island jutting out on the left adds a necessary reference point, making it recognisably Newport.

Plate 20

TOWARDS BRYNBERIAN, THE PRESELI HILLS

This is another of my earliest photographs. It has a simplicity to it, evoking a sense of freedom and optimism. It was a warm late spring day. I pulled the car over onto an open area just off the road, grabbed the camera and tripod and strolled aimlessly up a dirt track to look at the view. Sometimes, spontaneity can be so rewarding. The use of a high film speed setting has blurred the fine detail in the landscape, giving the image more of a painterly feel. After taking some photographs I remember lying down in the grass and gazing up at the clouds scudding past. Just one of those perks of the job I suppose!

Plate 21

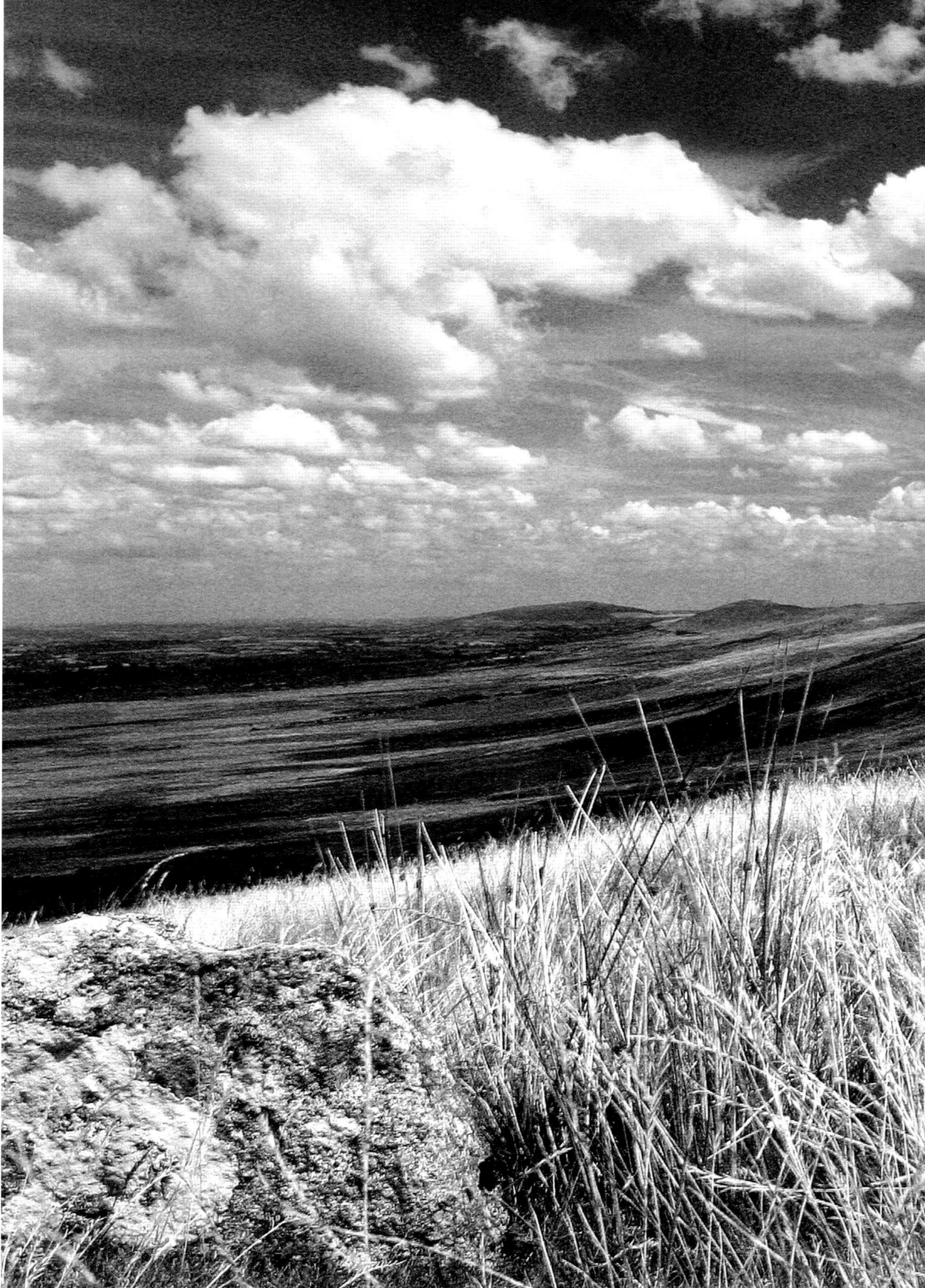

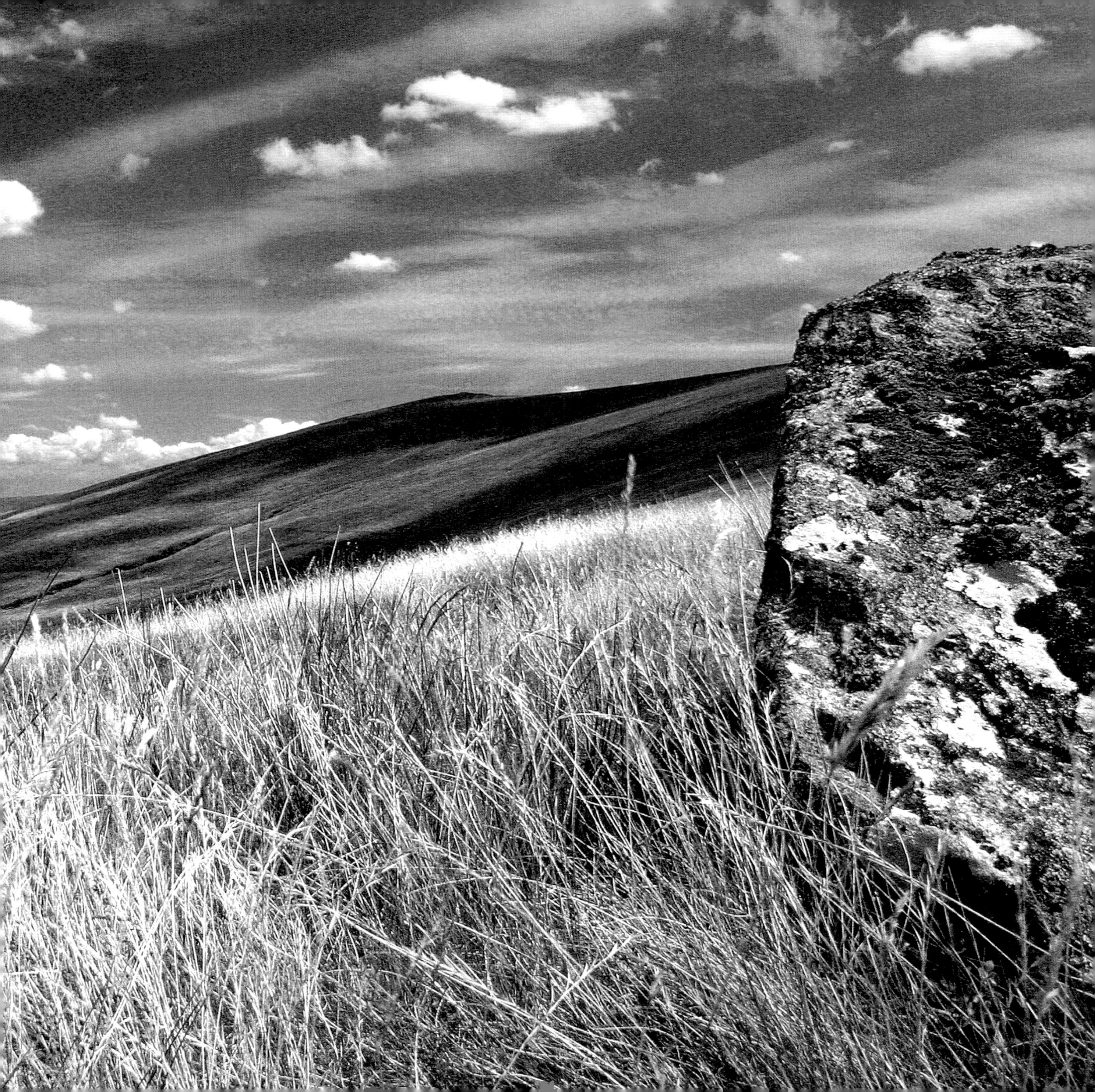

TOWARDS TRELEDDYD FAWR, NEAR ST DAVIDS

Heading towards Treleddyd Fawr on a late winter's afternoon, I spotted the crows in the field to the right. I stopped and saw that the road leading to the farm was wet after a recent downpour. Combined with the low, brooding clouds and the distant mountains of Carn Trellwyd to the left and Carn Penberry on the right, it comprised a wonderfully stark wintry landscape. The crows hung around while I composed the shot, taking in all the elements to make a dramatic composition. Very dark, grainy and bleak-looking – Pembrokeshire in the winter.

Plate 22

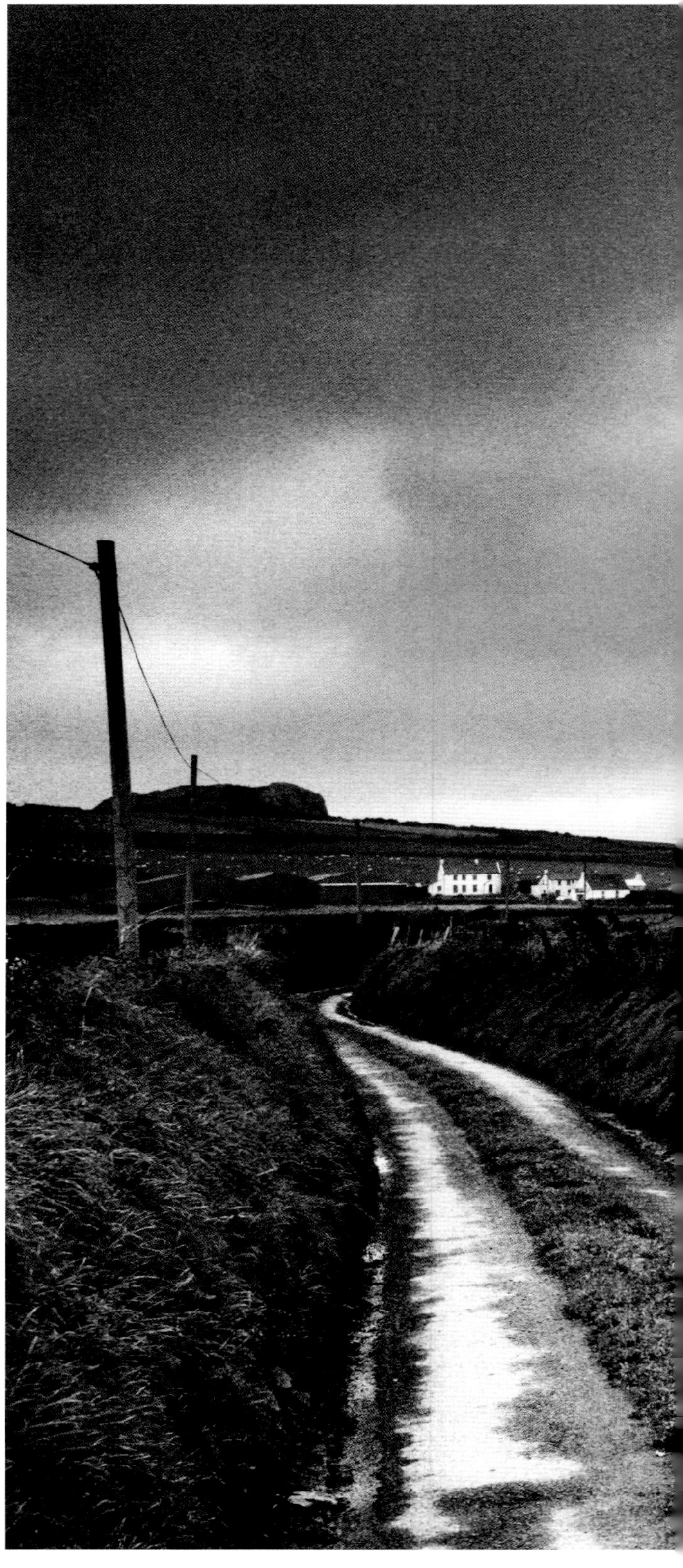

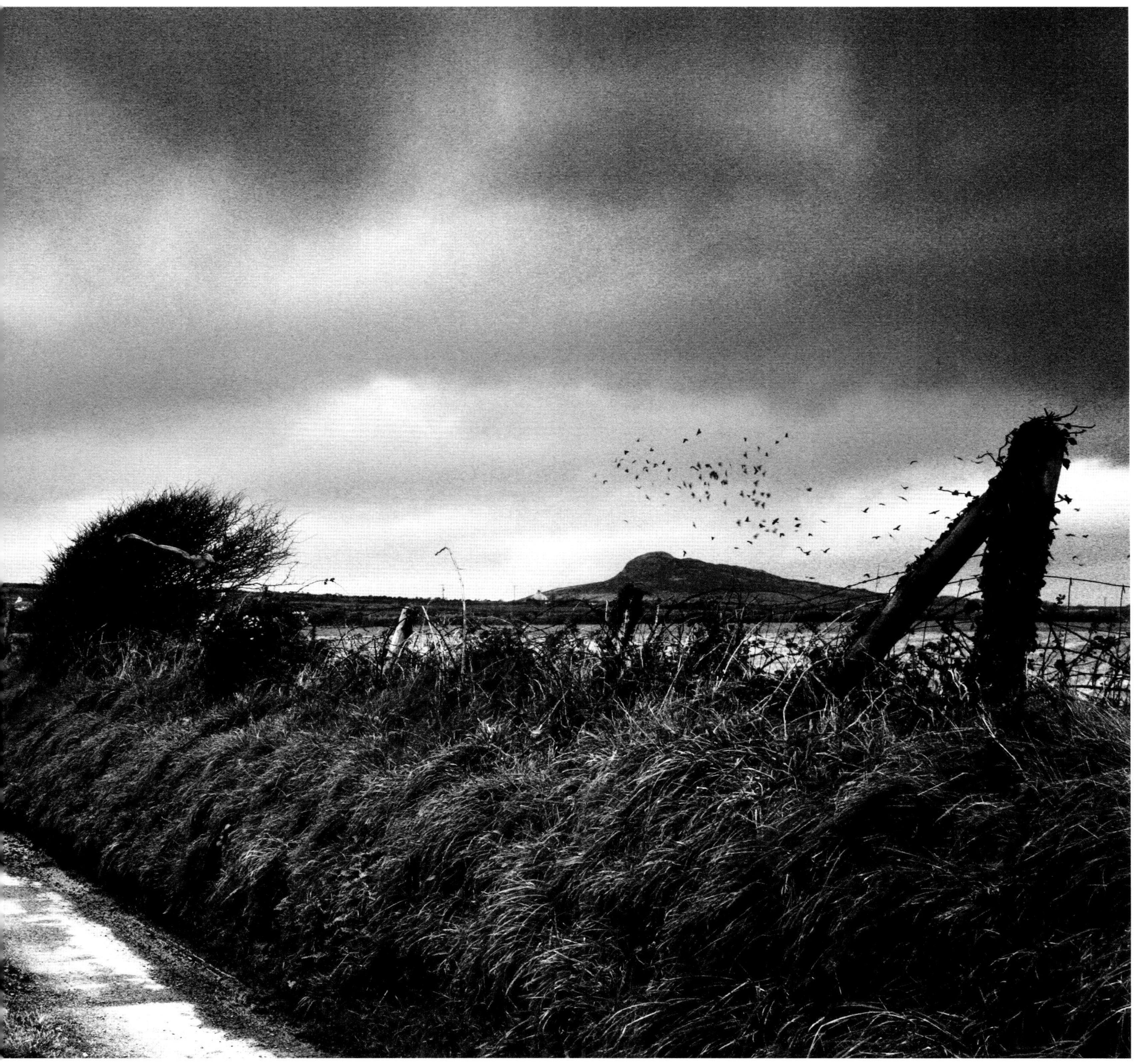

TREFIN

I found this spot overlooking Trefin about a year before taking this photograph and formed an idea for a dramatic and foreboding image where the village appeared under mortal threat from extreme weather. On the previous few occasions I had passed by, the sky and weather conditions did not match what I had envisaged in my mind's eye. This day, though, exceeded all my expectations. A storm cloud seemed to climb miles into the sky, drifting towards land carrying sheets of rain deluging everything in its path, and Trefin seemingly about to be swept away.

Plate 23

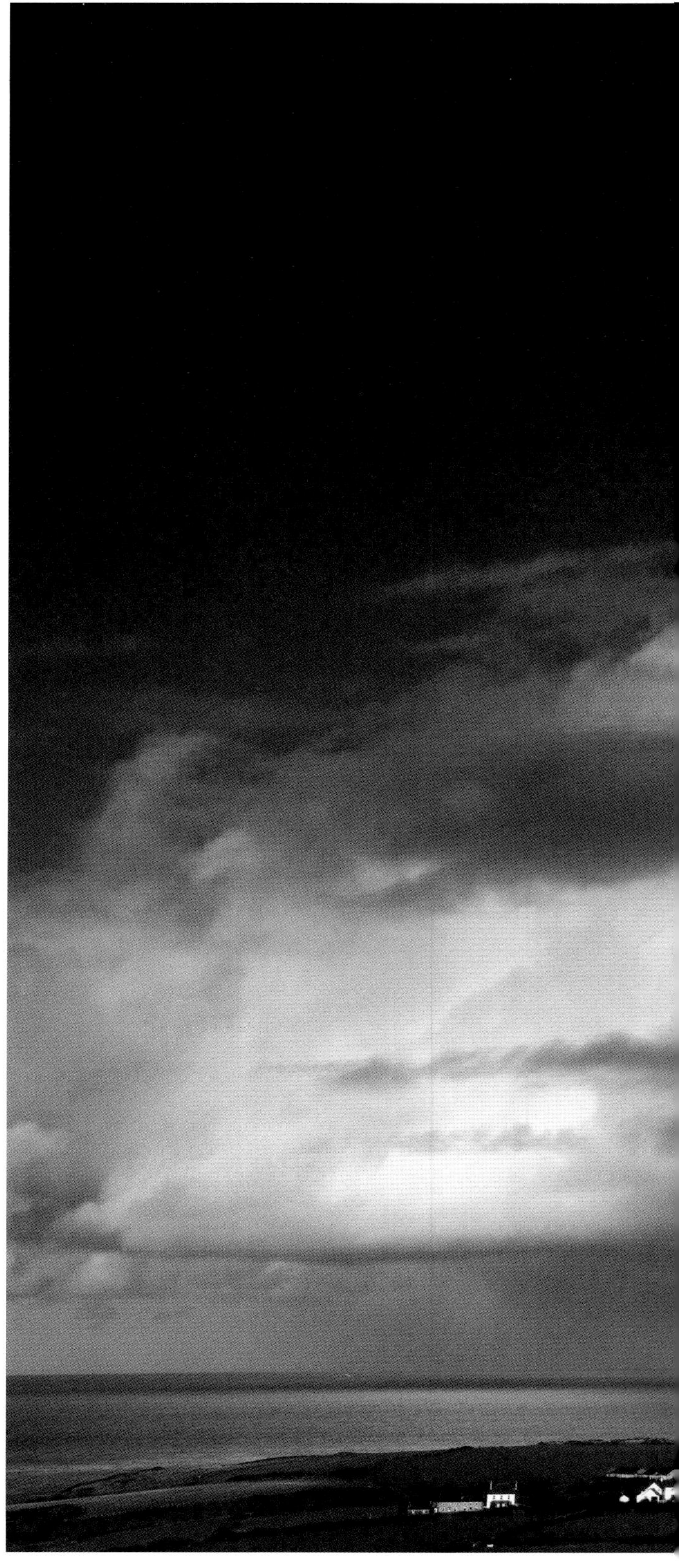

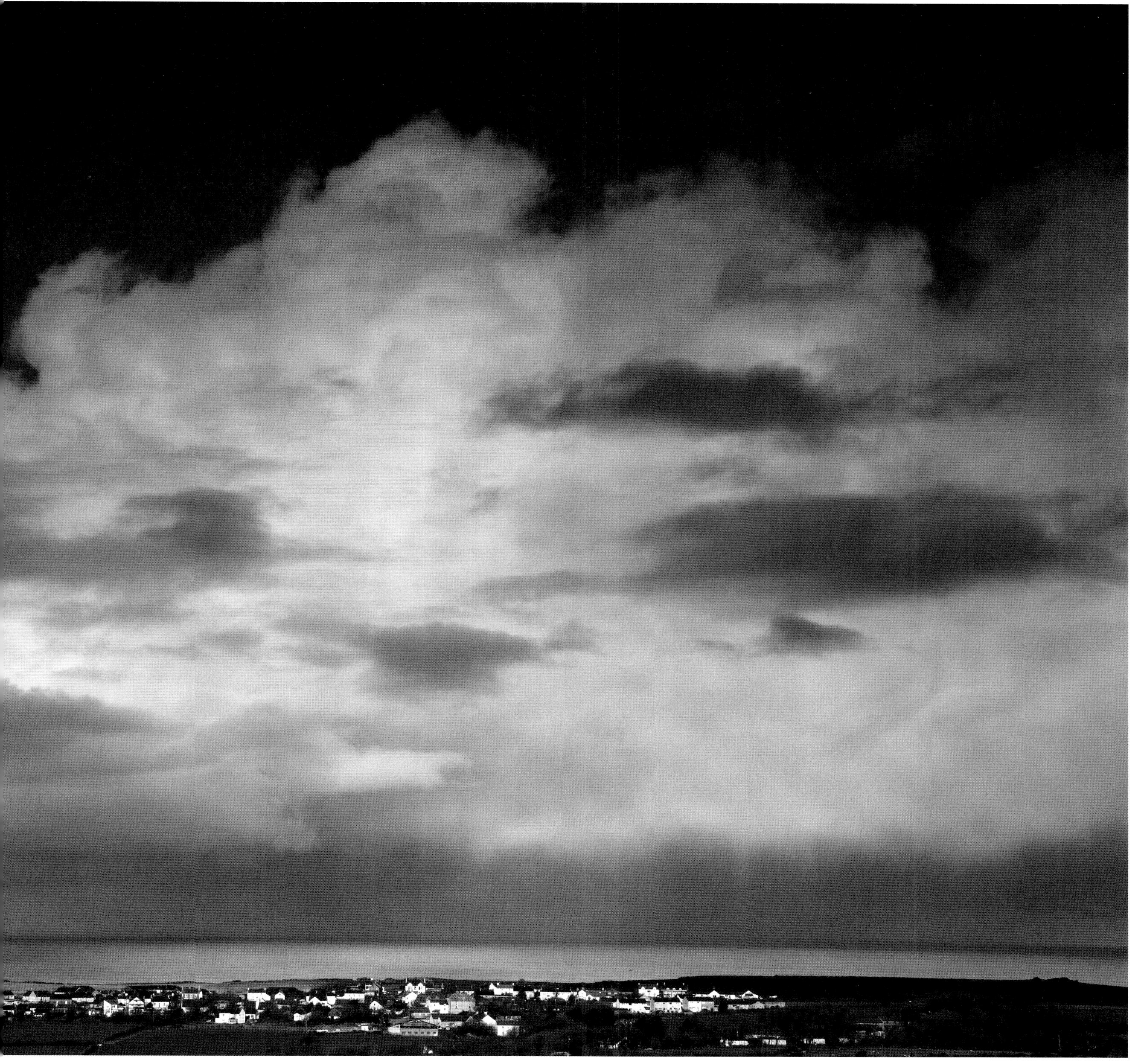

THE POINT, LITTLE HAVEN

From The Point you get the most breathtaking vista of St Brides Bay sweeping all the way round through Broad Haven, Nolton, Druidston and Newgale to St Davids Head. The coastal drive from Little Haven to Newgale is idyllic, taking in some of Pembrokeshire's most glorious beaches in the space of just a few short miles. The old cottage in the foreground, which must have taken some serious batterings from the weather in its time, provided the perfect lead into this image, with The Point over to the left. I particularly like the heavy, brooding menace of the sky.

Plate 24

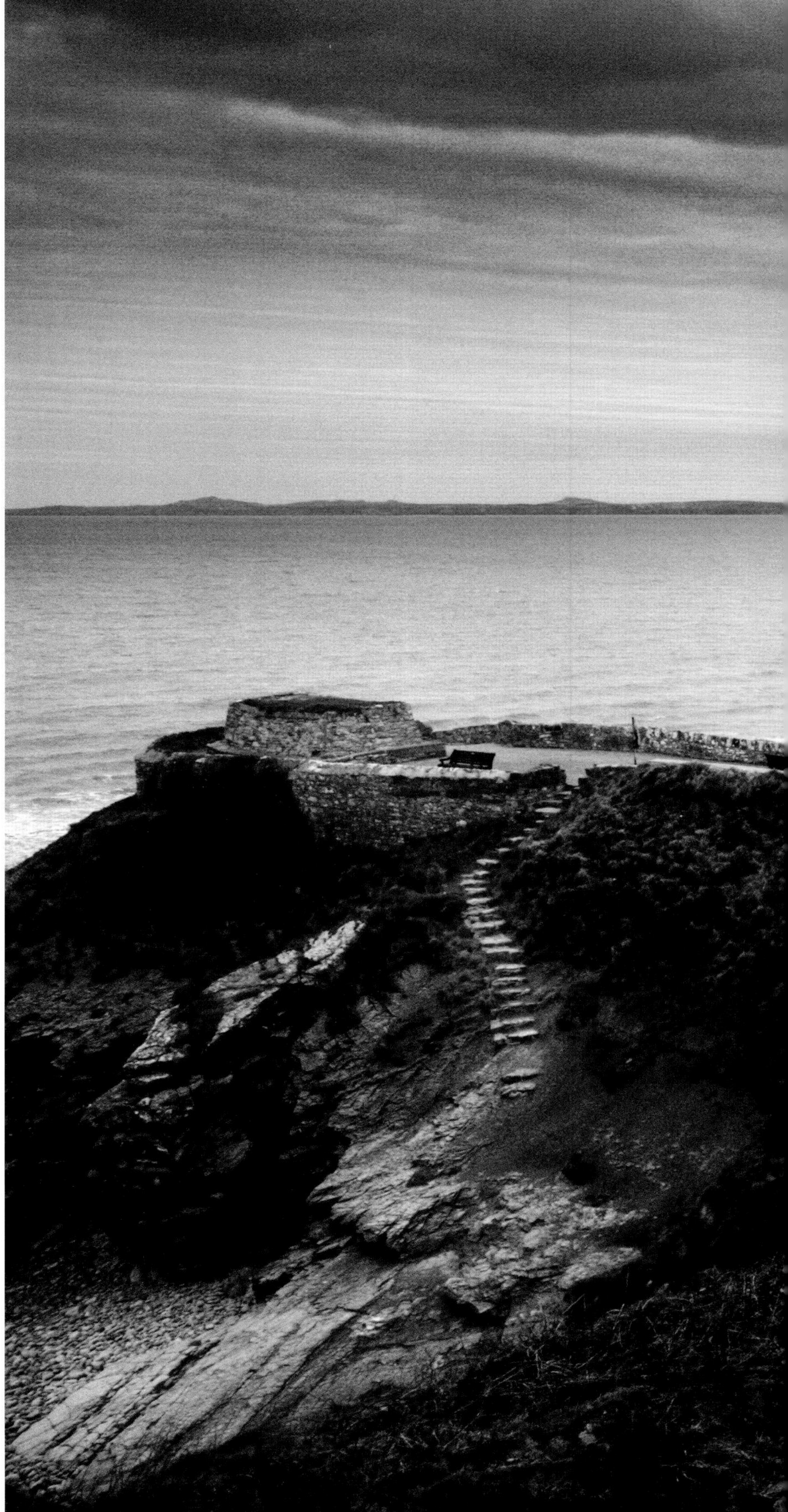

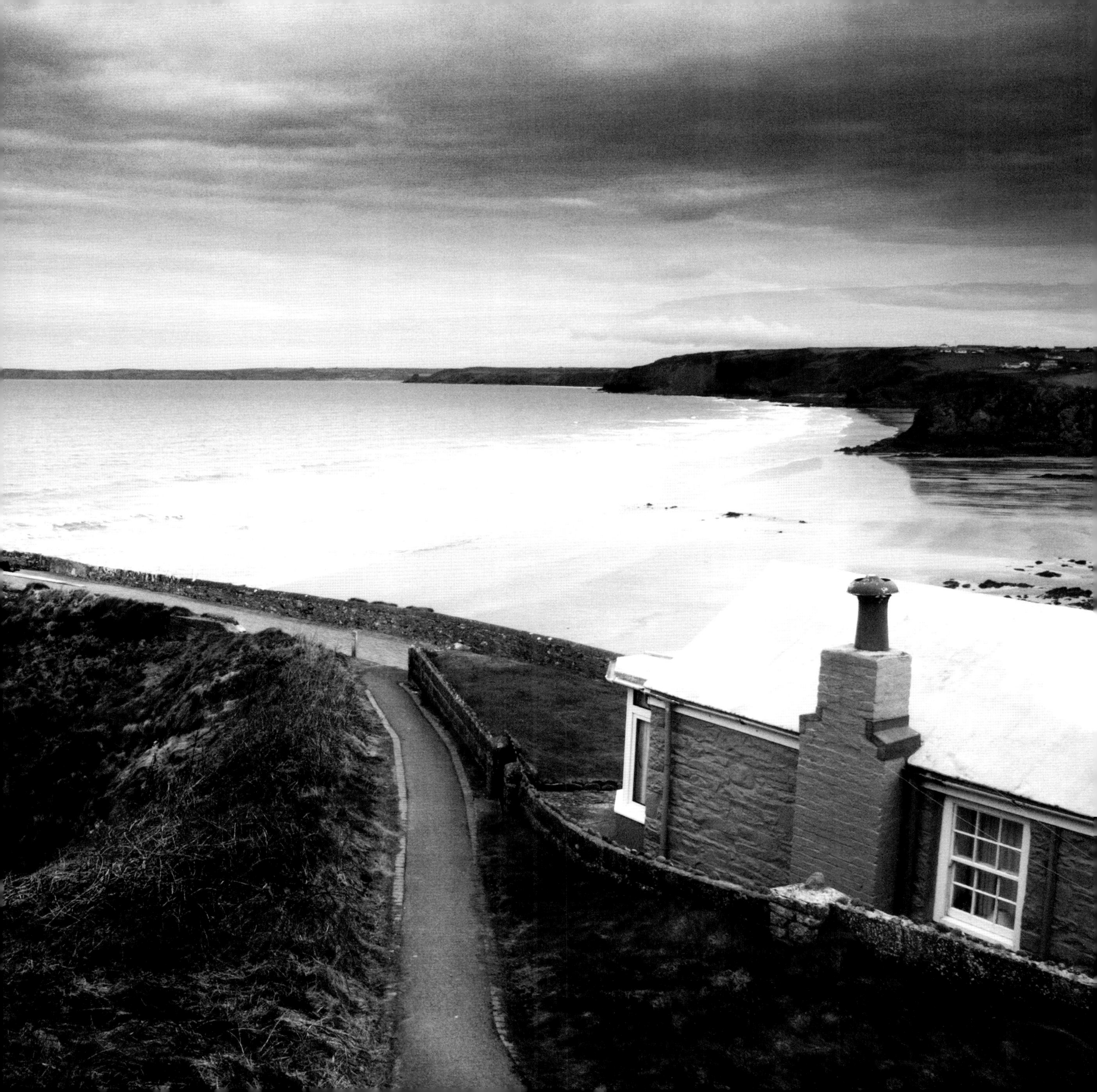

TRELEDDYD FAWR II, NEAR ST DAVIDS

This photograph gives you just a tantalising glimpse of what awaits at the top of the lane. It is a worn-out and ramshackle old place but a vitally important witness to our heritage and a physical reminder of the way our recent ancestors lived. When originally built it would probably have had a thatched roof, which was subsequently replaced with Abereiddi slate and a grout render to protect the slates, which were of inferior quality, from the harsh weather. Nothing is symmetrical and there are no straight lines – and it is all the more beautiful for it.

Plate 25

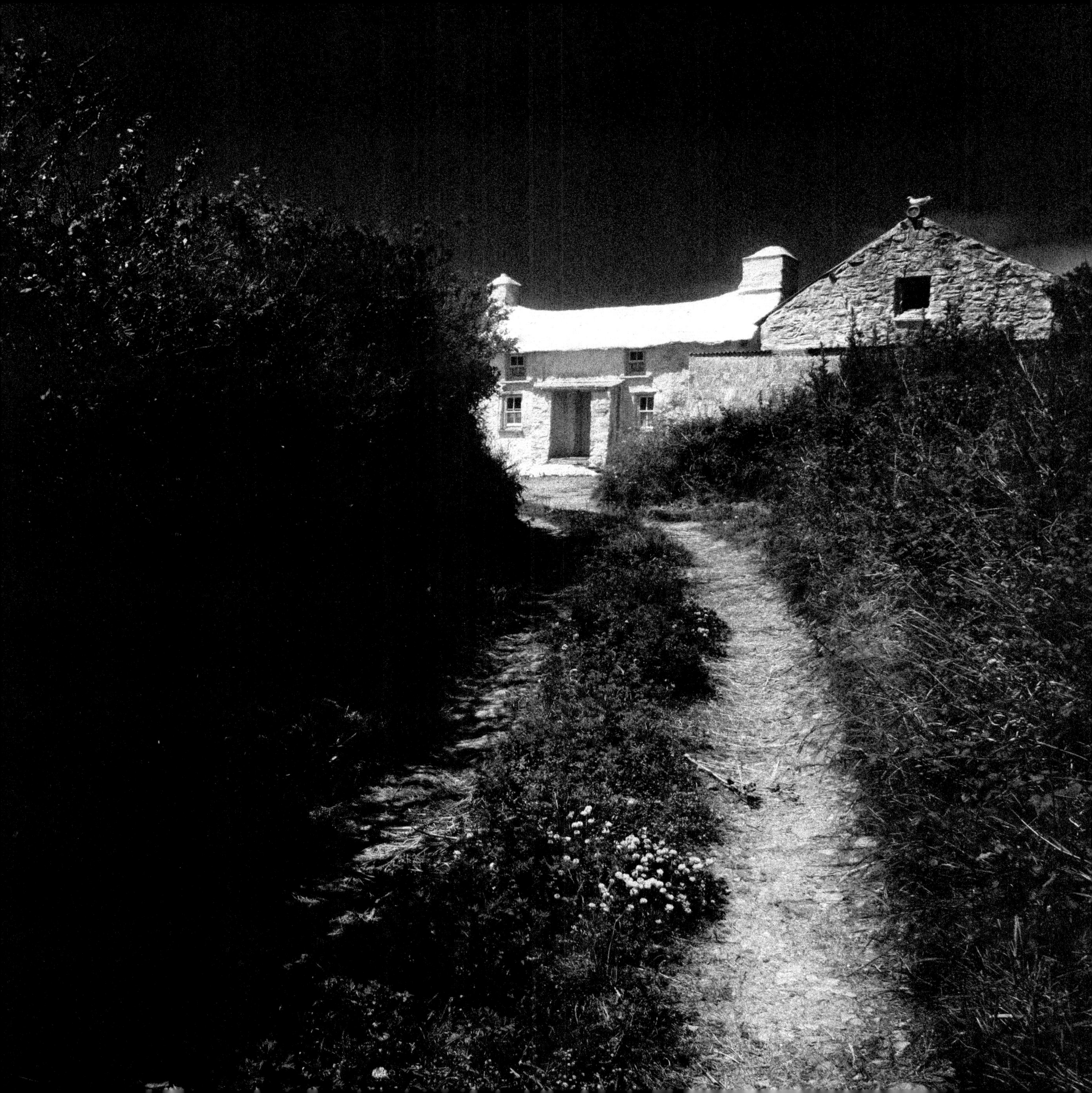

THE CROWS

Walking through woodland, I noticed lots of crows overhead making their usual excitable racket. I found a spot where a number of treetops converged leaving an area of open sky between them, lay flat on my back and waited for the crows to congregate. I set the camera on a high film speed setting to freeze their flying motion, which also adds an atmospheric graininess to the image. A duotone tint was applied to give some warmth. A simple yet evocative photograph.

Plate 26

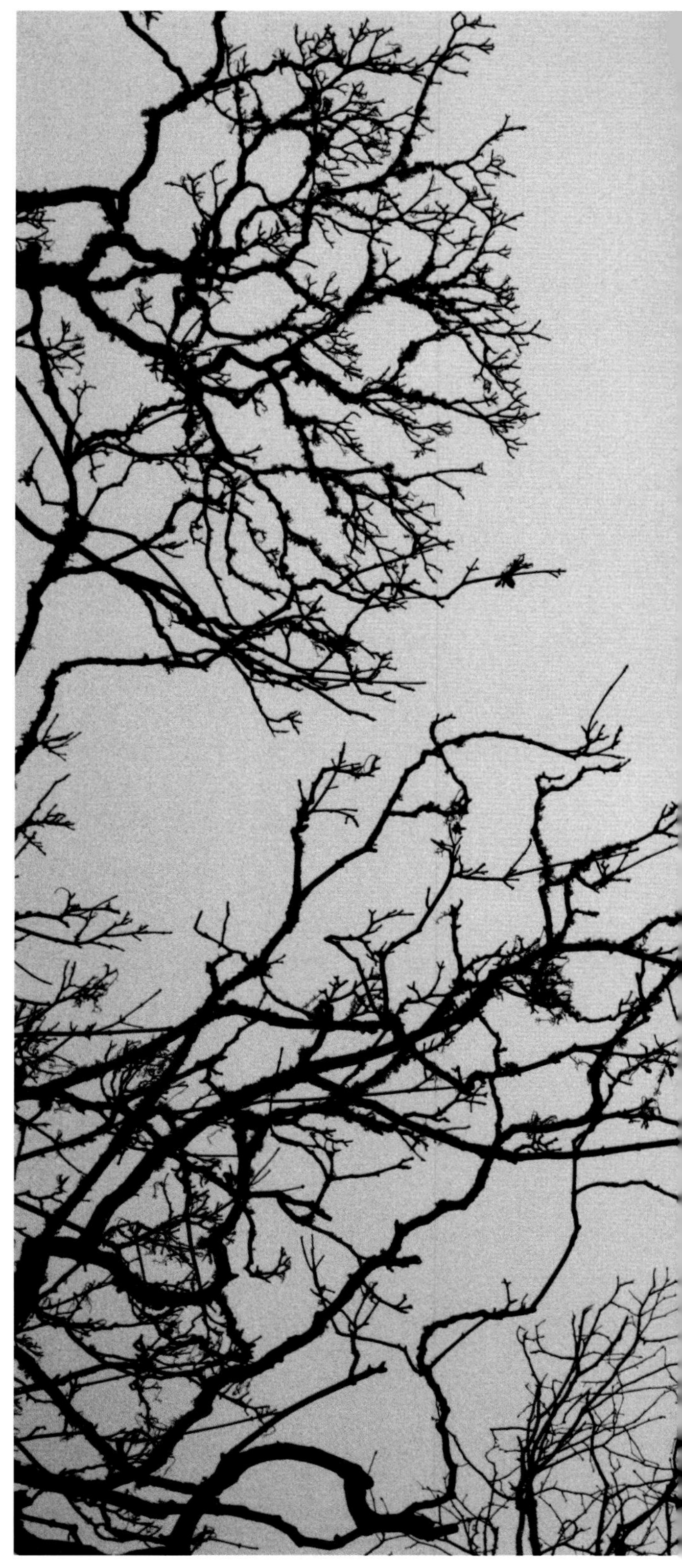

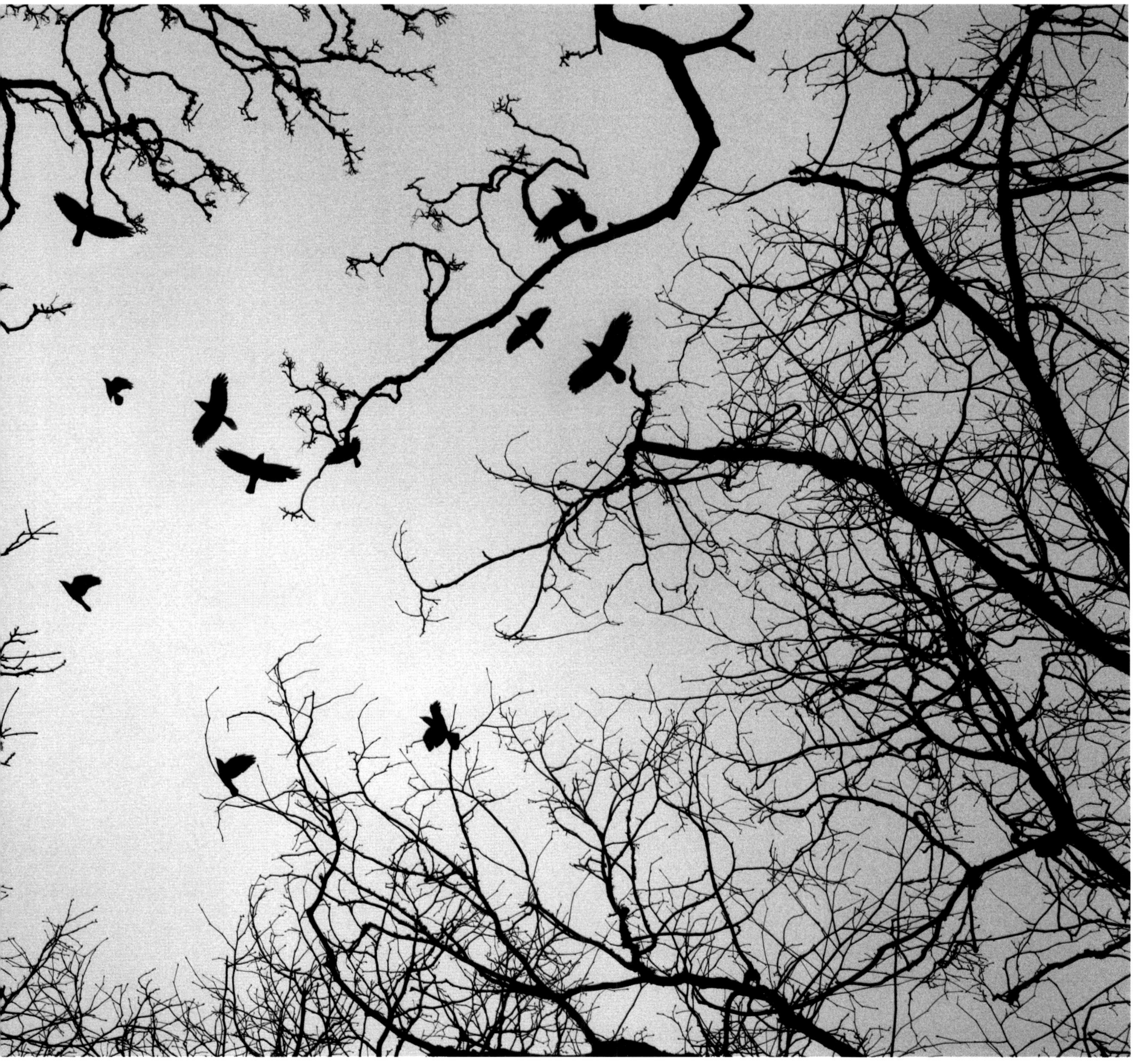

PORTHSTINIAN, NEAR ST DAVIDS

There has been a lifeboat station on this site since 1869 and the selfless volunteer crews from the St Davids area are reckoned to have saved 360 lives during that time. I like the broad sweep of this landscape from the jutting cliffs of Penmaen Melyn on the left, past the lifeboat station, and on to Ynys Dinas on the right. The treacherous swirling waters of Ramsay Sound separate the mainland from the nature reserve of Ramsay Island in the distance.

Plate 27

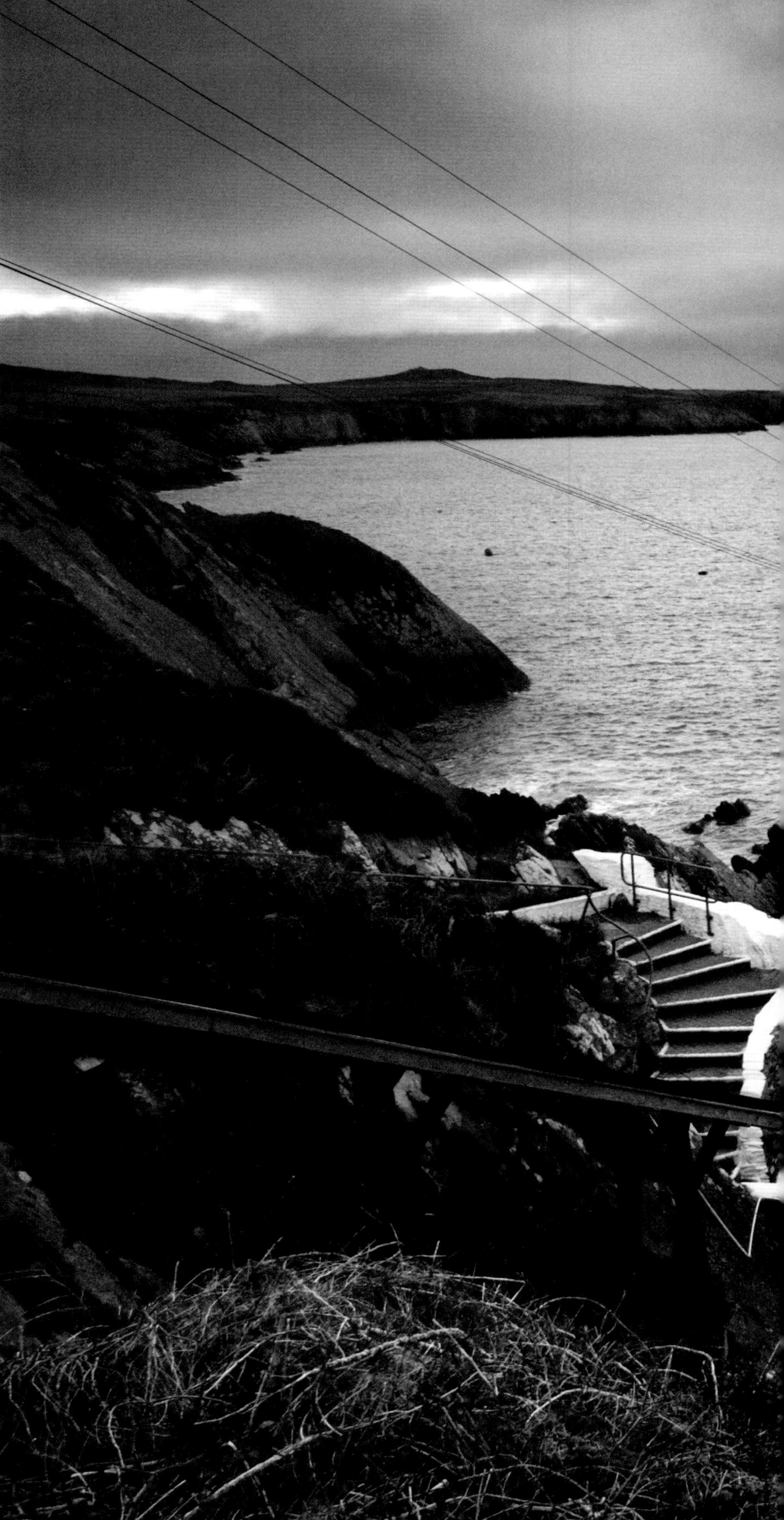

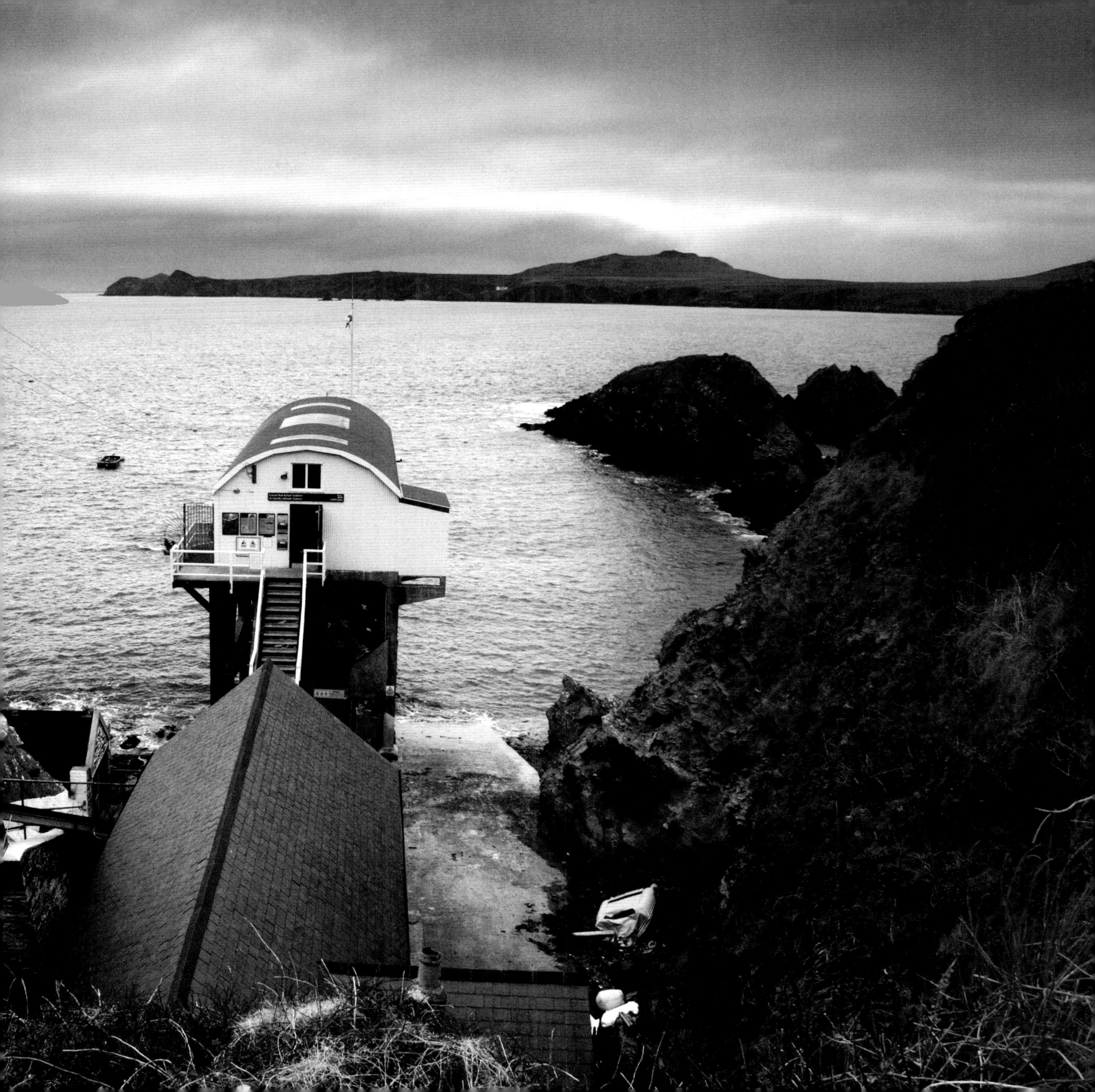

TRINANT, THE PRESELI HILLS

The inclusion of buildings in my landscape photography is very important to me. They lend a sense of 'being' to an image – that feeling of homeliness and belonging which appeals to the human spirit. The landscape is lived in and these buildings are part of that story. Questions abound, such as who once lived there, what hopes and aspirations did they have, and what caused them to leave. The moment that front door was locked for the last time, the process of decay began. In the course of a generation, a family home has degenerated into an empty ruin.

Plate 28

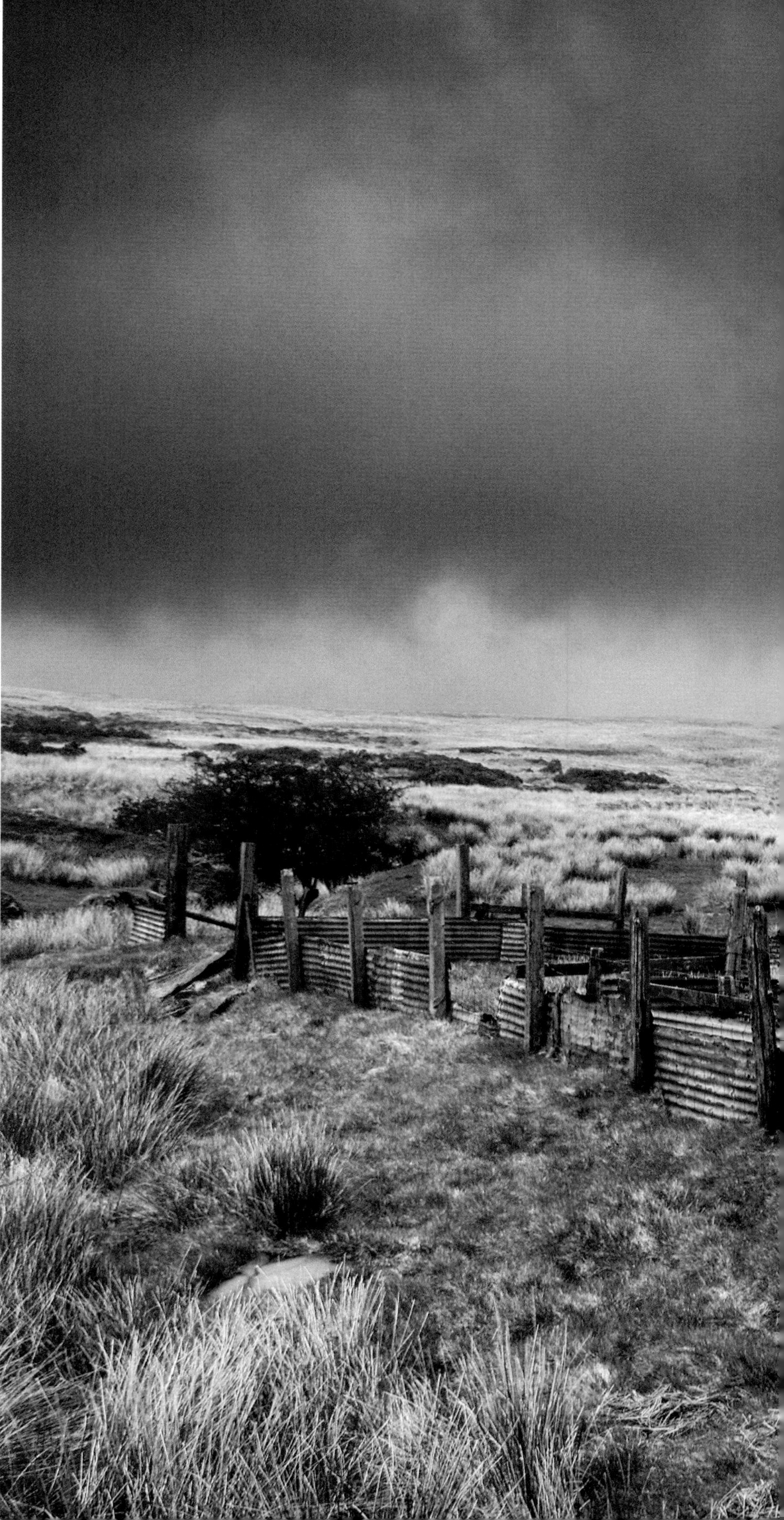

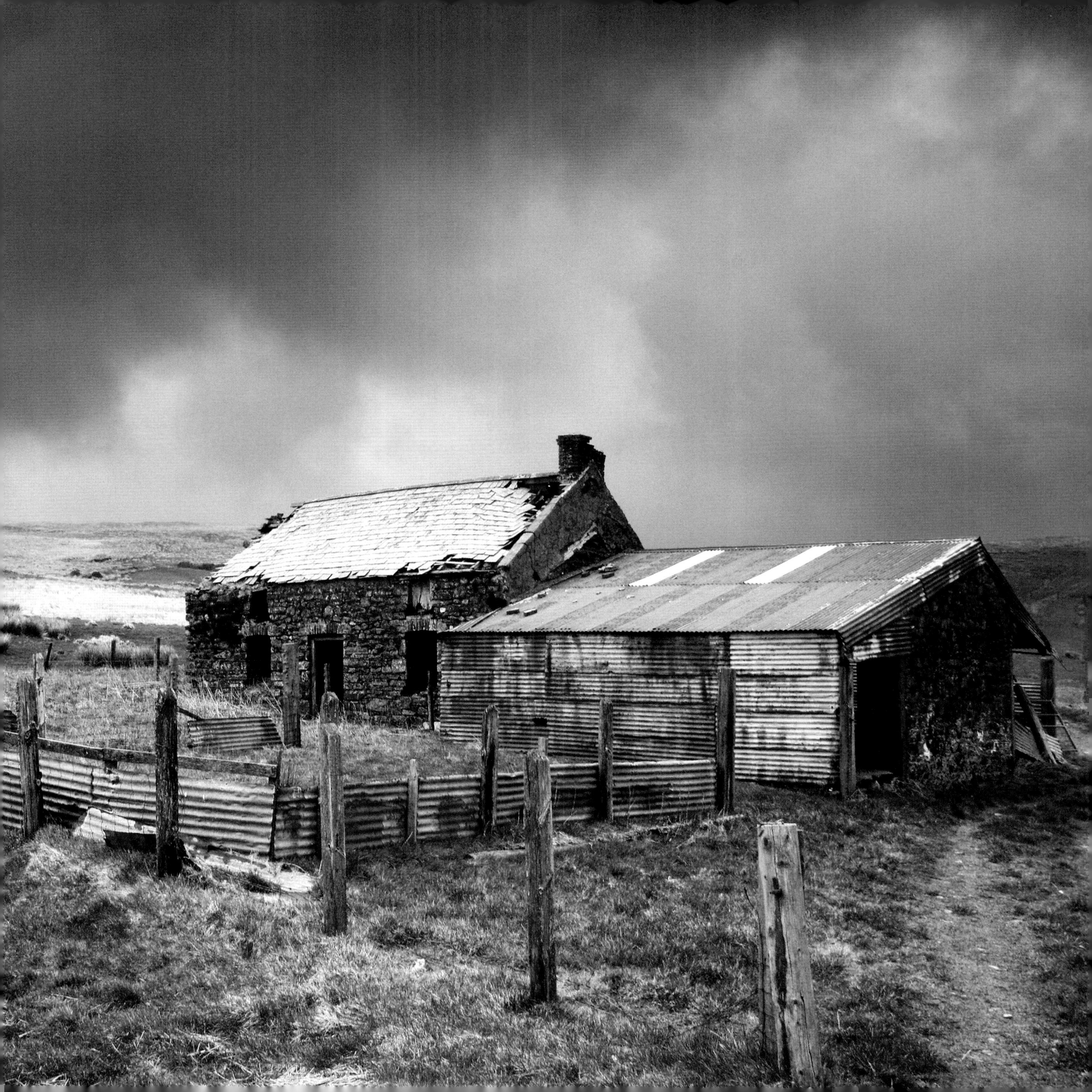

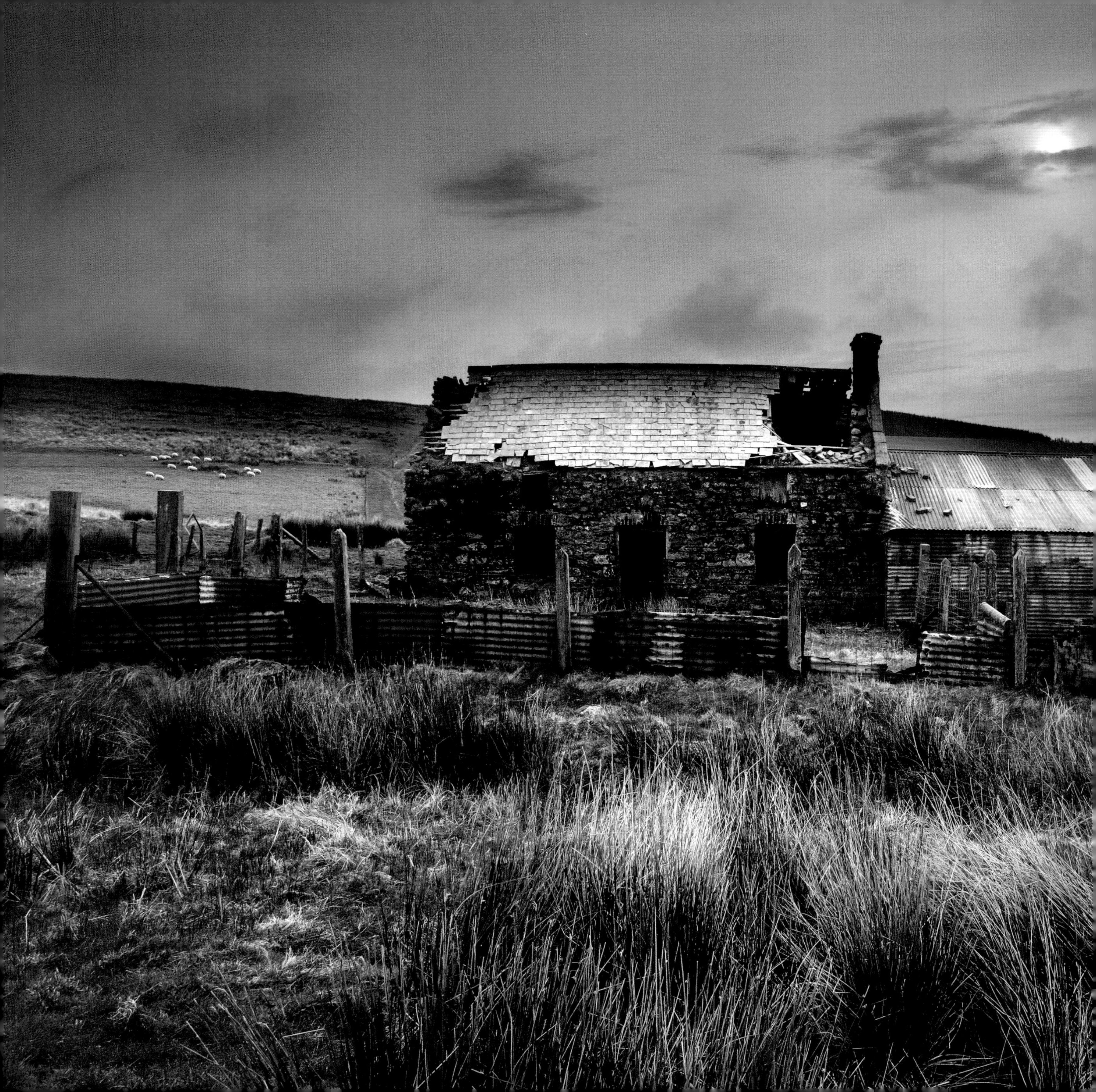

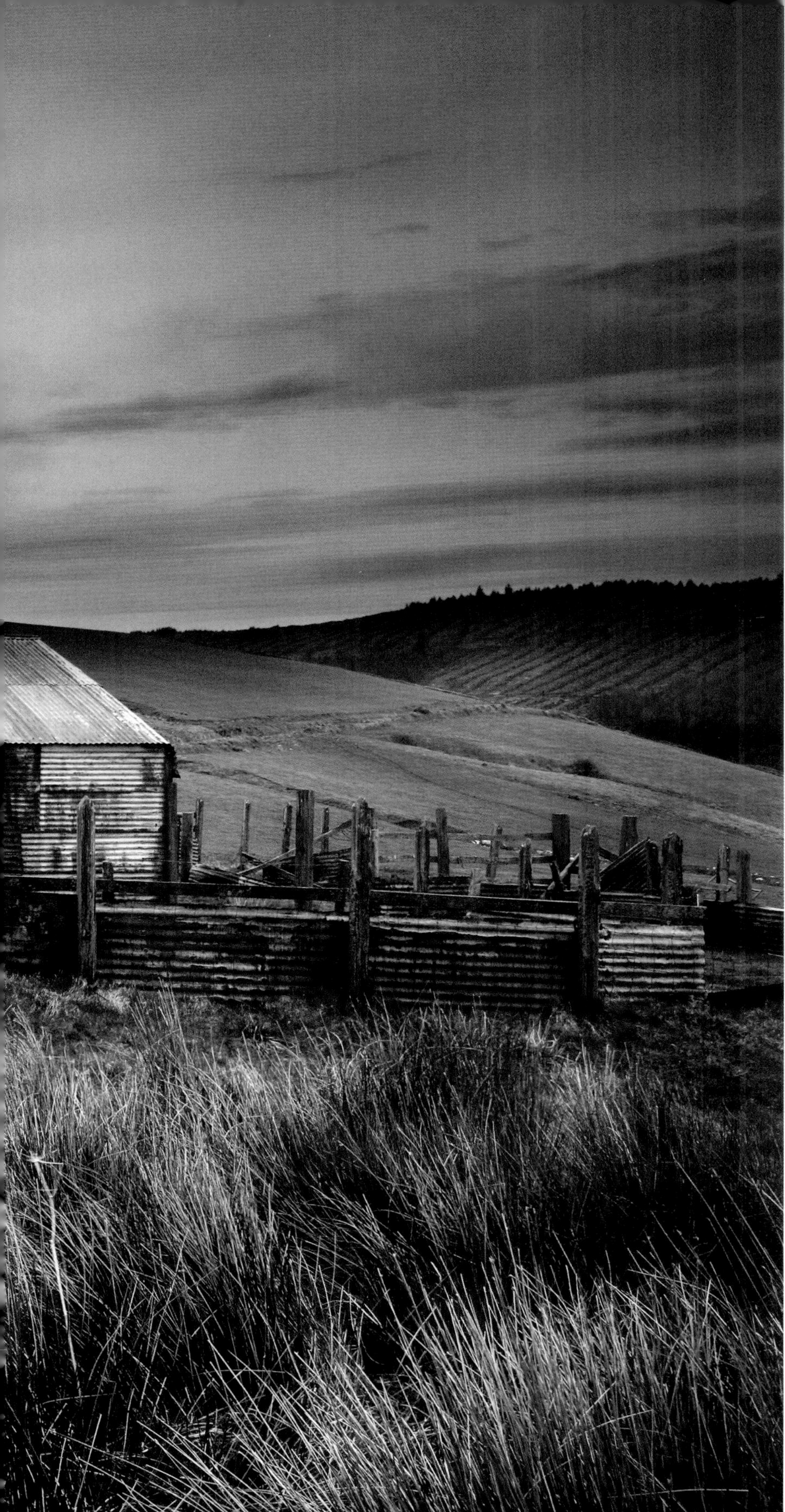

TRINANT II, THE PRESELI HILLS

A year after photographing Trinant for the first time I returned with a view to documenting its slow but inexorable descent into dereliction. This place had really got under my skin. I intend taking one photograph a year charting its collapse. In the year since the first photograph you can see that the roof has fallen in considerably on the right-hand side. I expect that without intervention, within our lifetime it will be reduced to a heap of stones. An archeological project a few hundred years down the line perhaps.

Plate 29

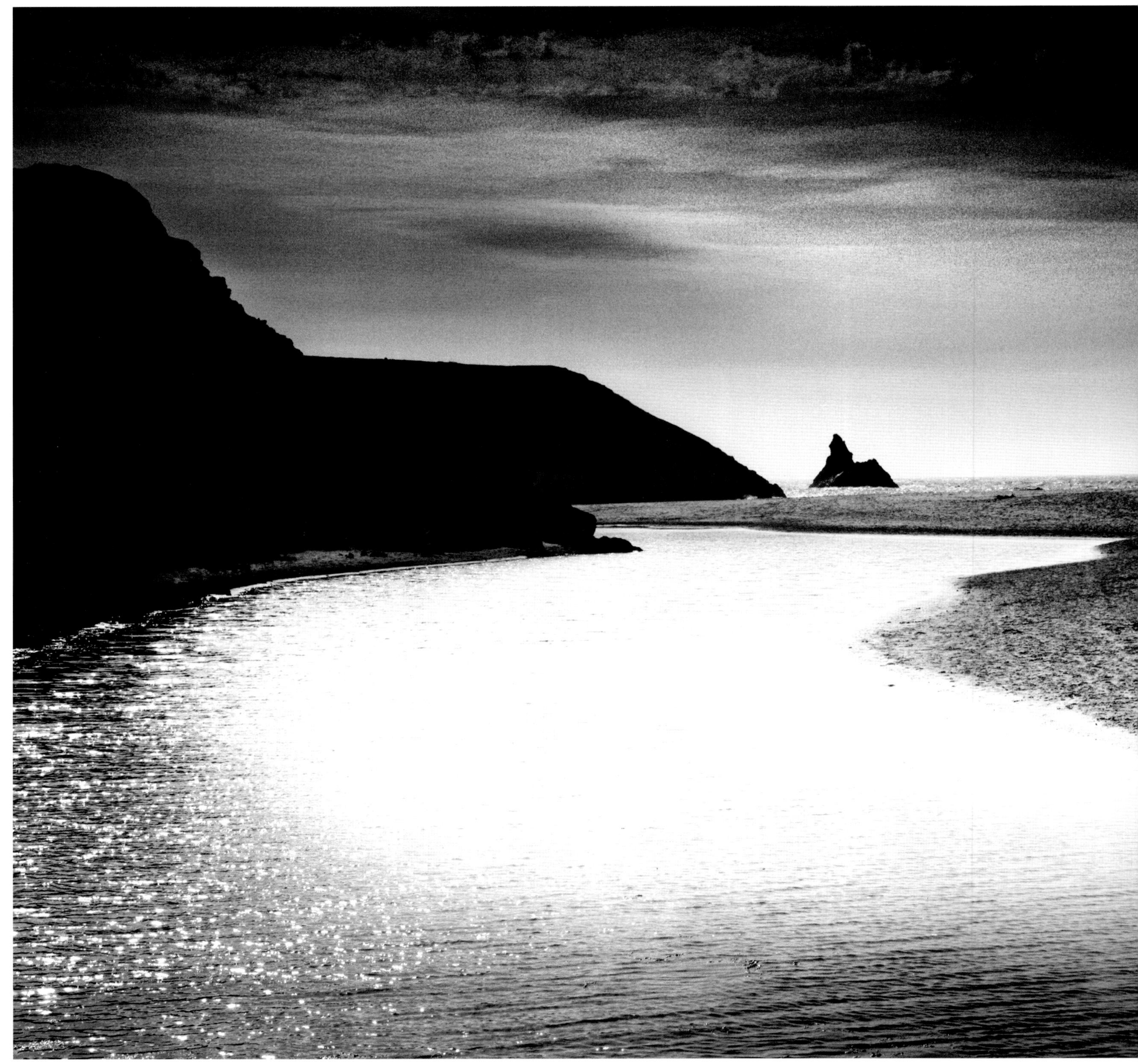

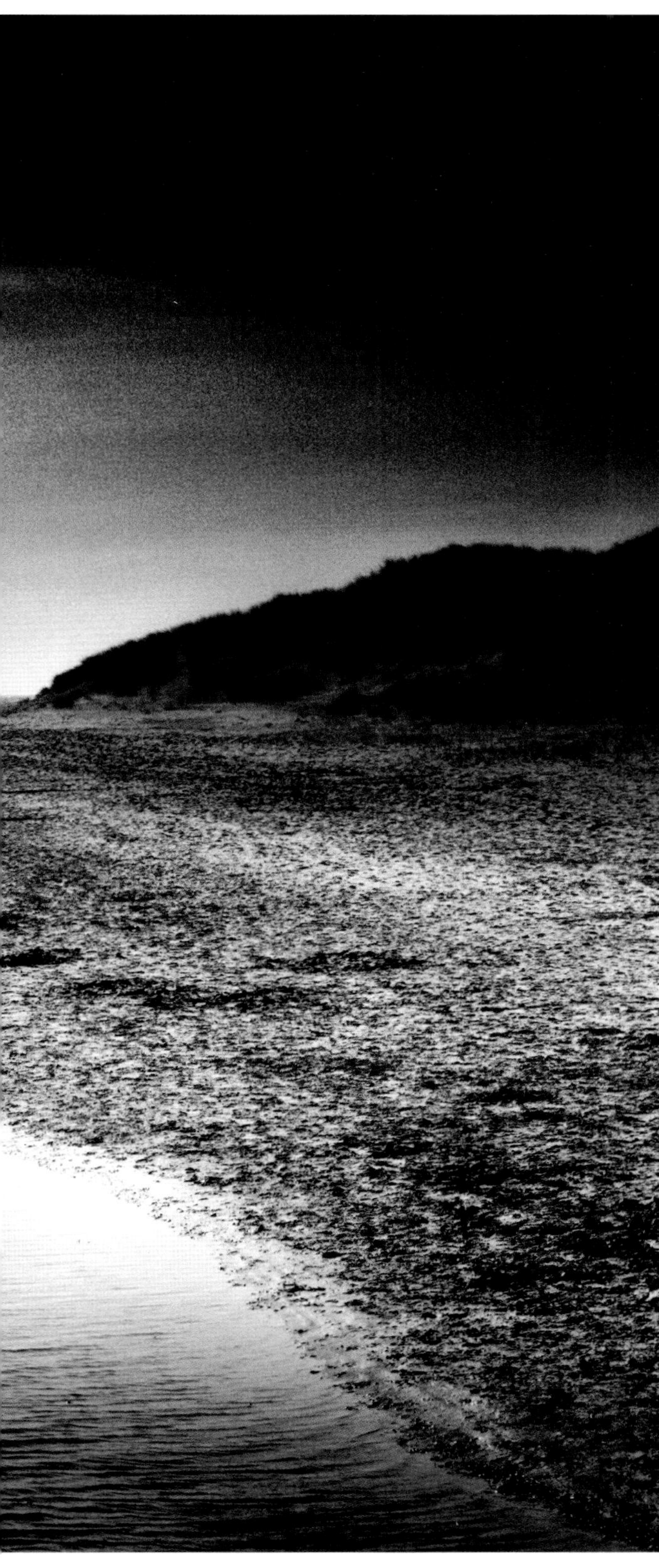

BROAD HAVEN SOUTH

Some subjects suit extremes of contrast. This image is a juxtaposition of rock shapes, water and sand. The high-speed film setting lends the photograph heaps of graininess and drama, with deep blacks, near whites and not a lot of tonal gradation between those extremes. The positioning of Church Rock dead centre gives the image a sense of focus and you are led from the foreground by the outflow of water from Bosherston lily ponds, a protected nature reserve.

Plate 30

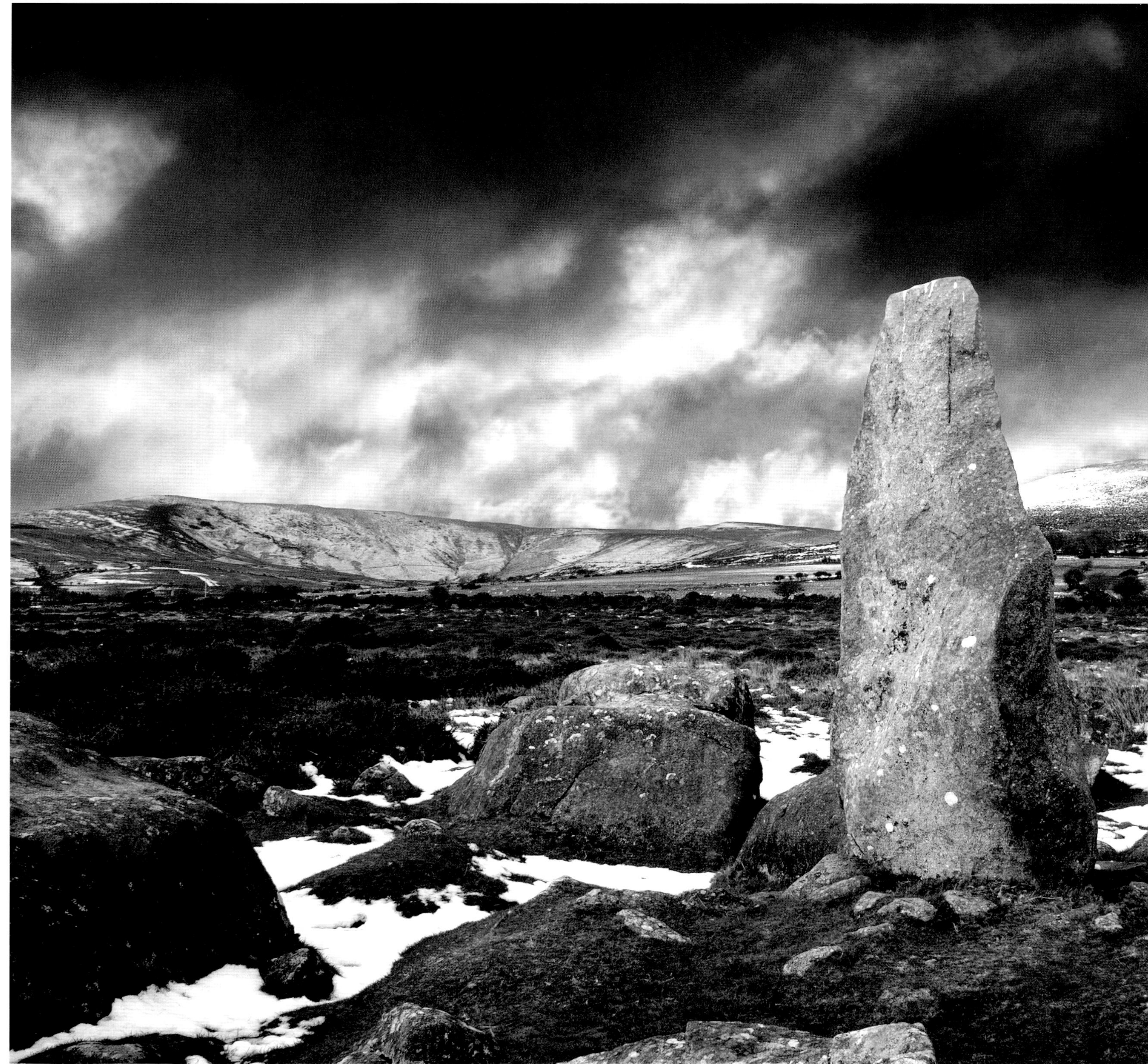

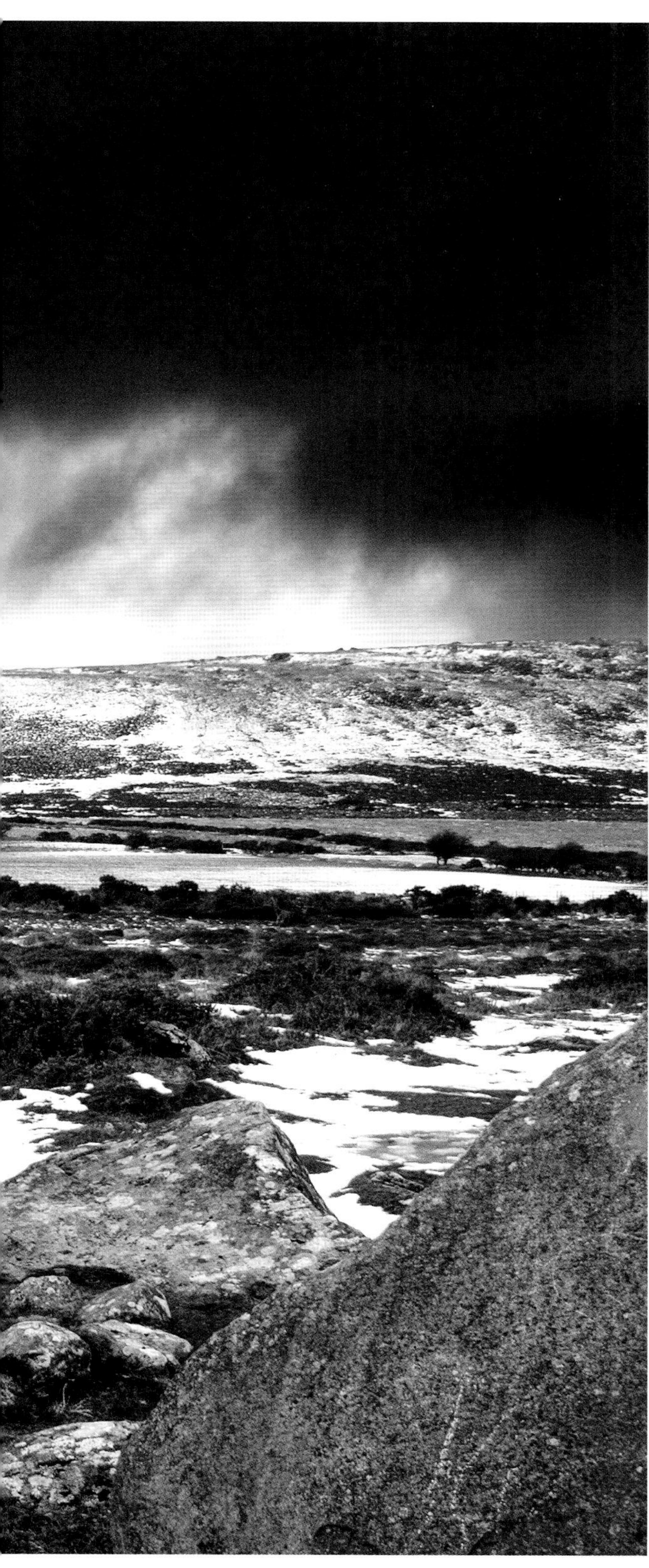

CARREG WALDO, THE PRESELI HILLS

Being a predominantly winter landscape photographer means getting wet or cold on a regular basis, quite often both at the same time. But I was in luck this day as it was dry and I only risked a mild bout of hypothermia from the snowy conditions. These stones are marked with a plaque to Waldo Williams, one of Wales' most famous Welsh-language poets, who found inspiration in this spot. Thankfully a flask of hot coffee was close by.

Plate 31

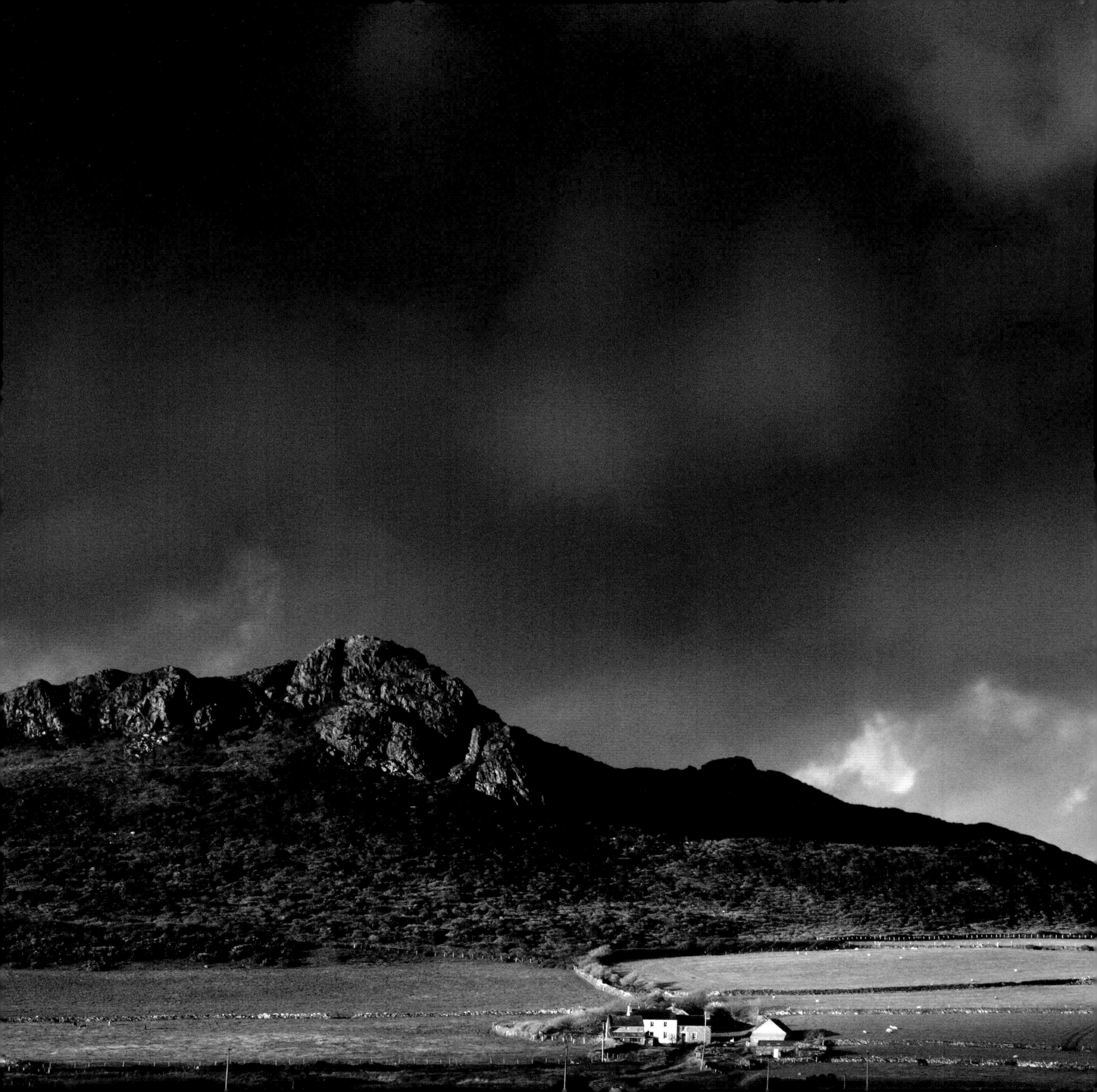

CARN LLIDI,
NEAR ST DAVIDS

Carn Llidi dominates St Davids Head, casting its imposing shadow over the nearby beach at Whitesands. I was drawn to this composition by the vulnerability of the farmstead at the mercy of the mountain in its backyard and with that very angry sky looming menacingly overhead. The often delicate tripartite relationship between man, the landscape and the elements is a common theme in my work and is demonstrated perfectly in this image.

Plate 32

GARN FAWR, STRUMBLE HEAD

This photograph has a timeless feel. If you had stood on this spot a hundred or so years ago the view would probably have appeared the same. Perhaps the roof may have had a grout render to protect the slates, which in all probability would have come from the nearby Abereiddi quarry. It is difficult these days to imagine what life at the base of this rocky outcrop must have been like back then. Pretty tough probably sums it up. Take a wander around any local burial ground and the common theme is death at a very young age by today's standards. Life was hard and middle age was considered a feat.

Plate 33

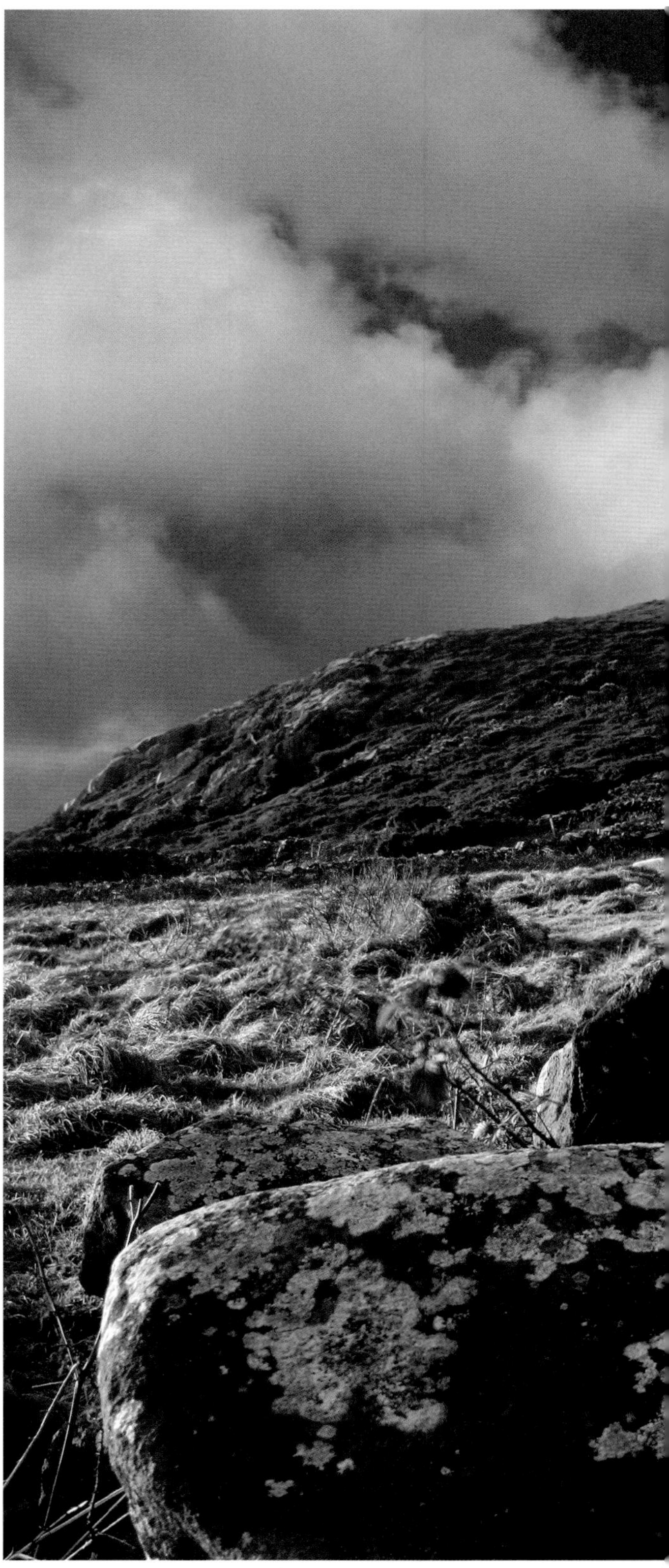

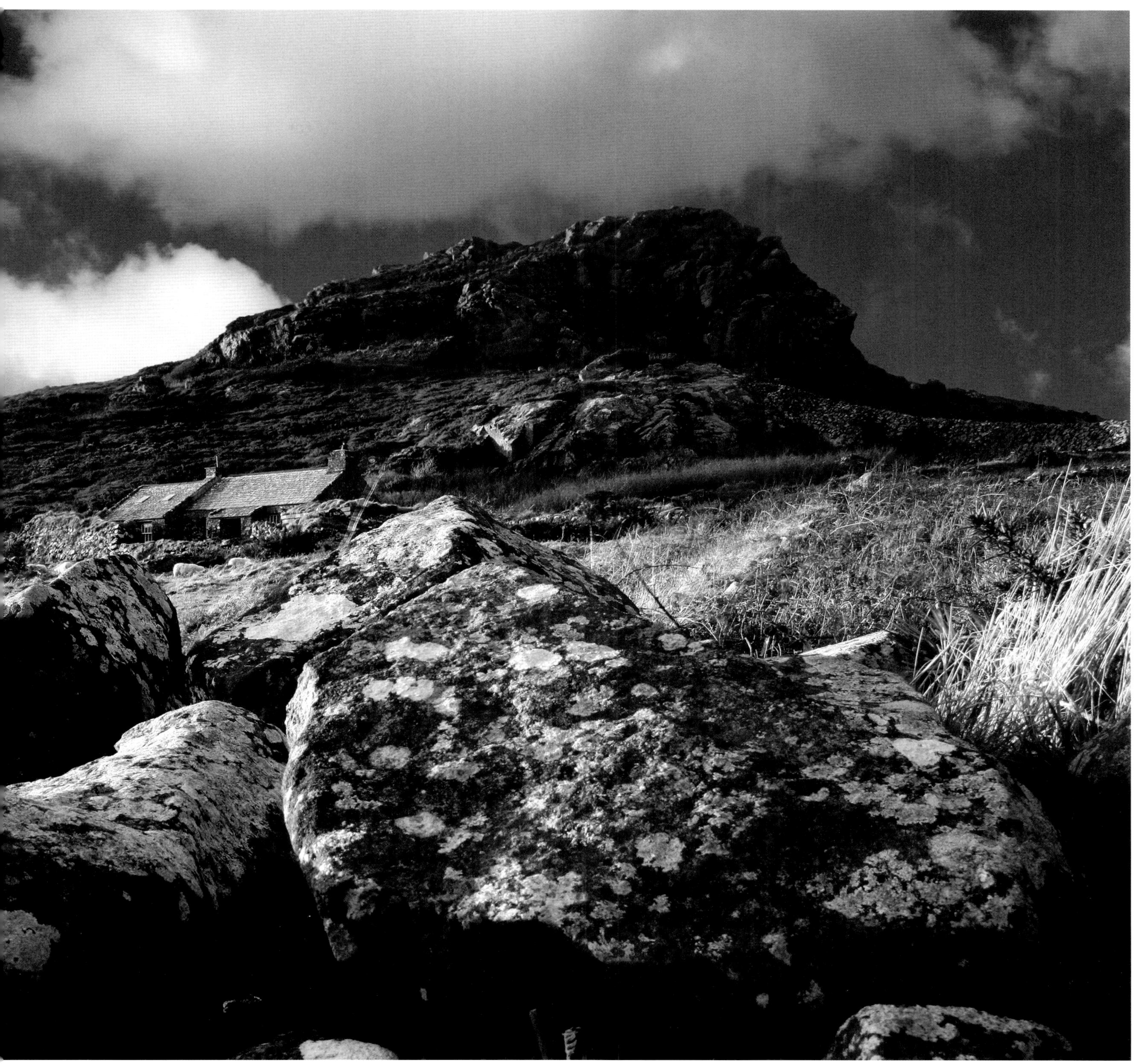

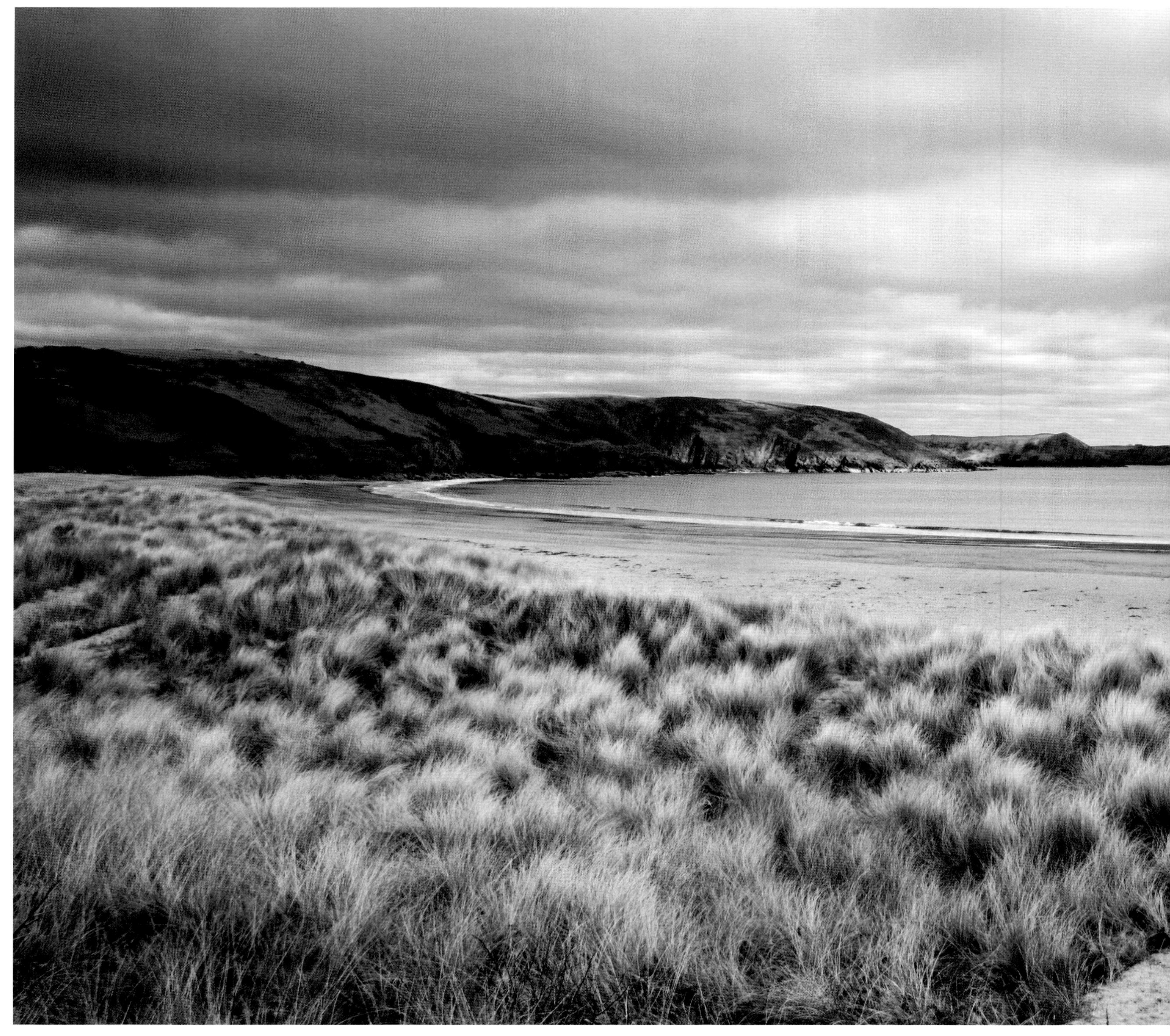

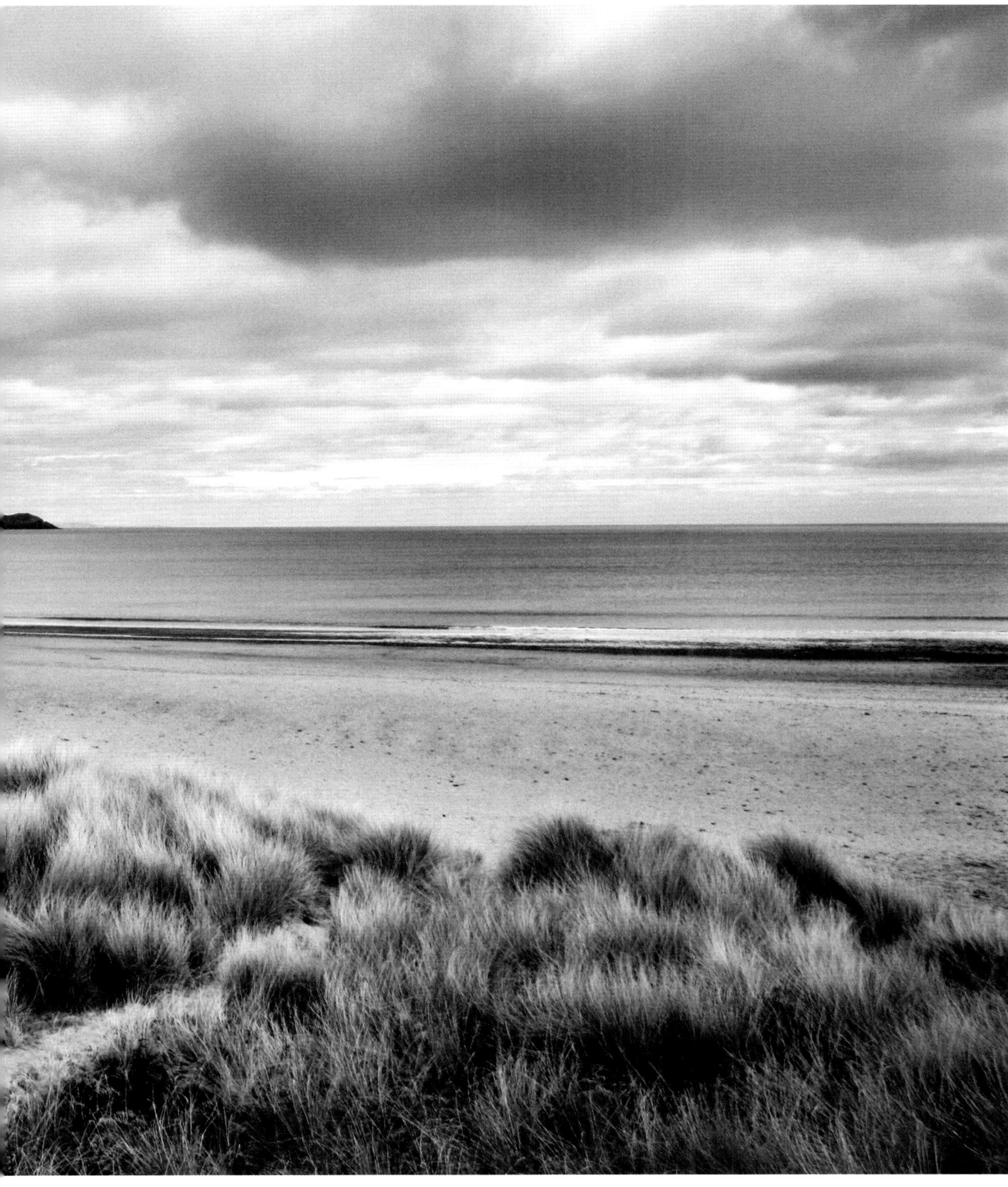

FRESHWATER EAST

Taken in early spring, I love the swaying grasses and full sky in this photograph. There is a hint of the heat and haze of summer just around the corner but without as yet the throng of visitors and locals who idolise this stretch of sand. Freshwater East and its neighbours Barafundle and Broad Haven South represent a magical trinity of Pembrokeshire beaches. Each has its own distinct character but all are truly stunning places to idle away a few hours on a sunny day.

Plate 34

GERNOS FACH,
THE PRESELI HILLS

As I approached this farm down a winding dirt track I could hear dogs barking. I pulled up by the house to be greeted by what seemed like a pair of rabid cross-breeds snapping at the driver's door. My inclination was to turn round and drive back the way I had come, but it had been a long and bumpy trek and I wanted something to show for it. I opened the door and put a leg out. It remained attached to my body, so out I got. I am glad I persisted. I love the feeling of isolation, the wonderful collection of old farm machinery scattered in front of the house and the family's old Fiat car parked dead centre.

Plate 35

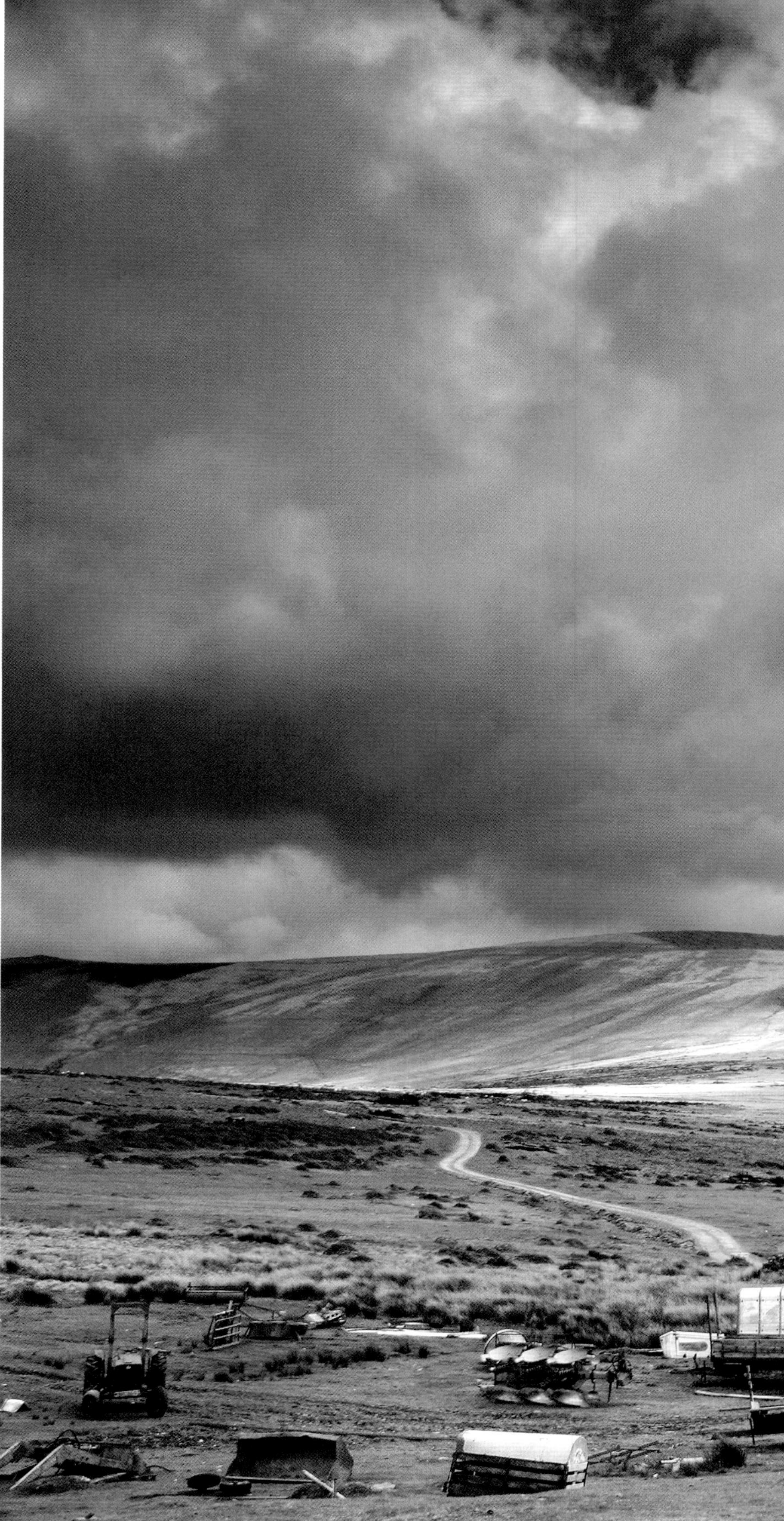

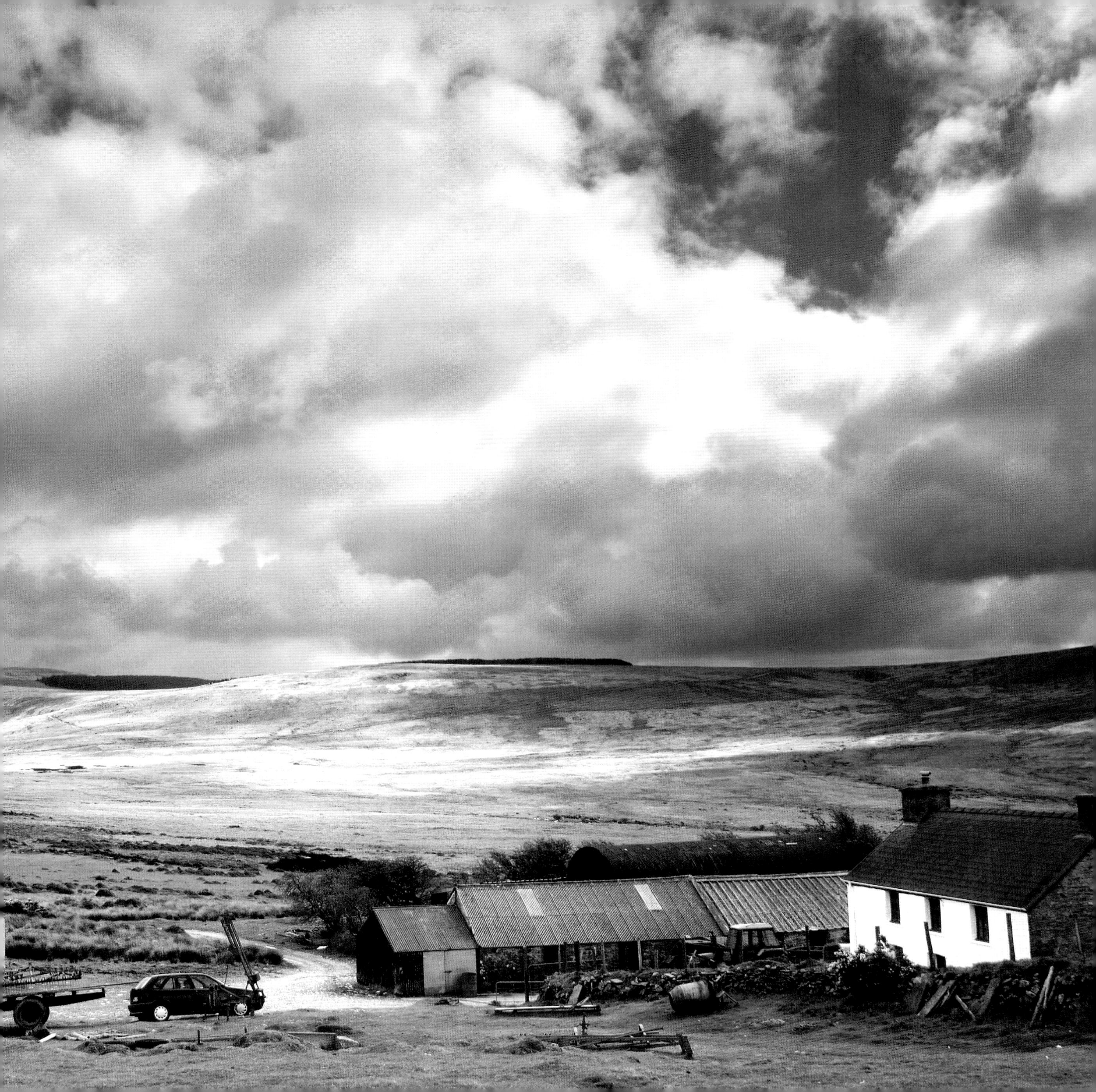

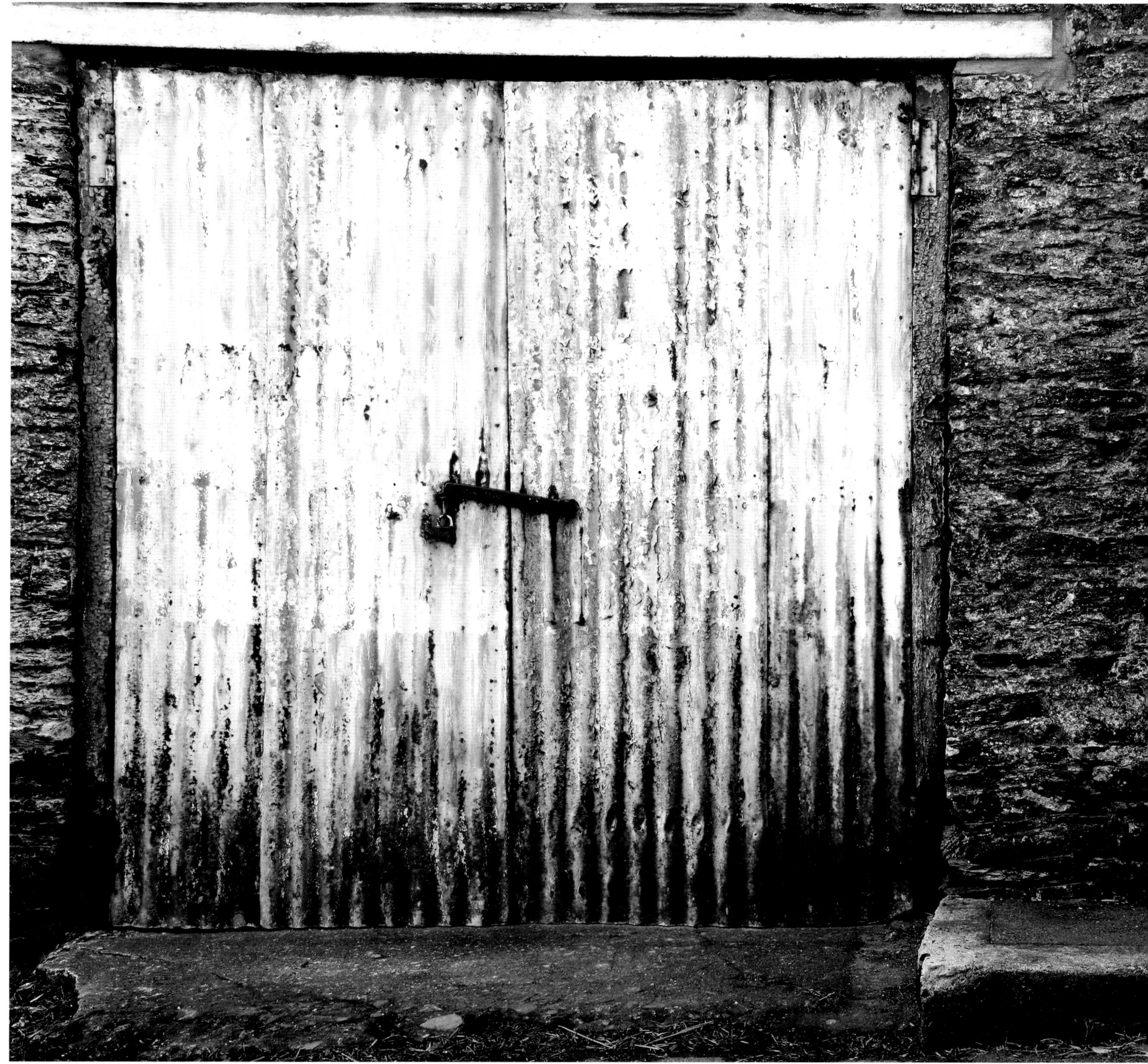

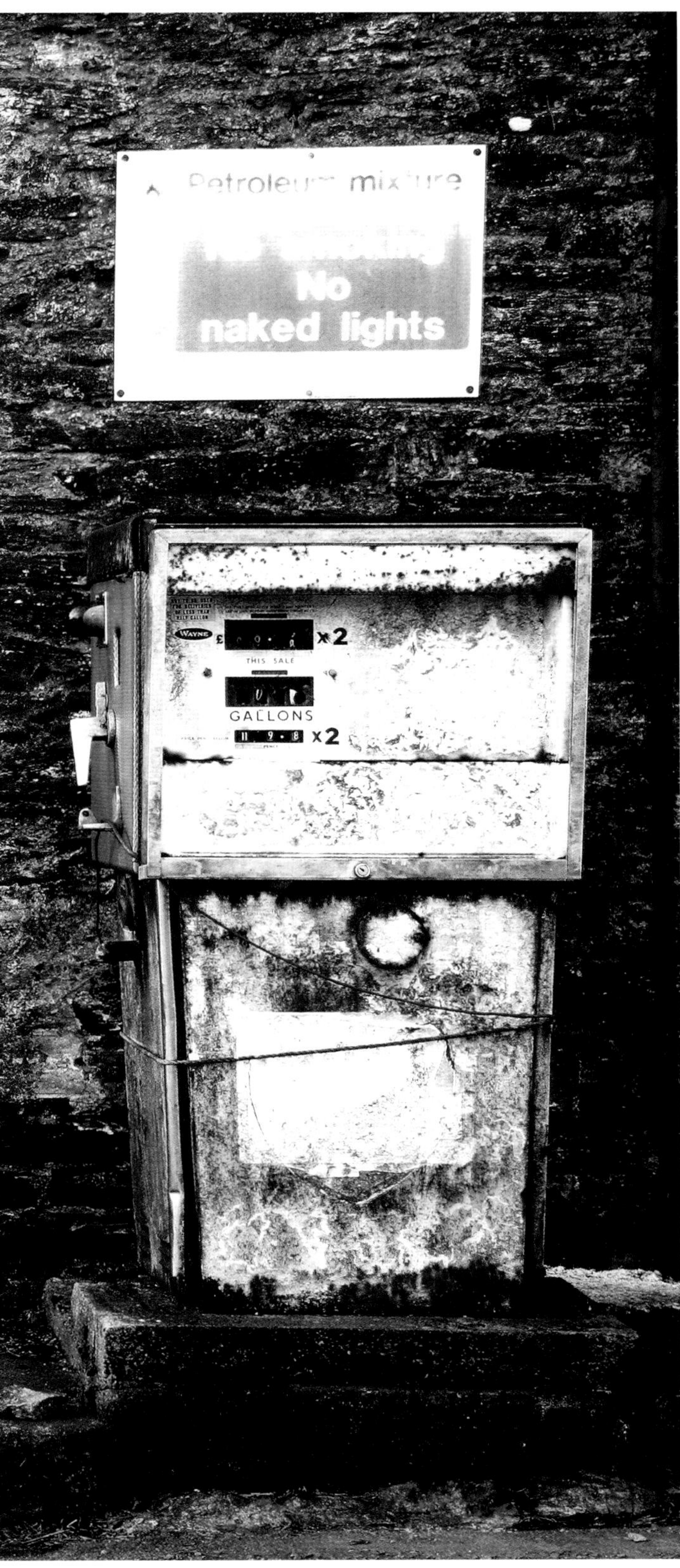

PETROL PUMP, MATHRY

There is a palpable sense of abandonment in this image. The last car to fill up must have called by a long time ago and the pump has been left to slowly rust and fall apart. The sign about switching your engine off is most definitely redundant. Businesses such as these were once the backbone of villages like Mathry. They fulfilled many functions, providing lifeblood to the immediate local economy, a social hub, and a sense of communal self-sufficiency.

Plate 36

PORT LION II

There is a particular smell to the river first thing in the morning when the tide is out and the mudflats are laid bare. A salty, almost acrid, scent that hits you right in the back of the throat. Combined with the fresh, crisp air of a new dawn, though, it is a truly intoxicating and heady concoction. If you don't believe me, try it. At that time of the day it's just you, deep gulps of salty mudflat-infused air and the birds. A great time and indeed an ideal excuse to do a bit of thinking and indulge in some quiet contemplation. Well worth getting up for and totally idyllic.

Plate 37

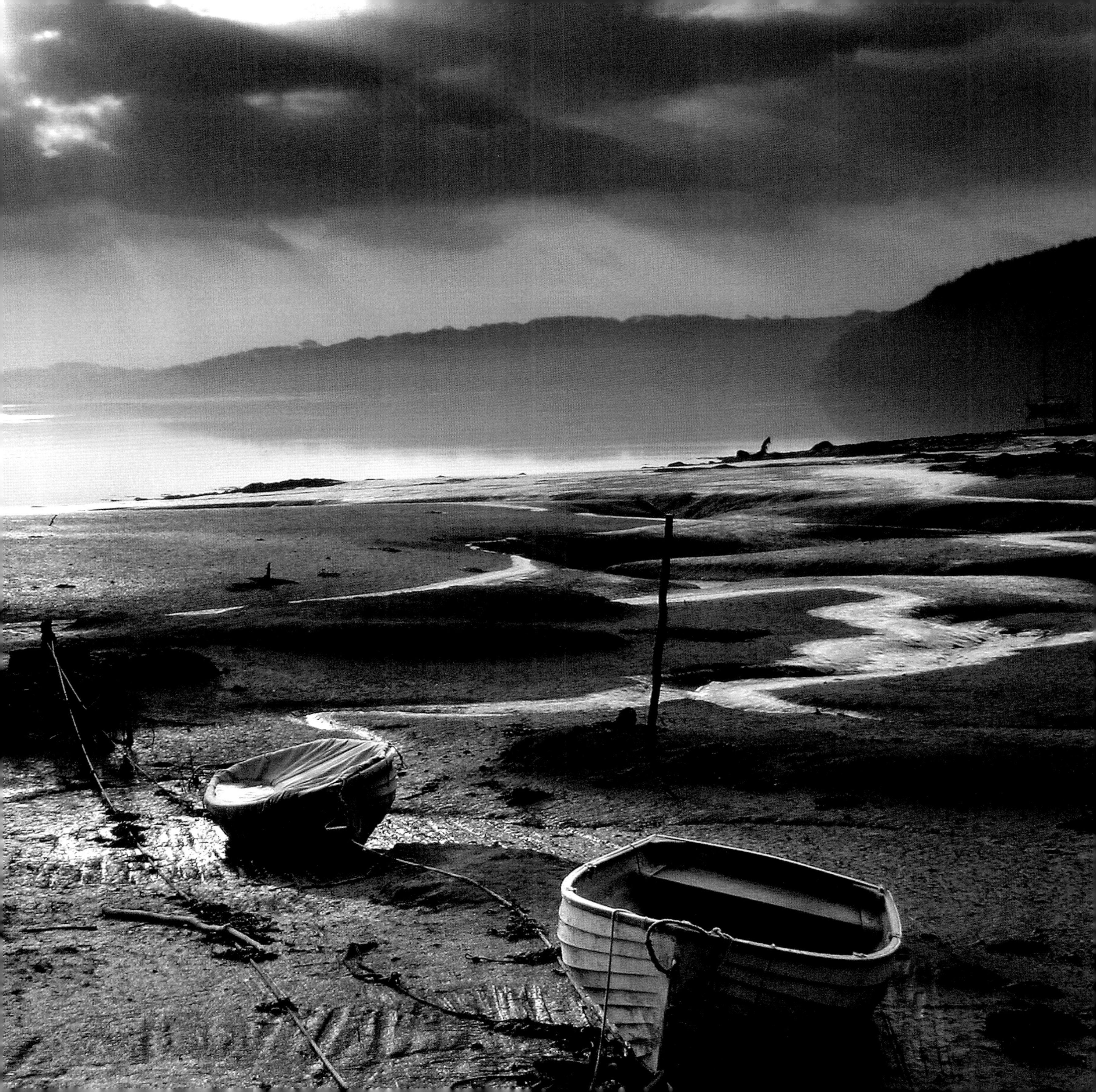

TOWARDS CARNINGLI, THE PRESELI HILLS

This was the third time I had returned to this spot. The previous occasions had been undermined by pretty ordinary skies but this time I was in luck. I used a medium focal length to compress the hills and create a meandering zigzag journey from the foreground through to infinity. But, of course, what makes this image is that huge billowing cloud rolling into view off the sea. Sometimes persistence does pay off.

Plate 38

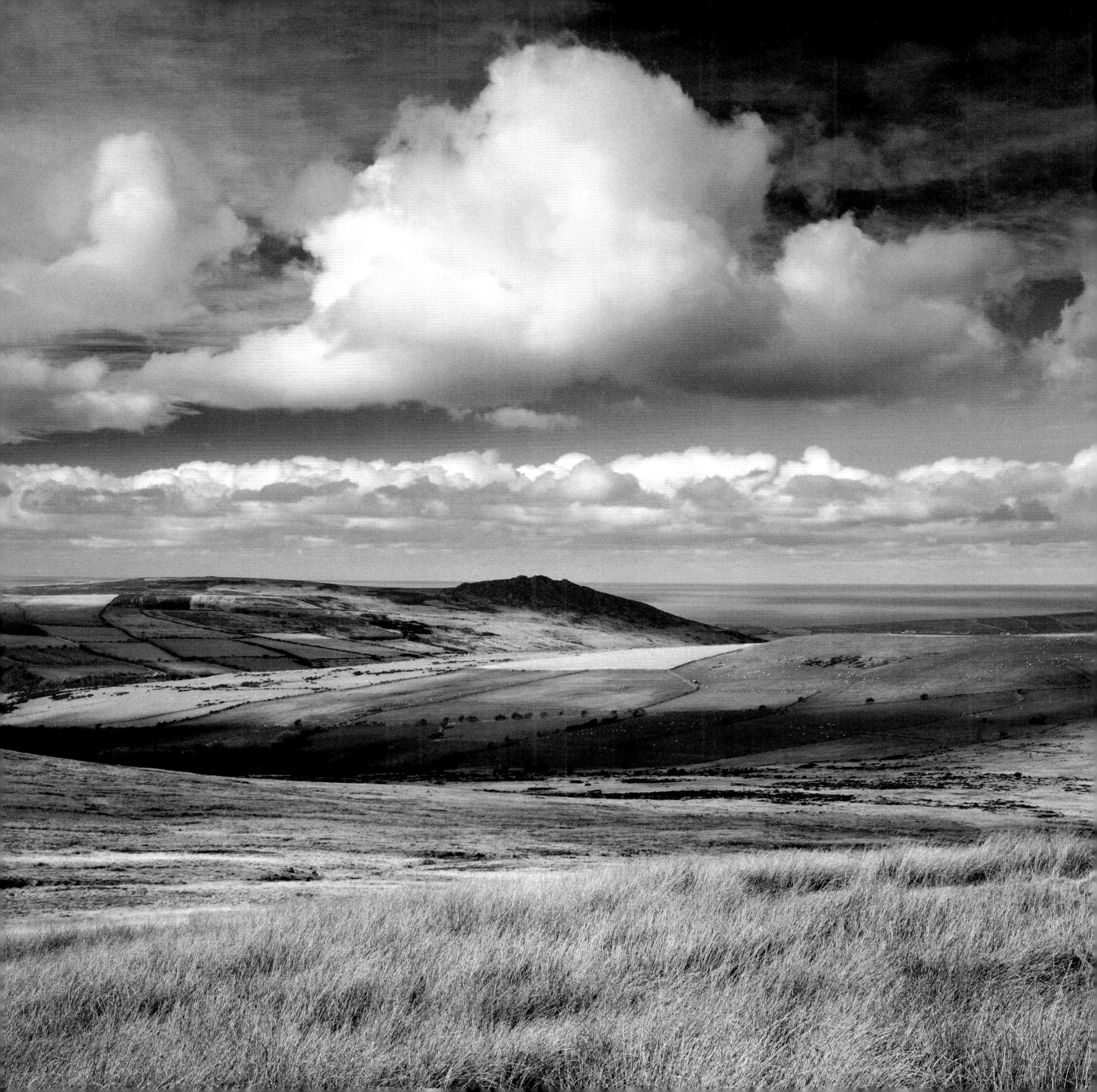

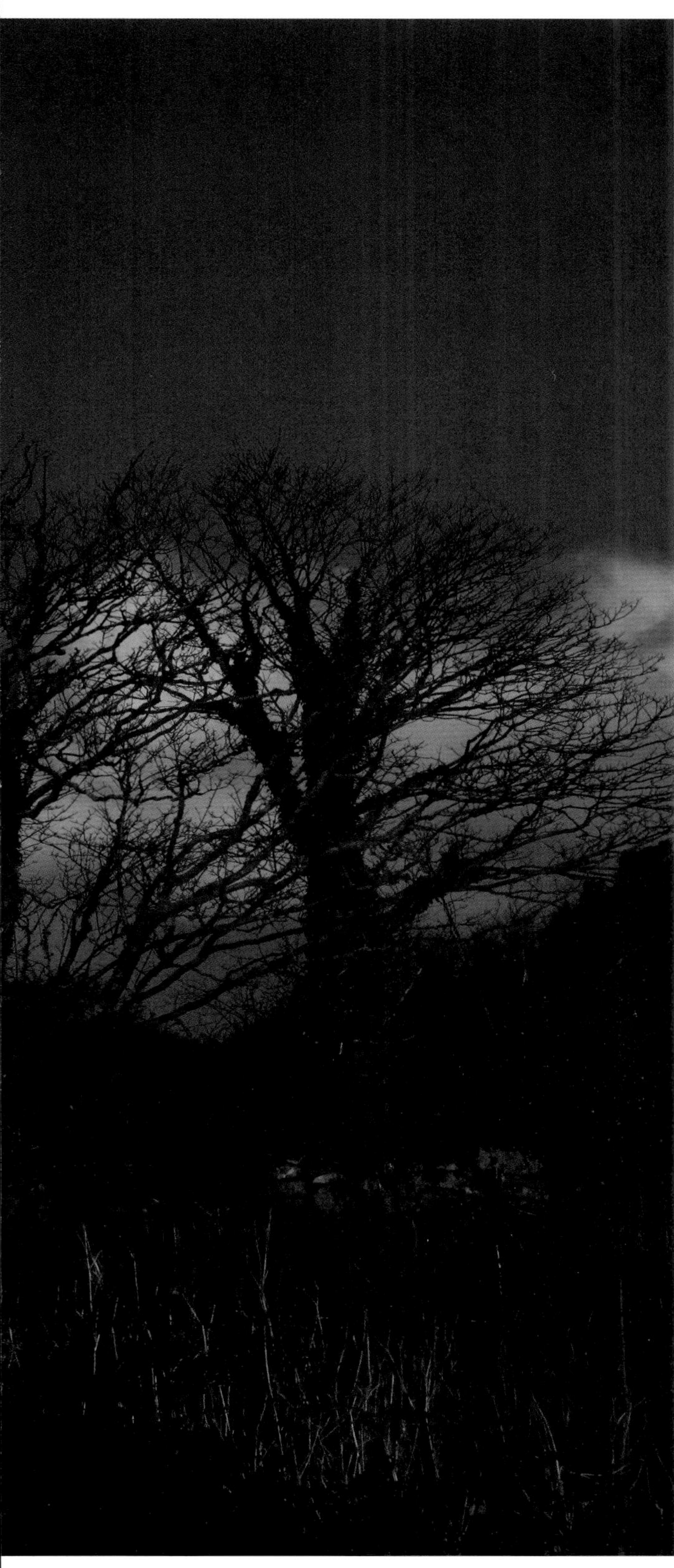

TRETIO,
NEAR ST DAVIDS

Tretio is a sleepy little cluster of
beautifully preserved cottages
just off the main road between
St Davids and Fishguard.
This stunning example of the
Pembrokeshire vernacular style
has been lovingly restored from
what was a derelict shell just a
few years back. The whitewashed
pine end projects a very powerful
and evocative shape in the
landscape, especially when set
in its ree-fringed surroundings.

Plate 39

TRELEDDYD FAWR COMMON, NEAR ST DAVIDS

I have a large tailgate on my car, which came in very handy for this photograph. I stood beneath it with my camera and tripod set up, sheltering from the driving rain. The foul weather was rolling in from the sea, partially shrouding Carn Penberry to the left. Compositionally, I was drawn to the drenched road and telegraph poles leading past the isolated farmhouse and over the horizon.

Plate 40

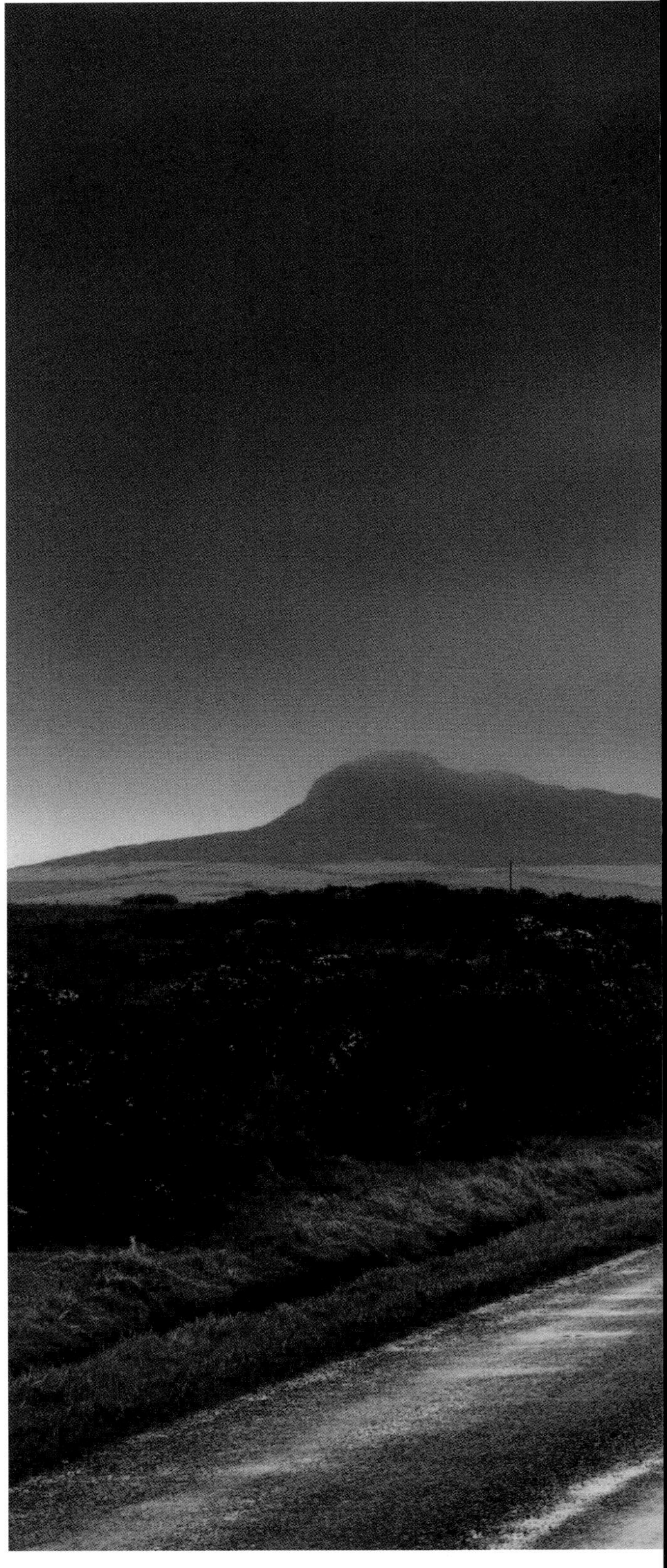

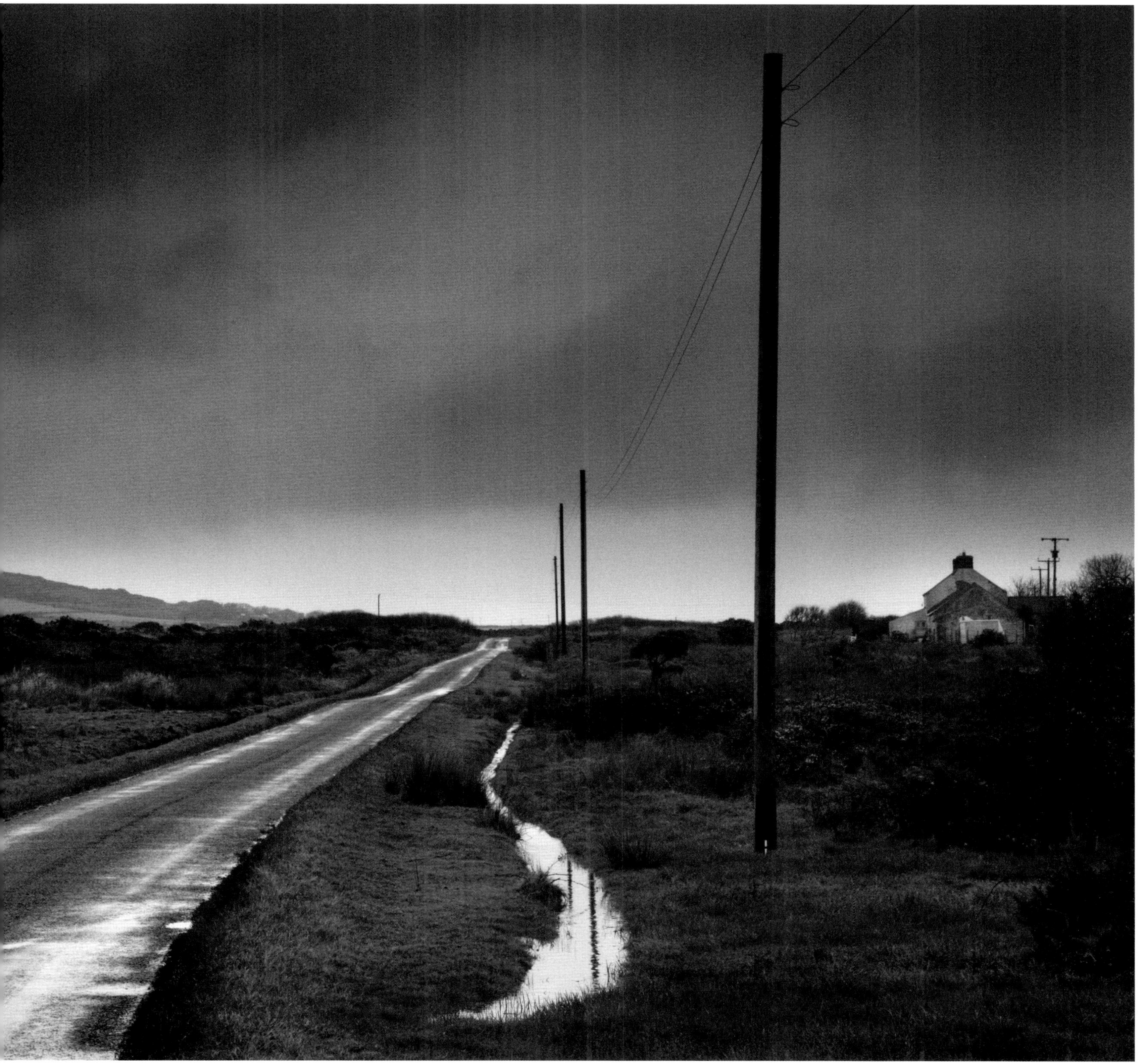

TOWARDS CARN MENYN, THE PRESELI HILLS

New Year's Eve 2004. Anna, who was heavily pregnant at the time, was with me. I certainly know how to show a girl a good time. Did she complain? Of course not – well, maybe just a little. What drew me to this composition was the sweep of the grasses in the foreground, leading the eye onto the rugged peak of Carn Menyn in the far distance. The village of Mynachlogddu is just out of sight to my right. When I'd finished we headed to Anna's grandmother's house a few miles away for some welcome coffee and cake.

Plate 41

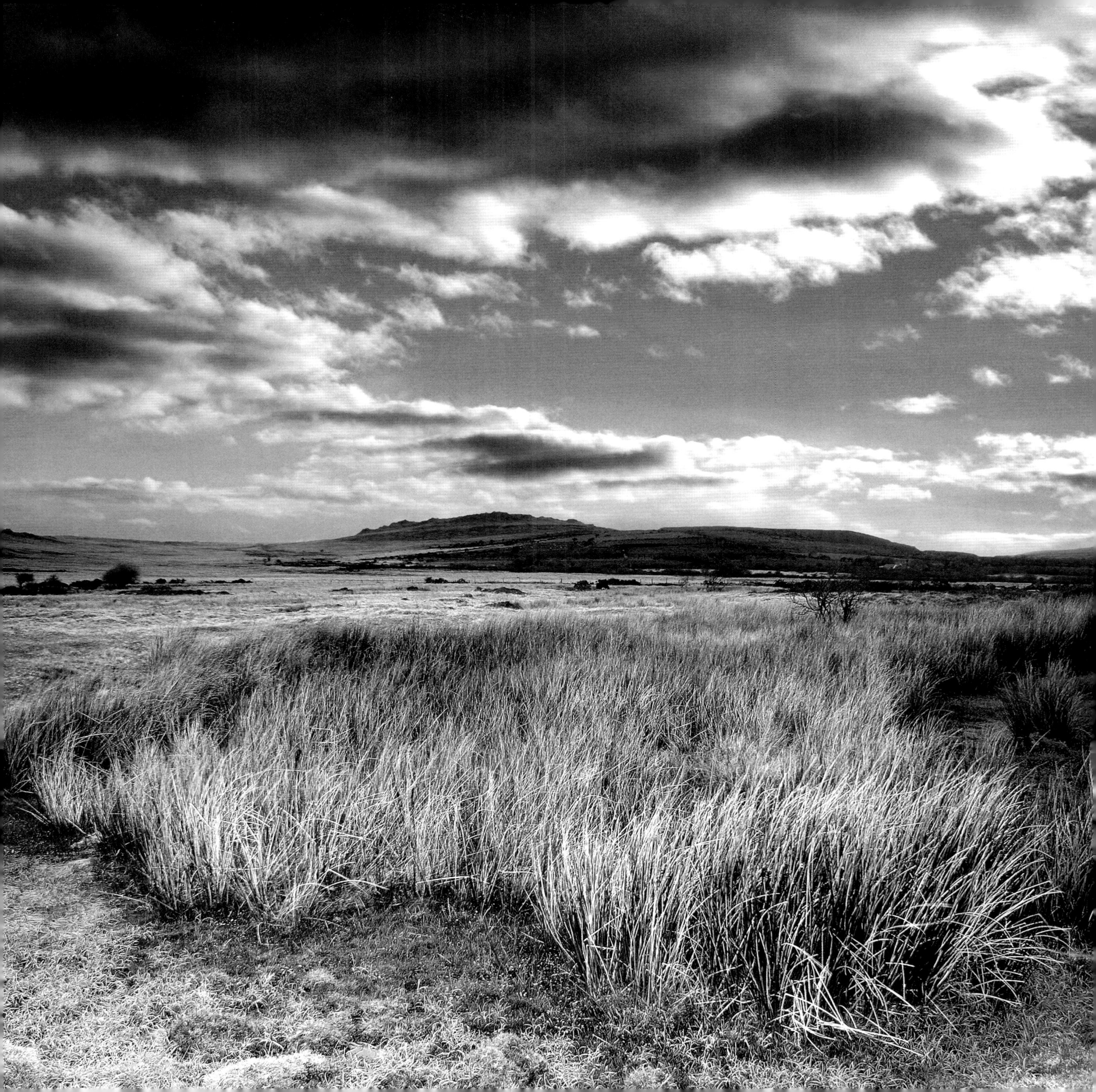

TOWARDS PONTYGLASIER, THE PRESELI HILLS

Looking down the spine of
the Preseli Hills towards the
Pontyglasier area, this image
is all about that mist cascading
over the top of Foel Feddau and
Mynydd Bach, tumbling down onto
the plain below. The placement
of the old, rusty gate and barbed
wire enclosure in the foreground
is a useful scaling device, giving
the viewer a sense of near and
far distance. Within ten minutes
that neat and compact carpet of
mist had lost its shape and form,
dissolving into an all-enveloping
foggy soup, reducing visibility in
all directions – the moment had
passed.

Plate 42

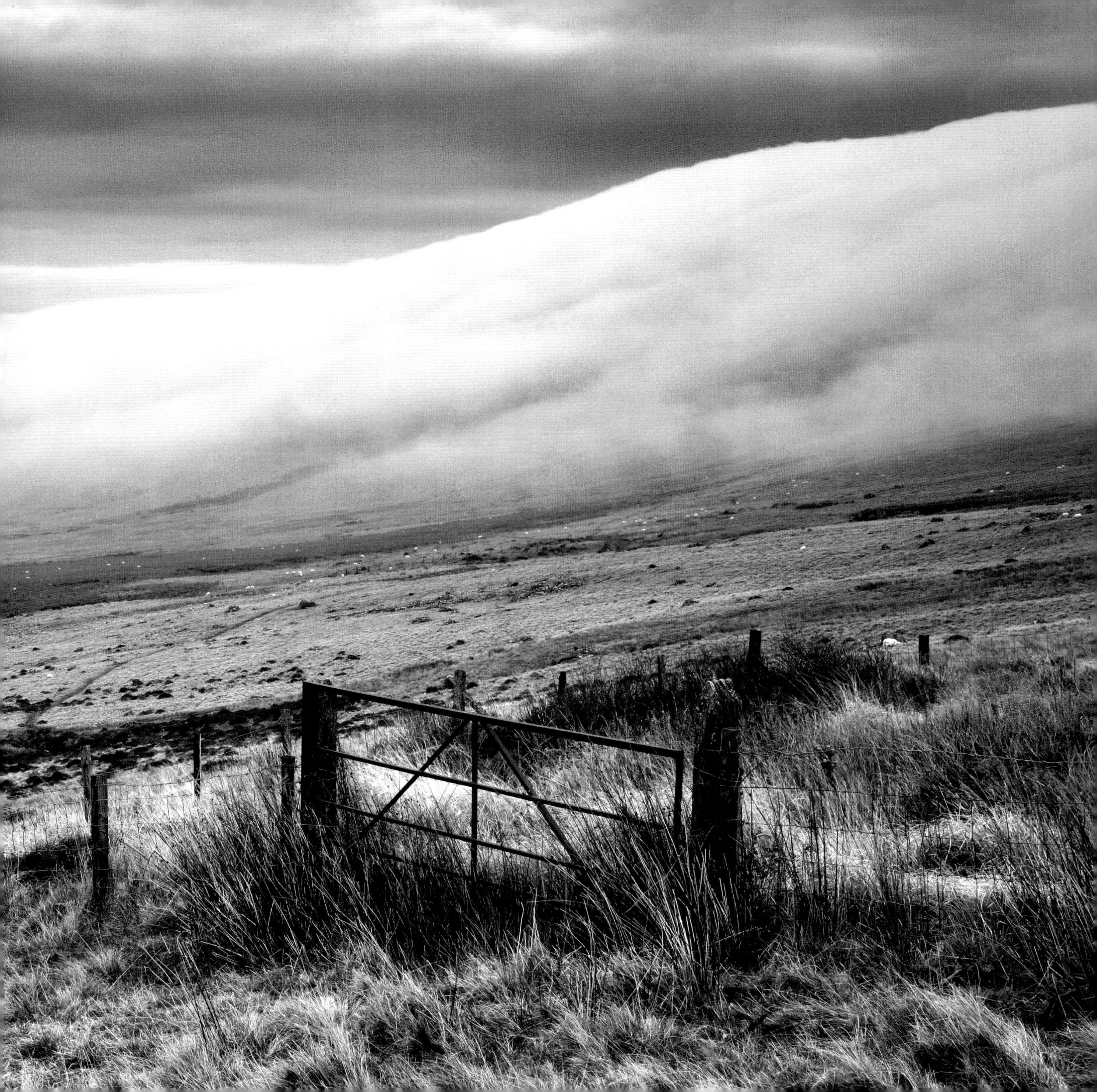

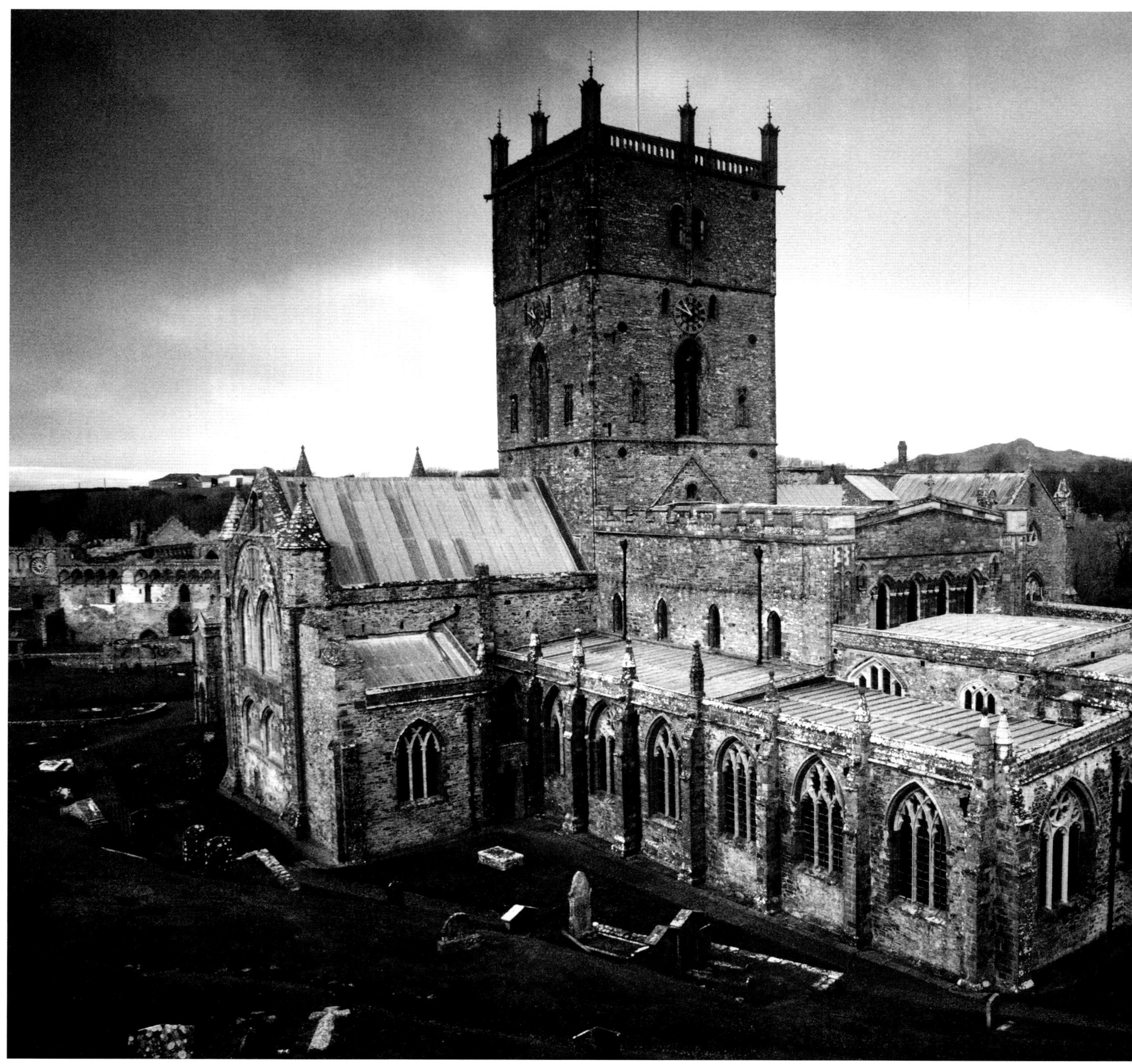

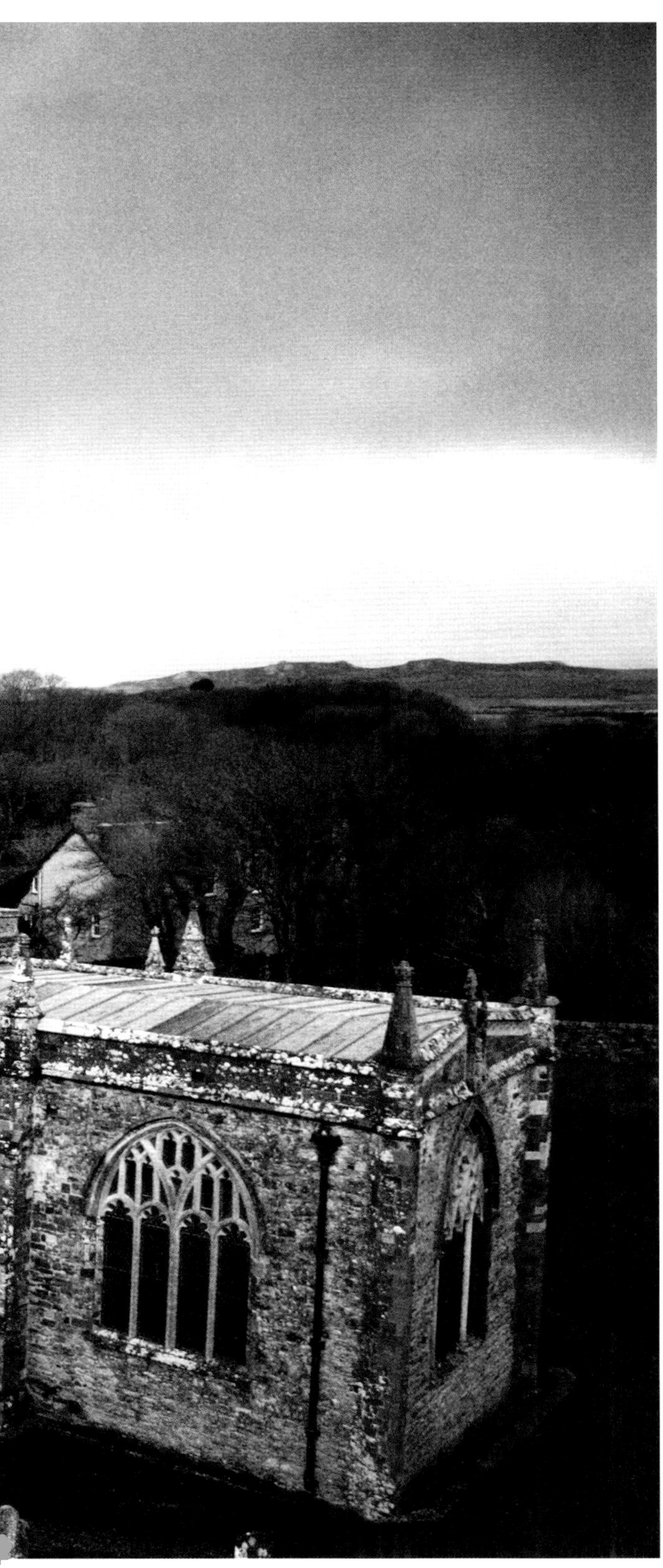

ST DAVIDS CATHEDRAL

Situated in St Davids, the UK's smallest city, the original cathedral was allegedly built in a hollow to obscure its view from marauding Vikings during the Dark Ages. Whether there is any truth in this is open to debate. The cathedral does sit in a tight-fitting natural bowl, protecting it from the elements. The ruin of the Bishop's Palace can be seen to the left at the bottom end of the cathedral. What I like about this image is the almost Victorian feel to the composition – this could be a photograph taken with a large plate camera on a gentleman's tour of the mid-nineteenth century.

Plate 43

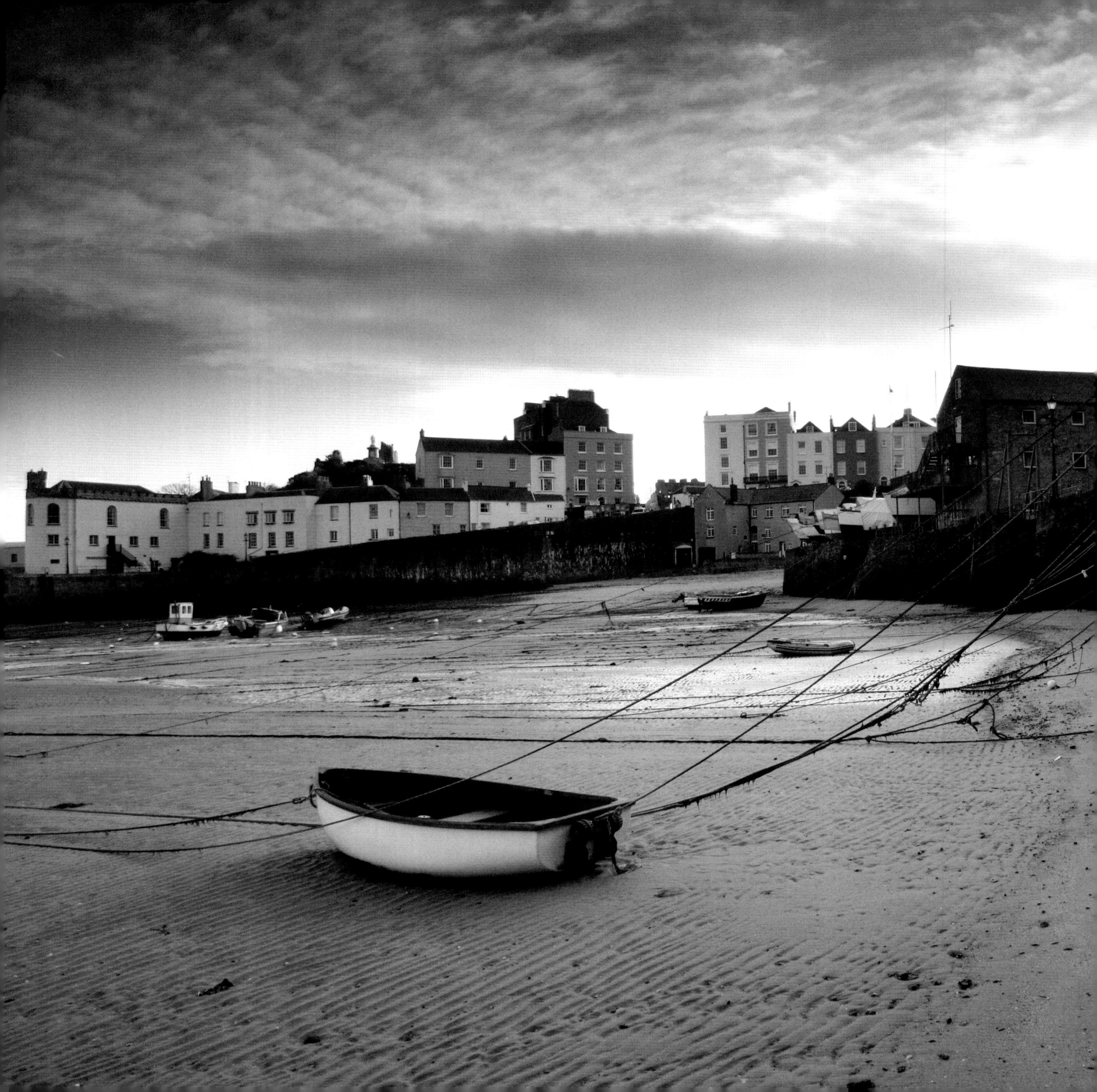

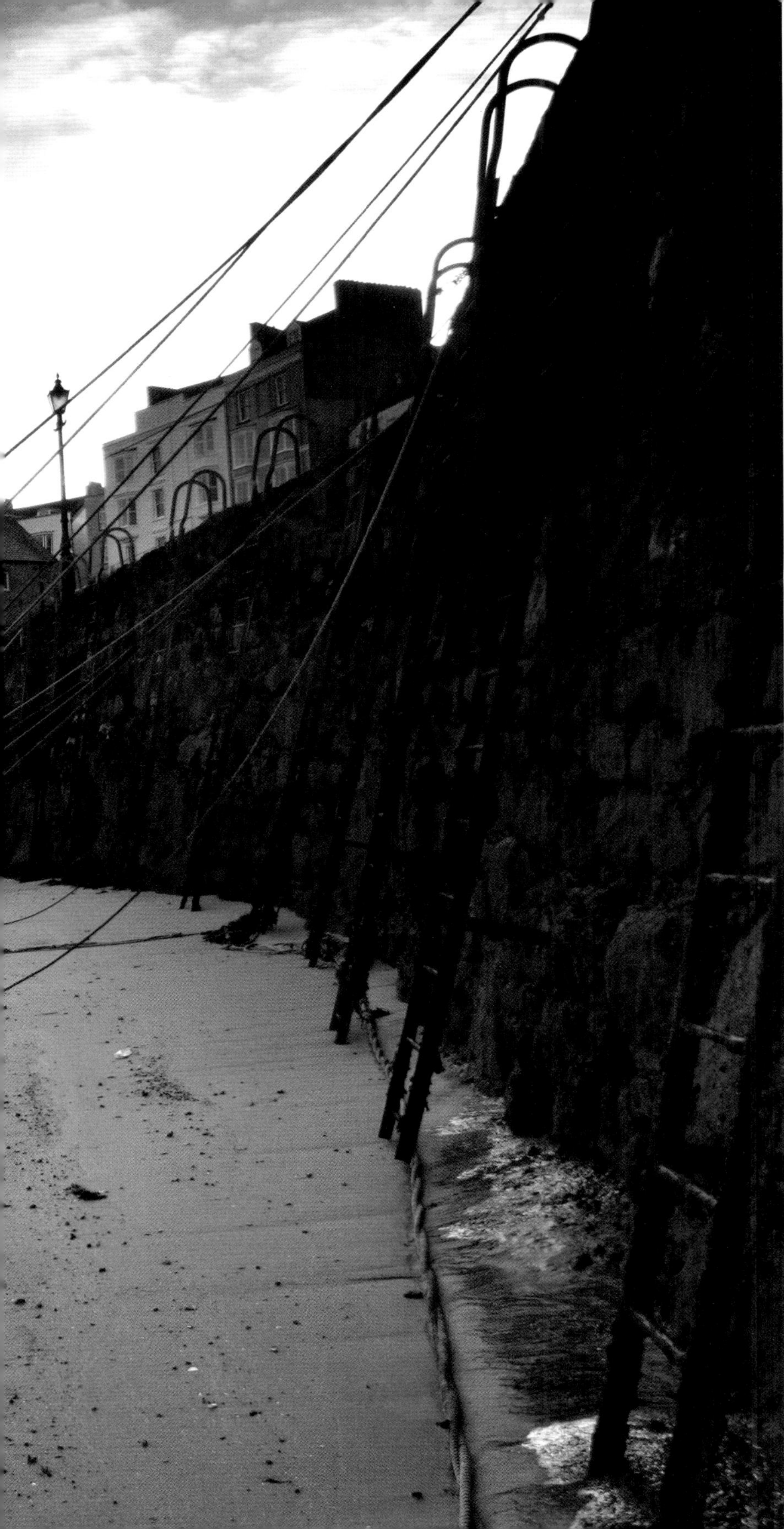

TENBY HARBOUR II

There is a huge contrast between the hustle and bustle of Tenby in the summer and the quiet out of season seaside resort. To me, this image perfectly encapsulates the stillness of the town in winter, with the harbour deserted of people and the mooring ropes for the most part missing their respective boats, which have been removed for maintenance and cleaning. I particularly like the sweeping arc of the harbour wall from the nearby ladder right round to the Georgian houses on the breakwater.

Plate 44

FRESHWATER WEST II

Some winter mornings I wonder what possesses me to get out of a lovely warm bed and head down to a freezing windswept beach at sunrise. But if I was bordering on mad then these two surfers were positively unhinged. As they gazed out into that violent heaving sea, I fully expected them to turn round and head back home. But no, in they went.

Plate 45

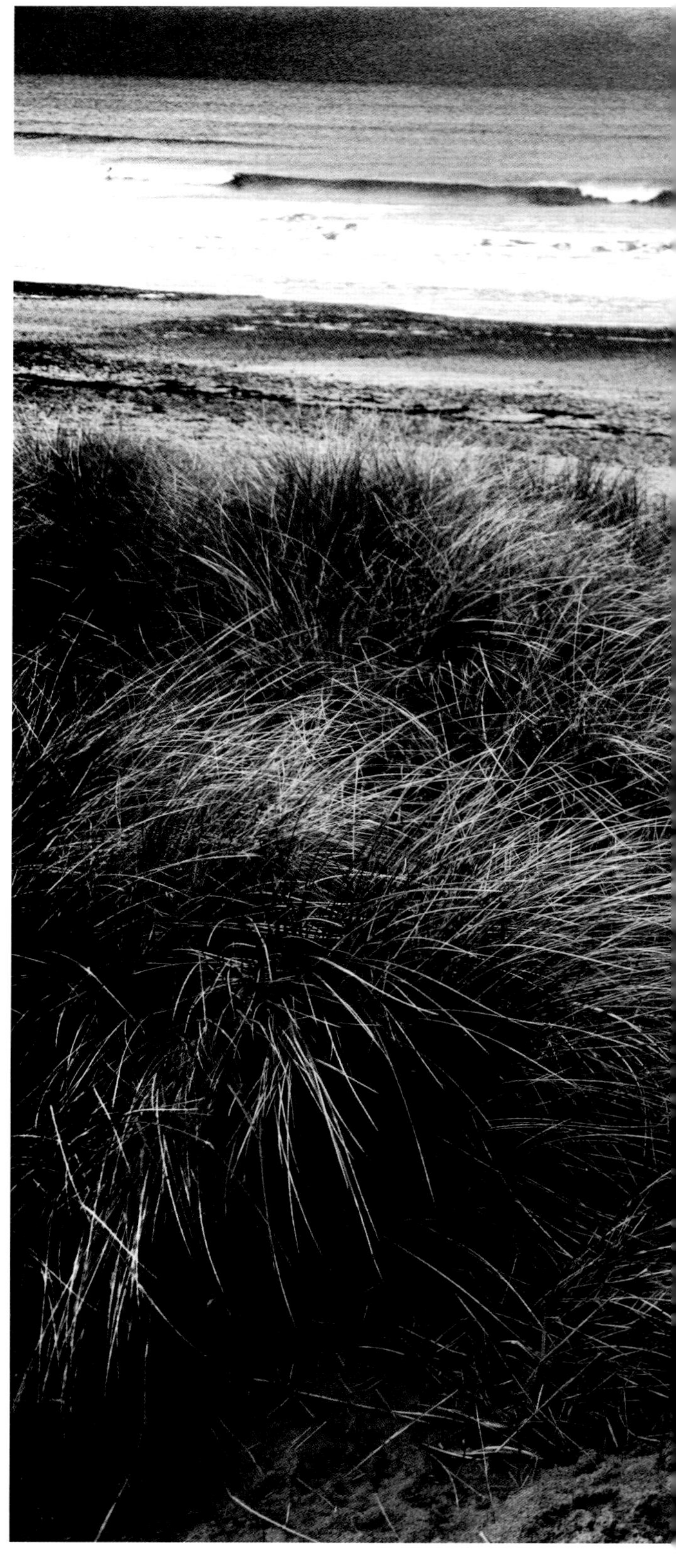

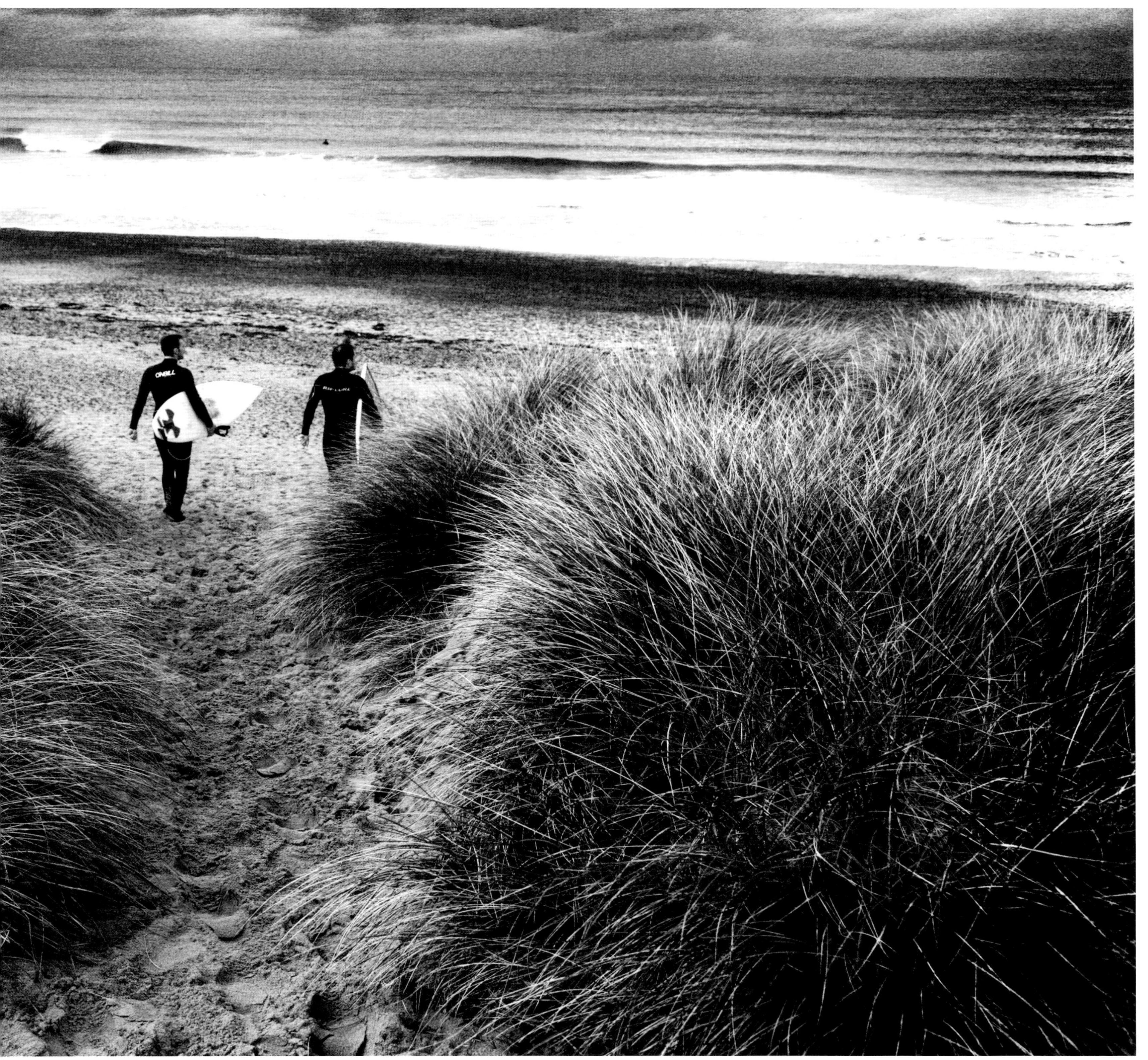

PENTRE IFAN,
THE PRESELI HILLS

The silhouette of Pentre Ifan
burial chamber is one of the
most recognisable outlines in
Pembrokeshire. A Bronze Age
megalithic site dating from around
4000 BC, it would once have been
covered in earth. With this image
I wanted to communicate some
of the aura and mystique that this
site emanates. The ghostly sky
with just that hint of winter sun
breaking through adds a certain
other-worldly feel. The inclusion
of the tree is a useful scaling
device and helps to position the
cromlech within its windswept
hilltop landscape.

Plate 46

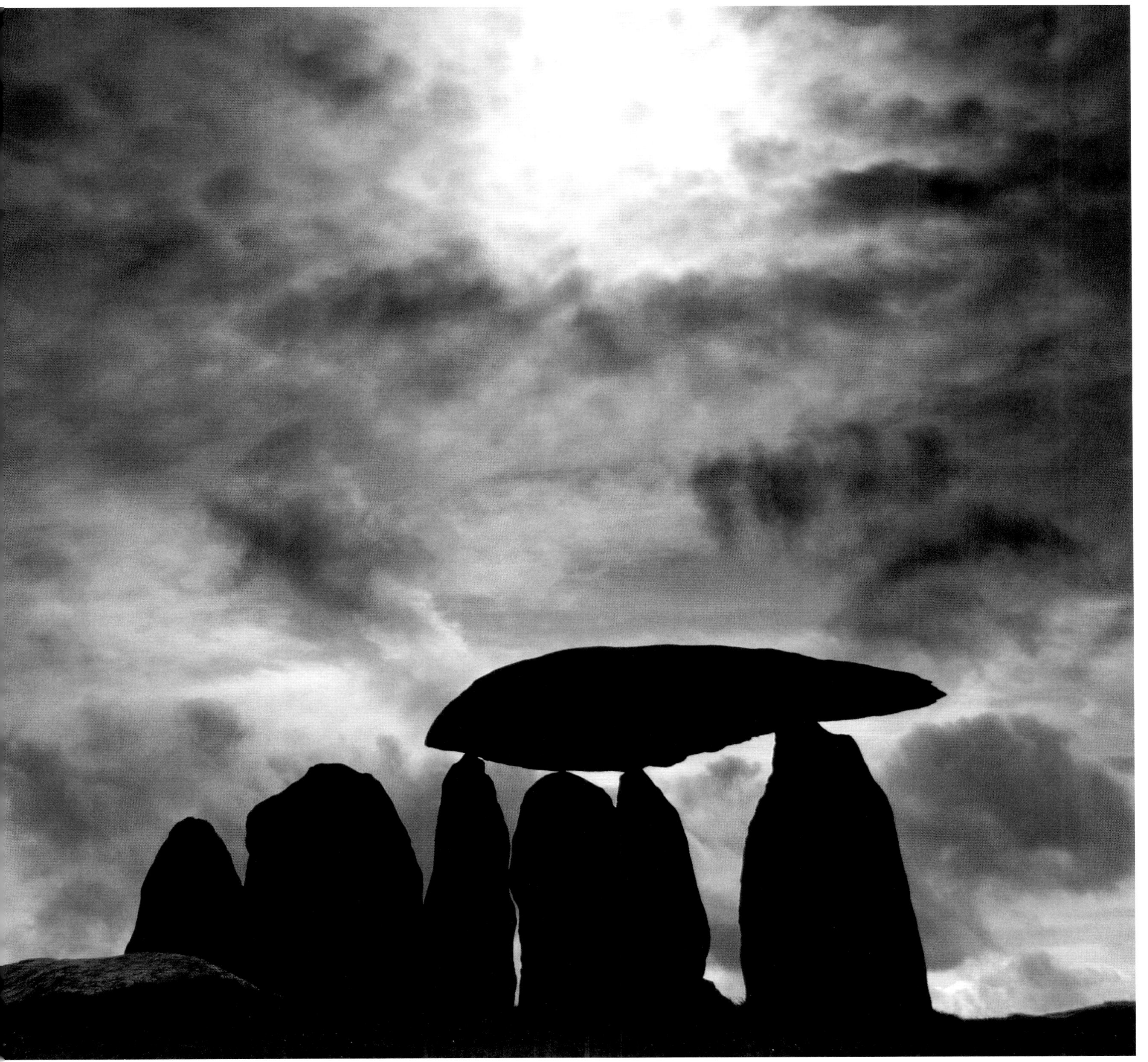

CATTLE, CARN LLIDI, NEAR ST DAVIDS

This was such an unremittingly damp and cold wintry day. Each time I got my camera out at various locations the lens was covered in speckles of rain. Then, in the deepening twilight, I passed this field and saw the cattle grazing. With a rainy Carn Llidi as a backdrop, I felt it made a striking and atmospheric composition. I used the highest film speed setting to extract every last ounce of useable shutter speed from the camera. The cow's dismissive backward glance probably sums up a pretty miserable day all round really.

Plate 47

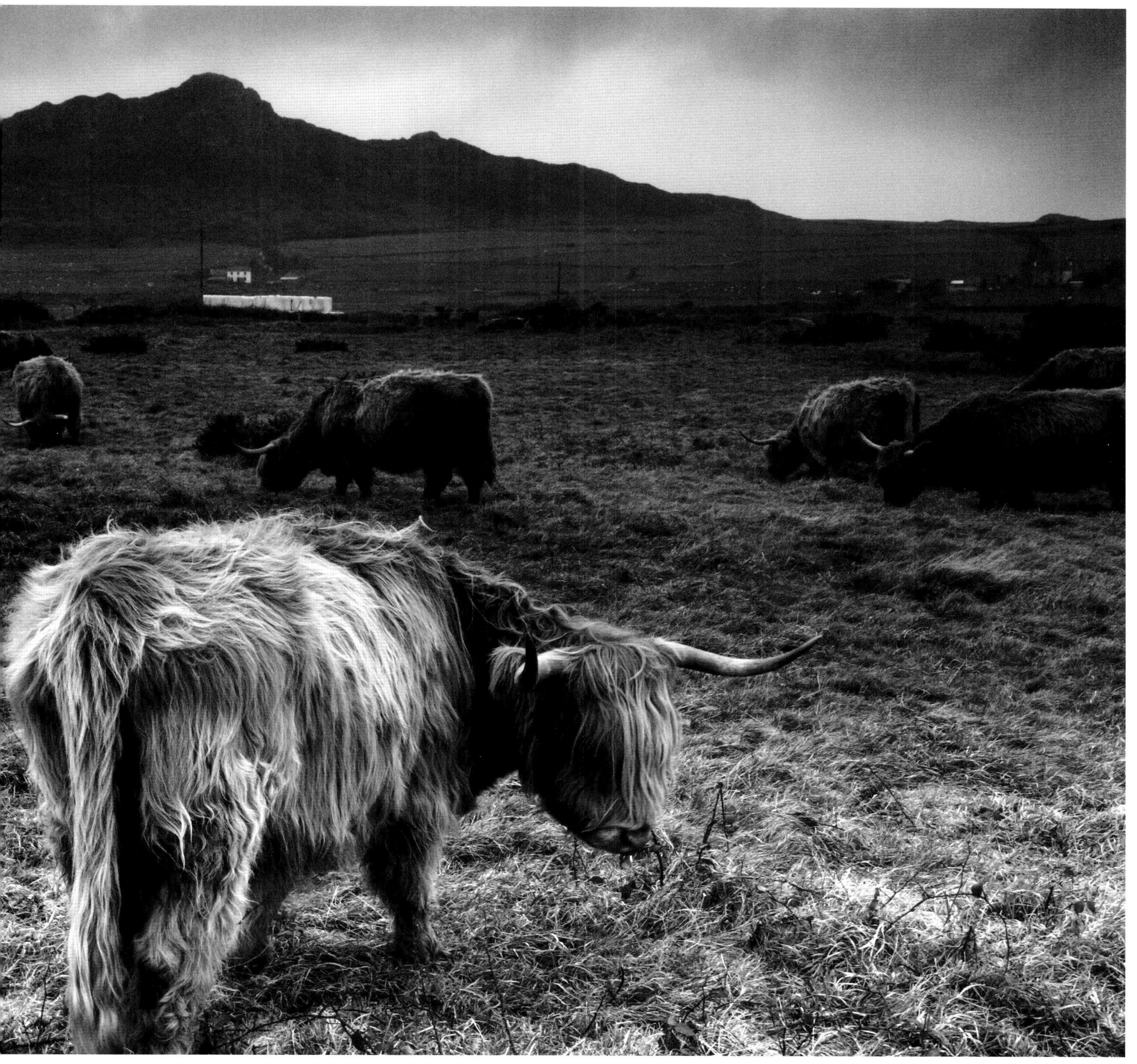

CEIBWR BAY II

The contrast between this image of Ceibwr Bay and the earlier photograph in the book could not be starker. This one is all calmness and tranquility, whereas the earlier image is storm-lashed and blustery. Taken in late September, I adore this sky with its wispy cirrus clouds and the bleached, almost high-summer ambience of the image.

Plate 48

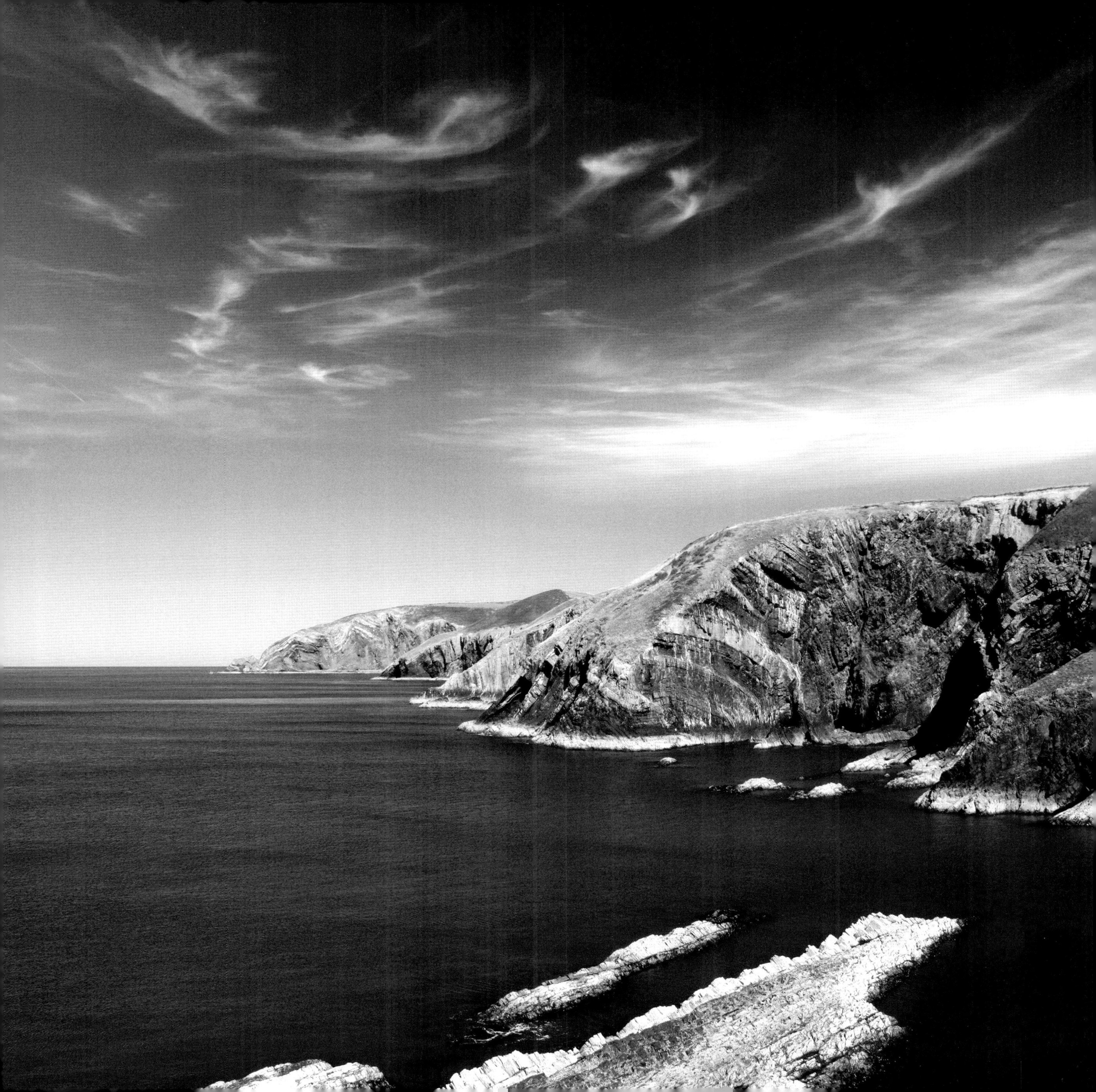

MANORBIER CHURCH

Driving through Manorbier one late winter's afternoon I noticed the church tower lit by the sun and isolated from the remainder of the building, which was in shade. The white tower provides a powerful focal point. It is an unusual architectural feature these days but would once have been a common sight when whitewash was used extensively throughout the county, even on churches. The composition is enhanced by the illuminated cross and bench in the graveyard. The cross is redolent of death while the bench is used by the living. I applied a duotone tint to add some warmth to the image.

Plate 49

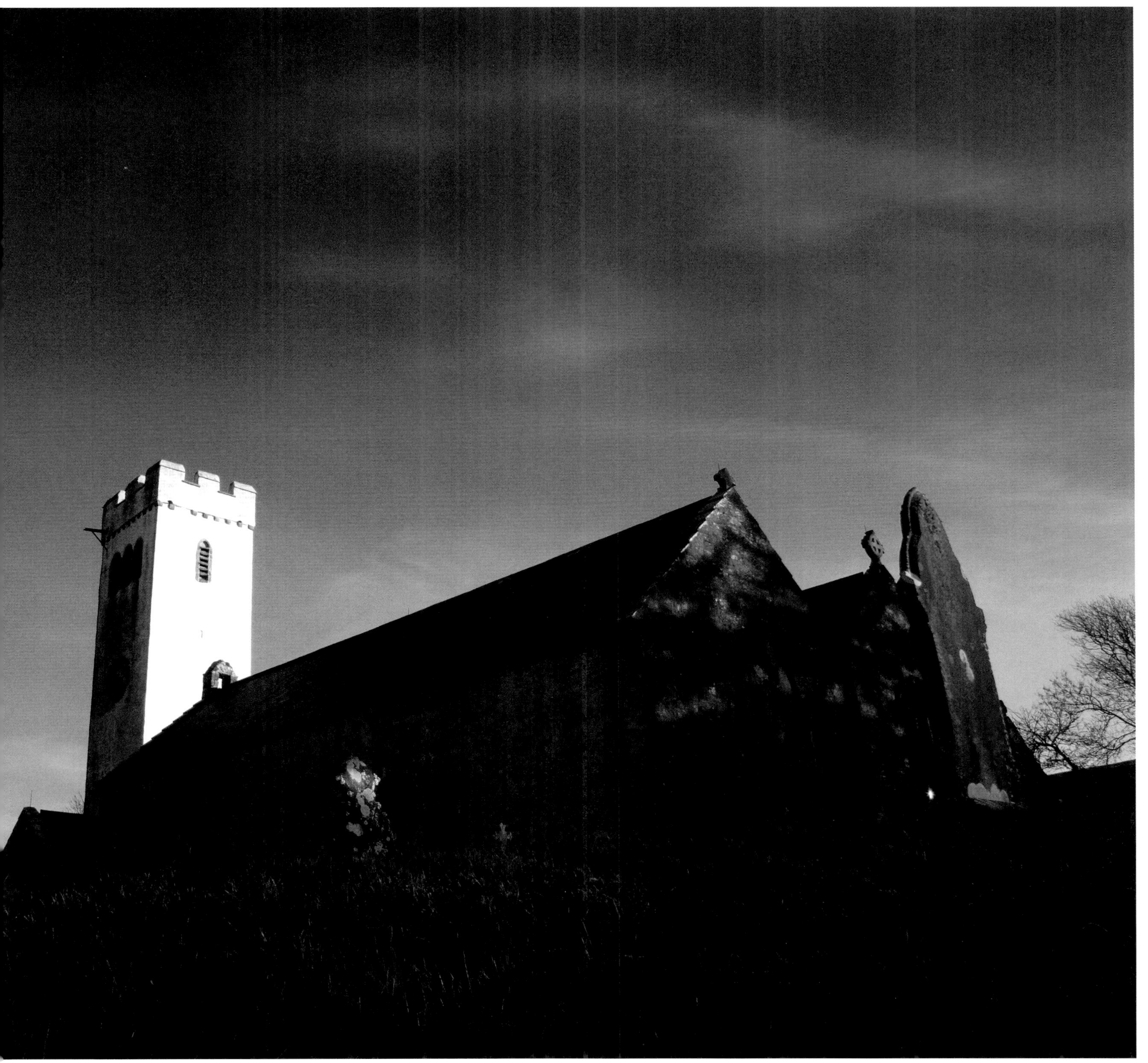

ENTRANCE TO SOLVA HARBOUR

How to photograph popular locations in a novel way – a recurring challenge. I feel this image is representative of Solva's great seafaring tradition. Facing out to sea, the buoy and its seaweed-draped mooring remind me of the many thousands of boats that have departed this harbour over the centuries. The tide was at its lowest point, with a rippled carpet of sand leading to the water's edge.

Plate 50

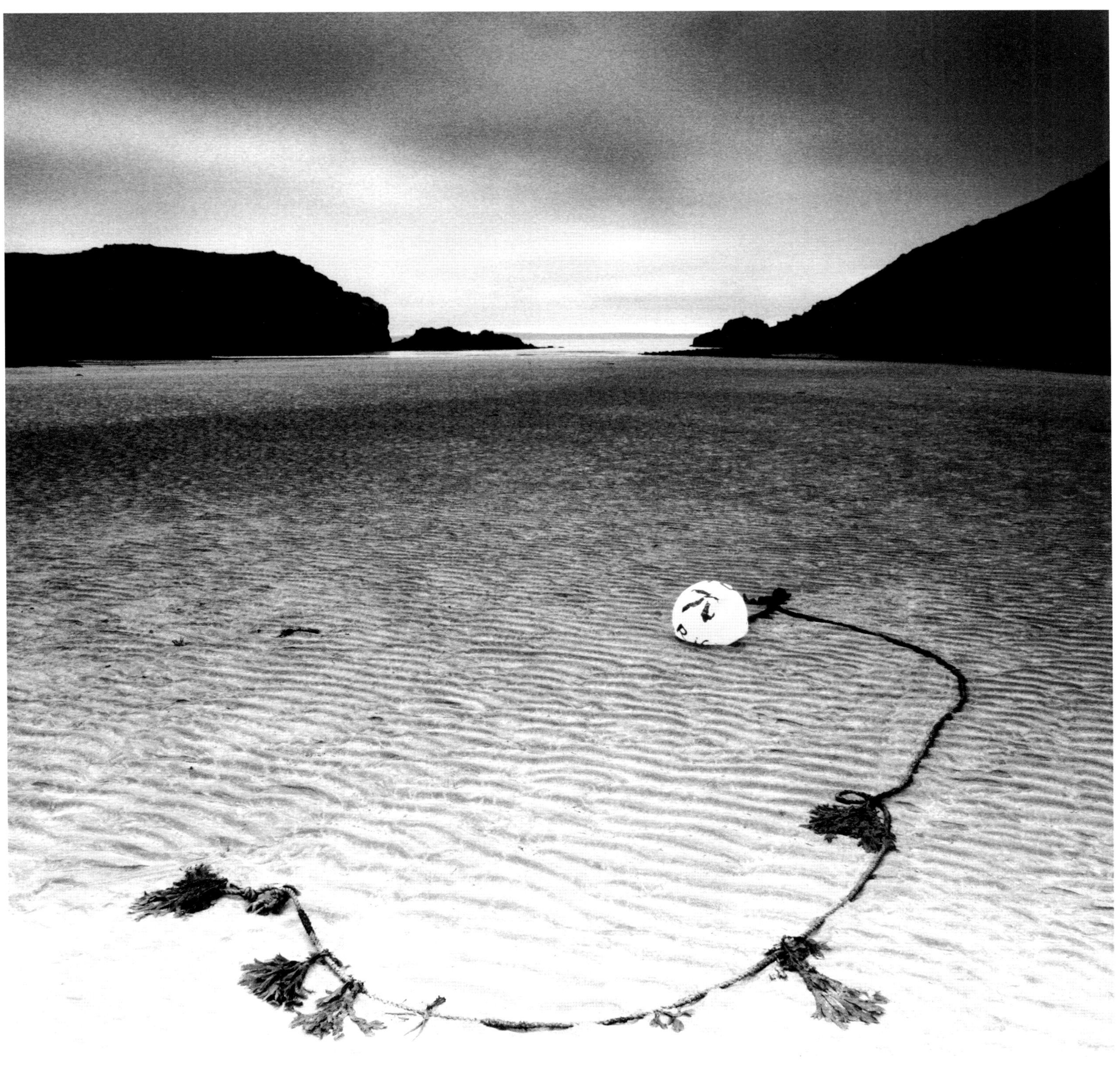

PORTHGAIN II

There are certain locations in
Pembrokeshire which I never
tire of, and Porthgain is up there
on my list of favourites. Clues
all around allude to its former
industrial heyday as an exporter
of slate and hardcore. Today,
the imposing breakwater offers
protection to fishing boats and
leisure craft, the pace of life
quickened by the countless visitors
that flock to this idyllic harbour.

Plate 51

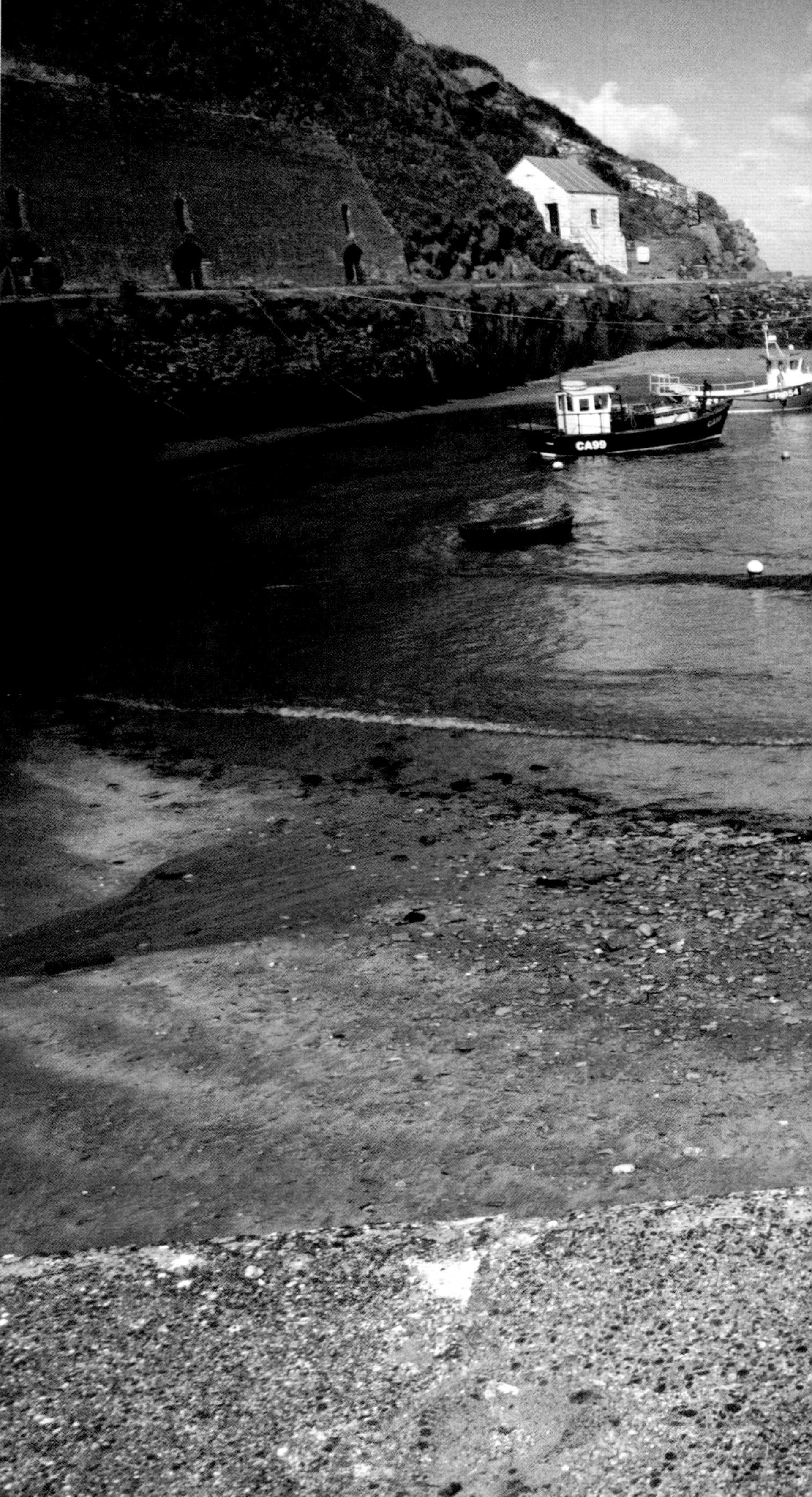

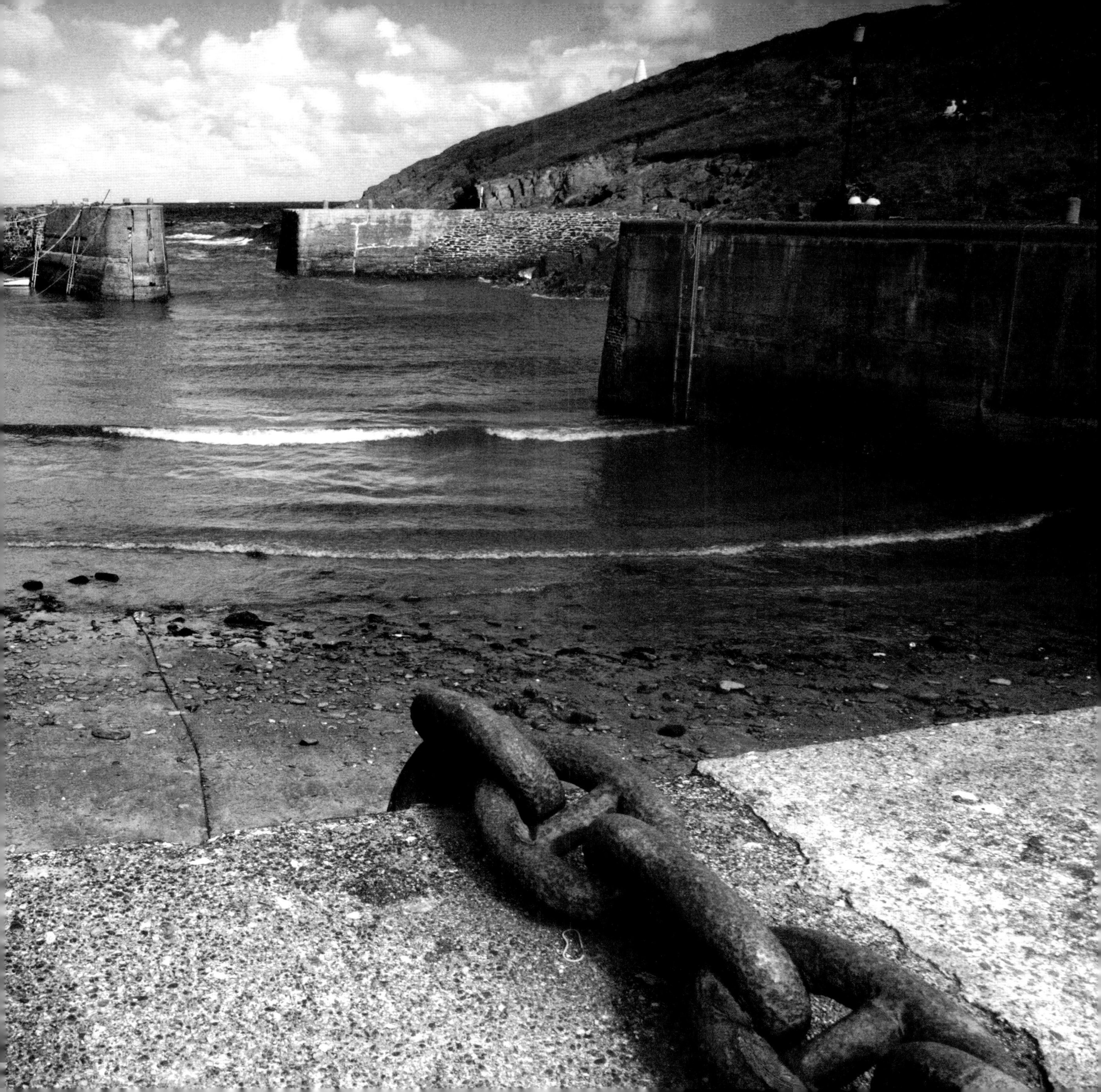

GOODWICK HARBOUR

Mist is the landscape photographer's friend; a welcome prop that softens harsh edges and imports atmosphere into an image. Goodwick Harbour is enclosed by a large breakwater, and to the right you can just make out the faint outline of Dinas Island. The three trawlers seemed almost becalmed by the tranquil sea.

Plate 52

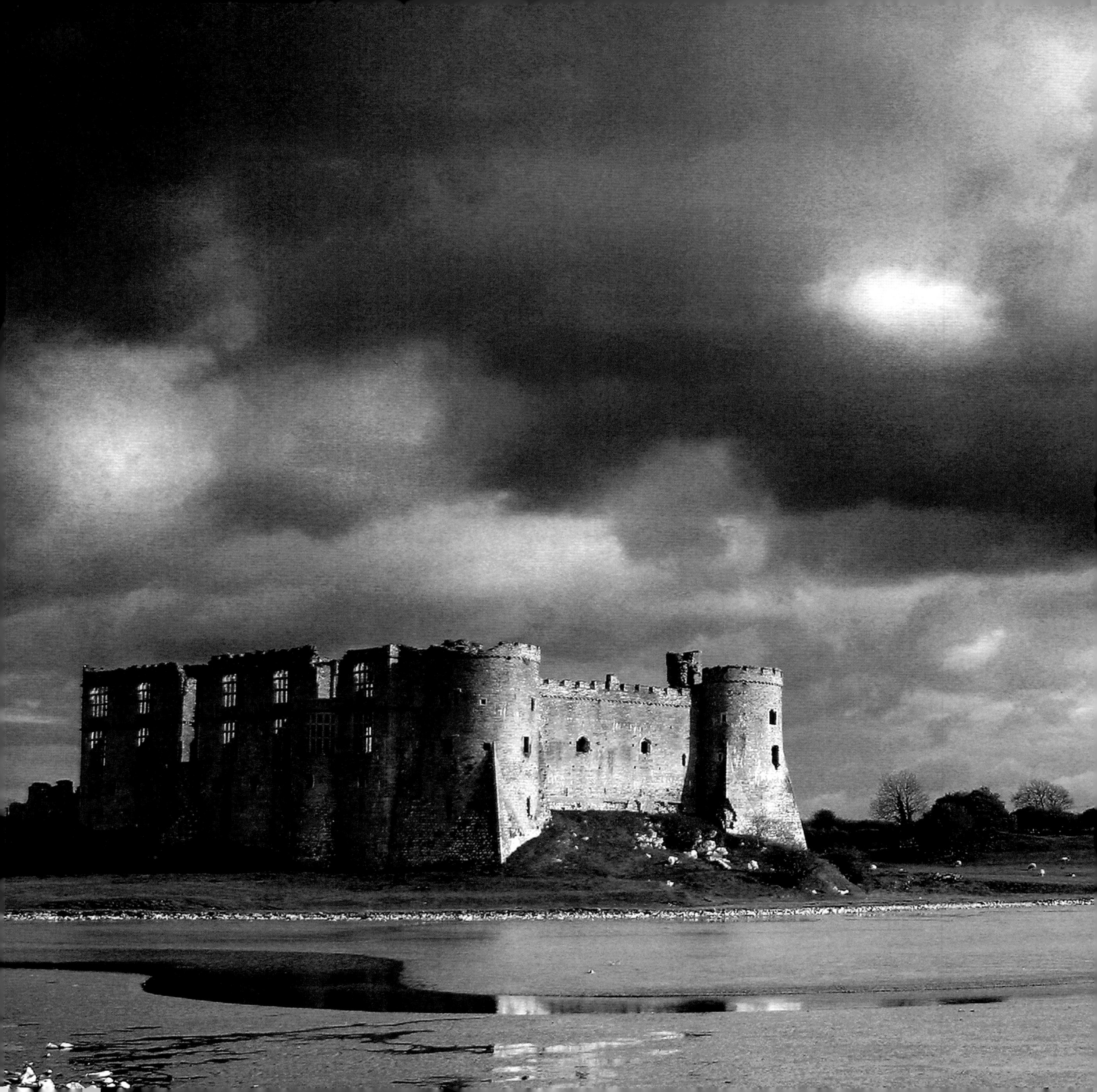

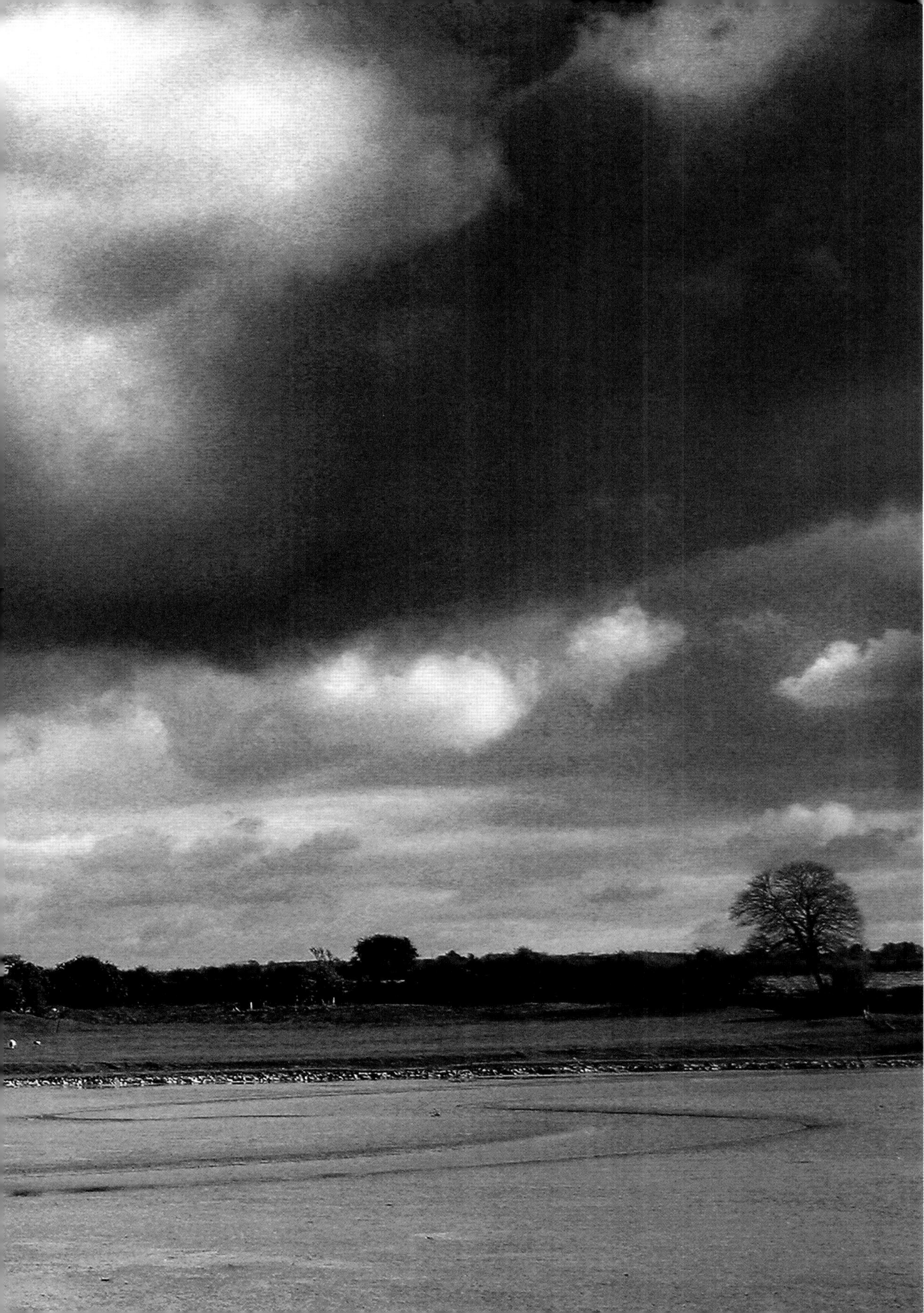

CAREW CASTLE

In 1507 Carew Castle hosted the last jousting tournament in Wales, a medieval celebration of men-at-arms on horseback. A few decades later and Sir John Perrott, illegitimate son of King Henry VIII, took up residence. An infamous character with a dangerously loose tongue, he ended his days in the Tower of London, having allegedly made disparaging remarks about Queen Elizabeth I.

Plate 53

CWM YR EGLWYS

I was drawn to this composition by the way in which the clouds seem to imitate the outline of the headland. The solitary windswept tree breaks the ridgeline. It was a very blustery day so I used a high film and shutter speed, giving the image a grainy feel.

Plate 54

NEWGALE II

Pages 108–109

A disparate scattering of walkers heading across the open sands into a fierce wind; a life-affirming experience while being battered by the wilds of the West Wales coast. There is something elemental about beaches in winter as opposed to the comfortable certainties of summer sunshine. I have to admit that the car's heating system was very welcome on my return though.

Plate 55

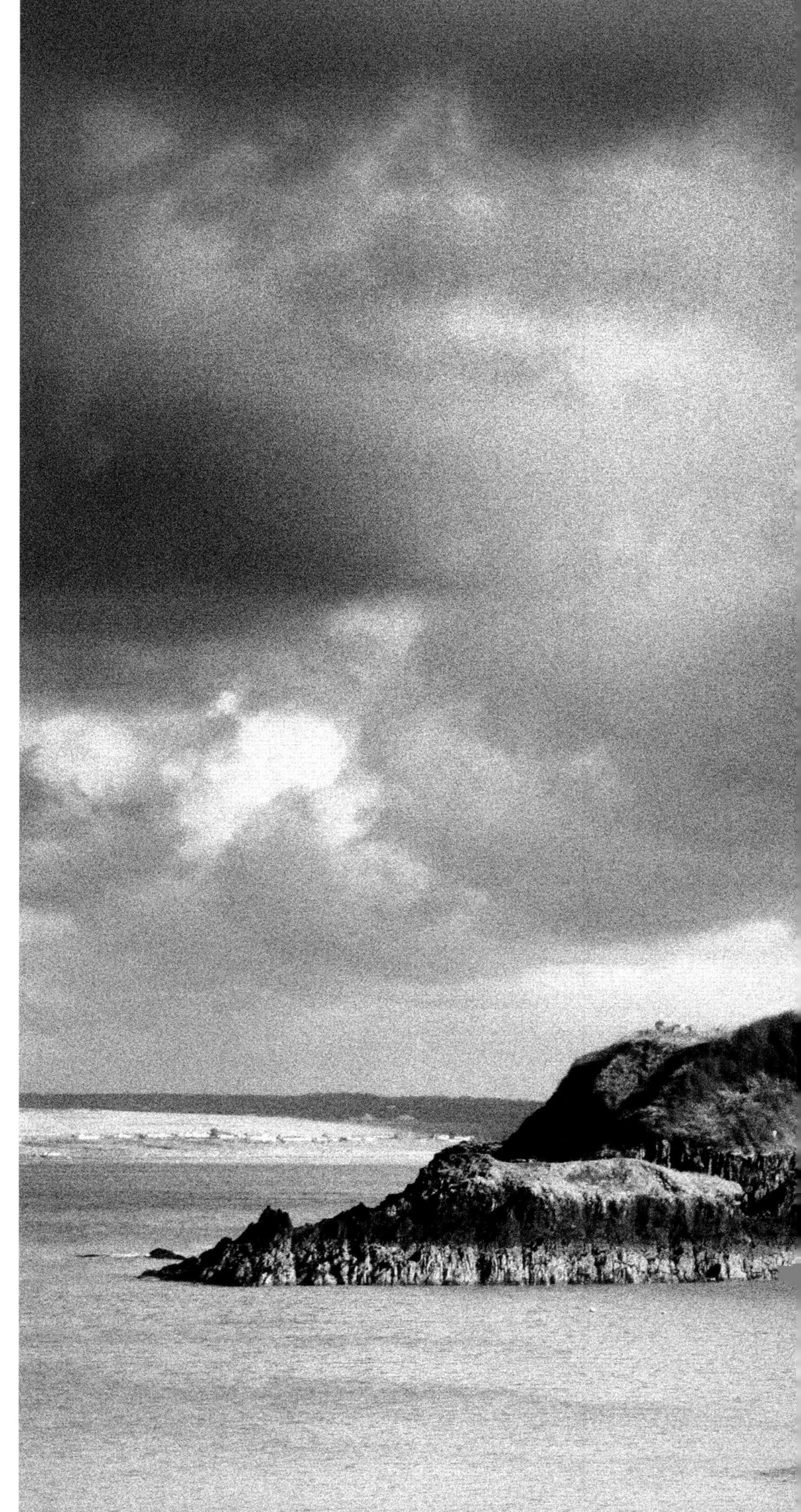

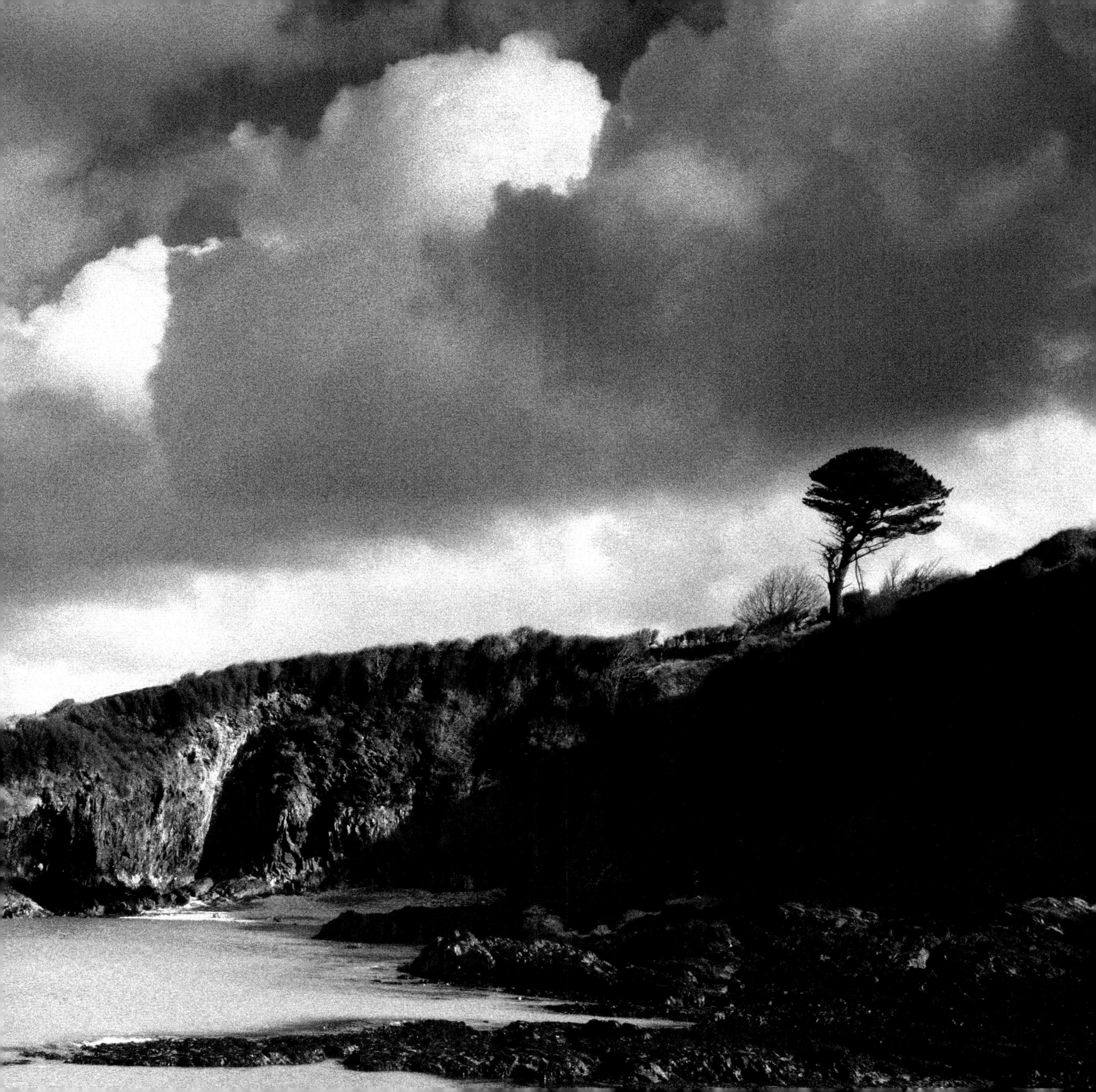

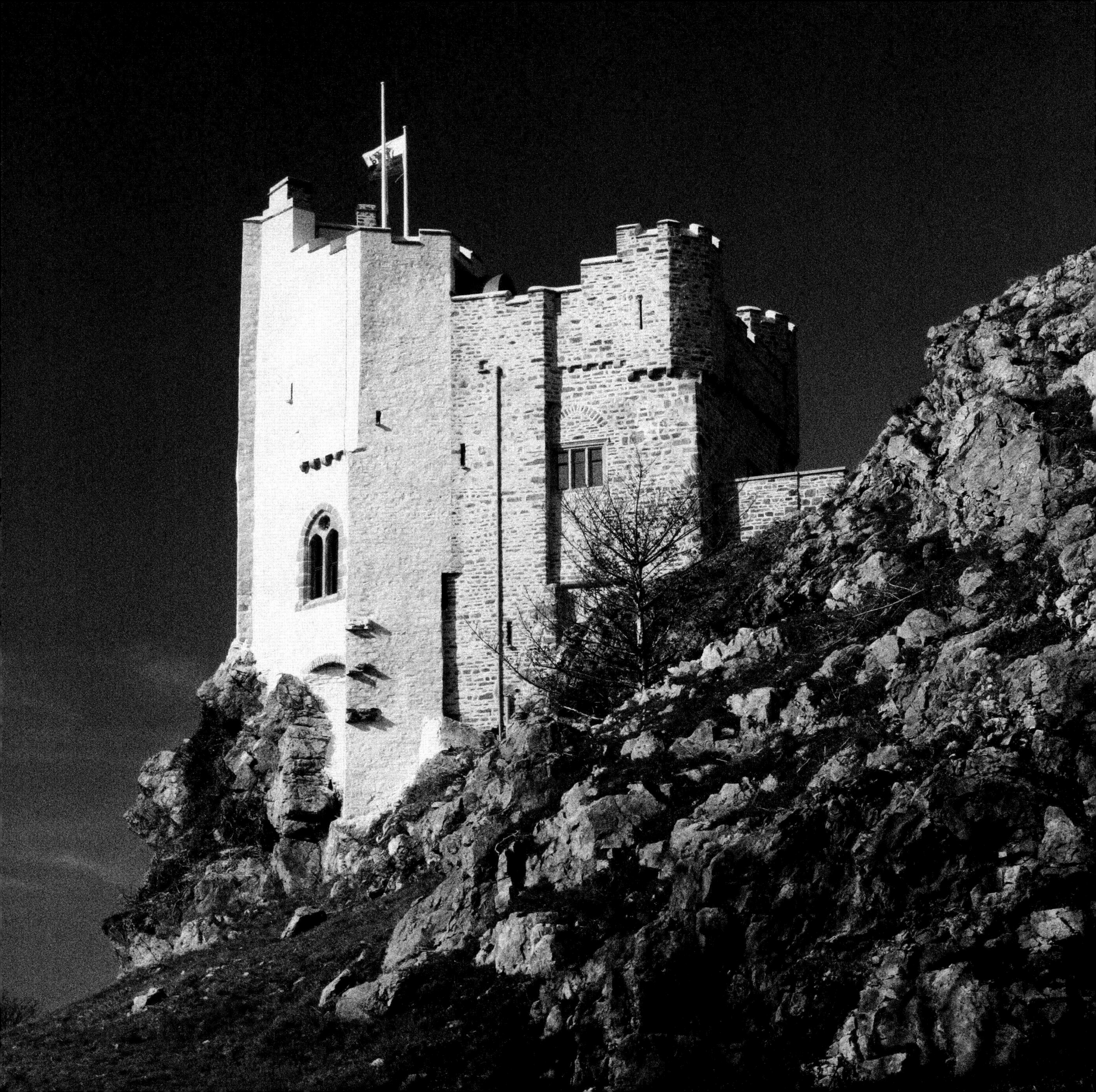

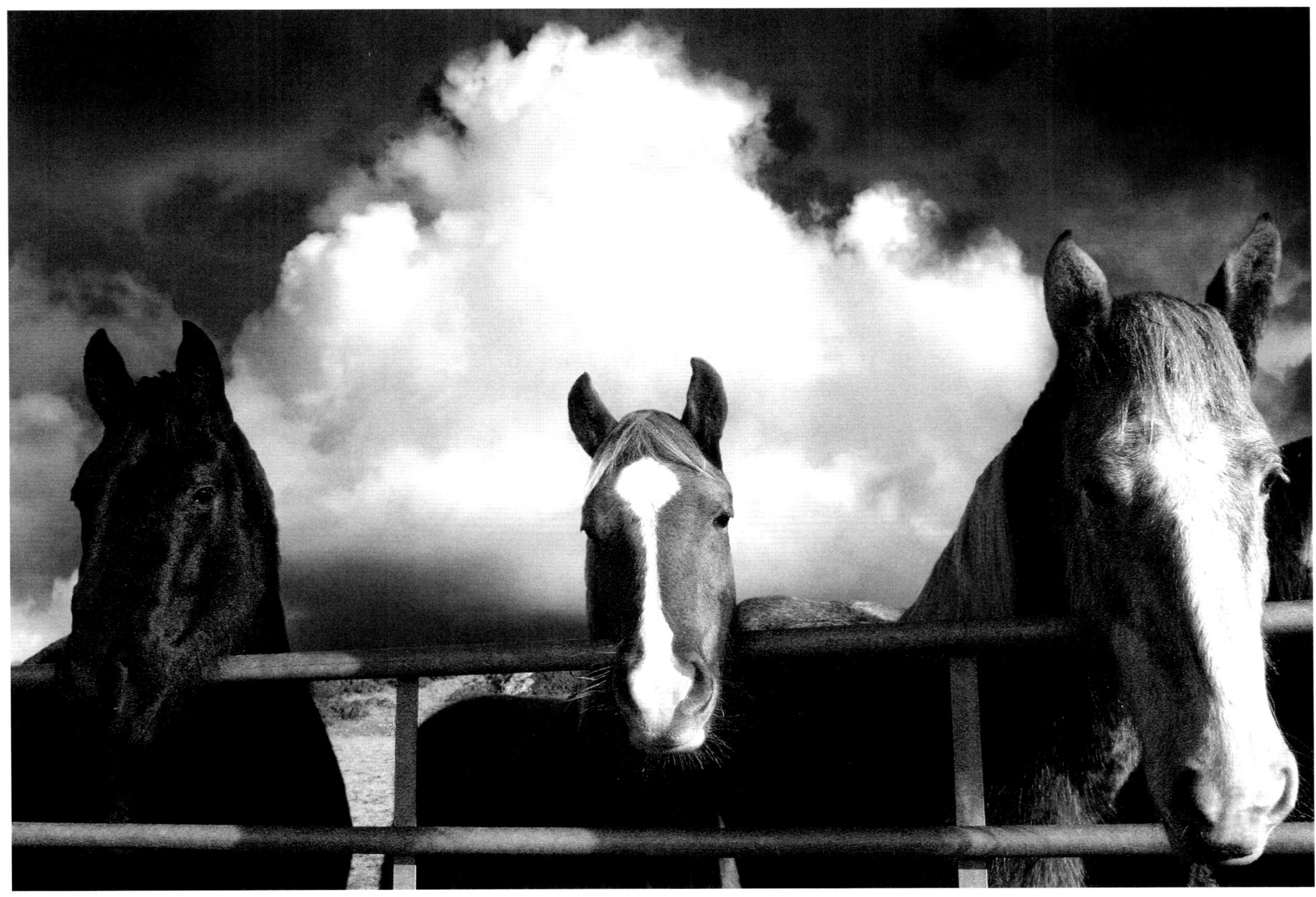

ROCH CASTLE

Built astride a rocky knoll, this castle affords 360 degree views of the surrounding countryside. Roch Castle is one of numerous fortifications built on or near the Landsker line, the medieval linguistic demarcation between the former Flemish-Norman occupied south of the county and the indigenous Welsh-speaking north. This border ebbed and flowed over the centuries but is still very apparent to this day; South Pembrokeshire is predominantly English speaking (Little England beyond Wales) while the north retains its Welsh-language heritage.

Plate 56

STRUMBLE HEAD

Trundling down the twisting lane from Garn Fawr towards Strumble Head lighthouse I stumbled upon this cheery trio. A grey, black and brown, all gazing attentively into the lens. Ordinarily, I would use a tripod in my work, but not wanting to lose the moment I simply grabbed my camera and shot this portrait before they wandered off, which, of course, within seconds they had.

Plate 57

PRESELI HILL FARM

A blanket of snow brought a quietness to the landscape; an icy stillness. I came across this rough track leading to a cluster of sheds and trees, a semblance of shelter in an otherwise barren and exposed environment. A tractor had recently been up the track, perhaps to deliver feed to livestock. Britain may grind to a halt at the first sign of snow but farming continues.

Plate 58

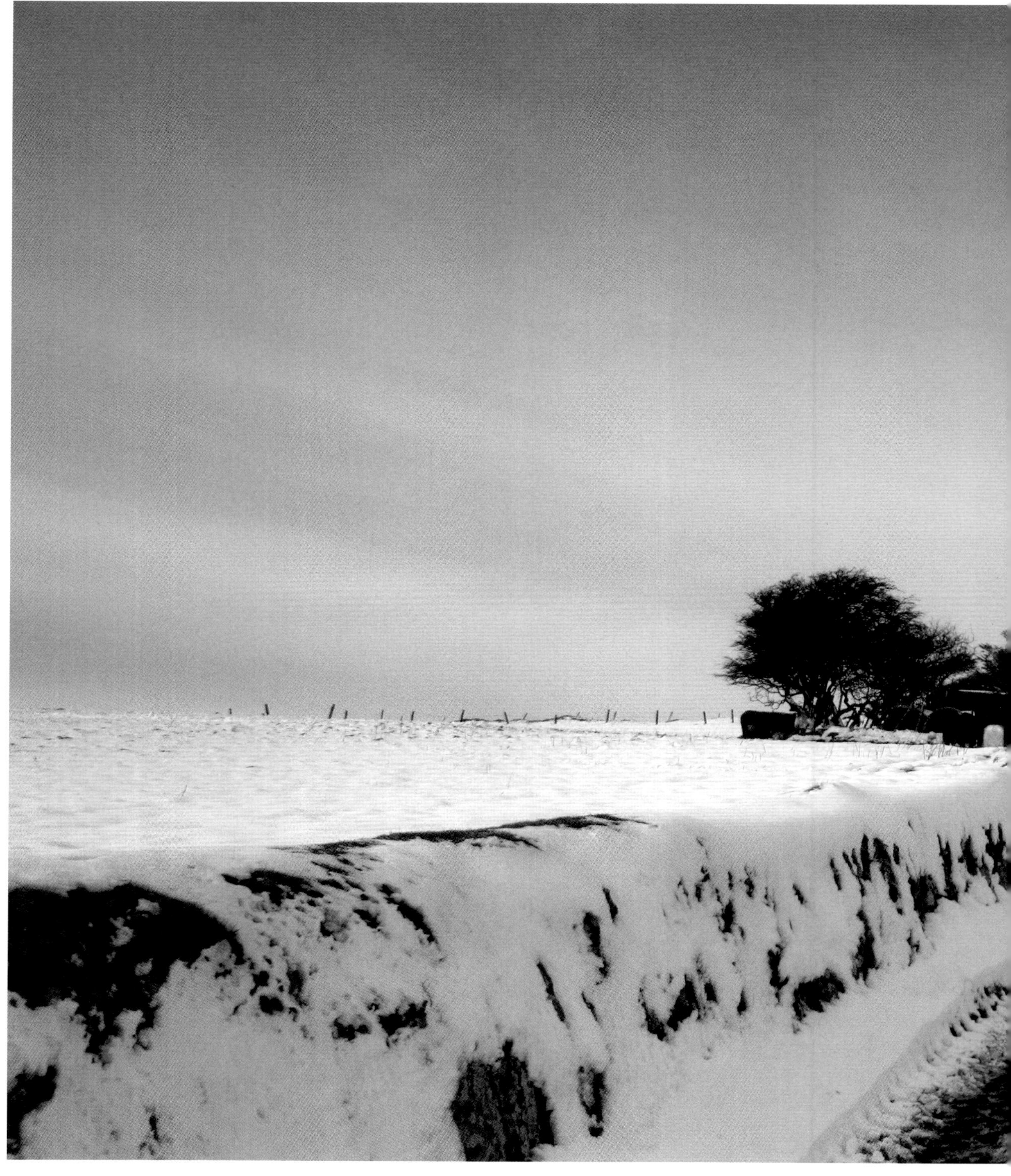

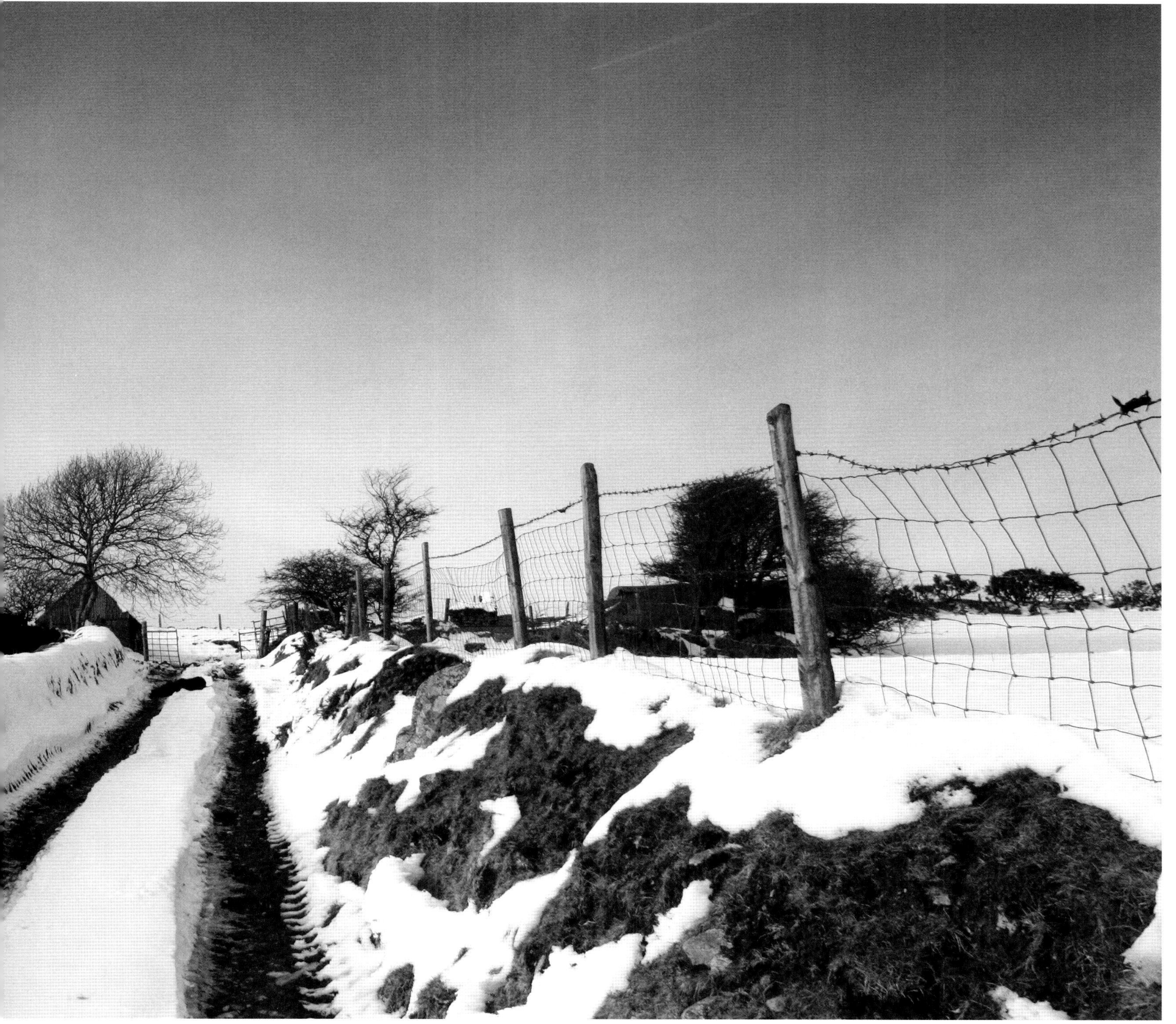

PLATE INDEX

The vast majority of my photographs are taken with the use of a tripod, an electronic cable-release and the mirror-up facility on my camera. I also use graduated neutral density filters and occasionally a polarising filter.

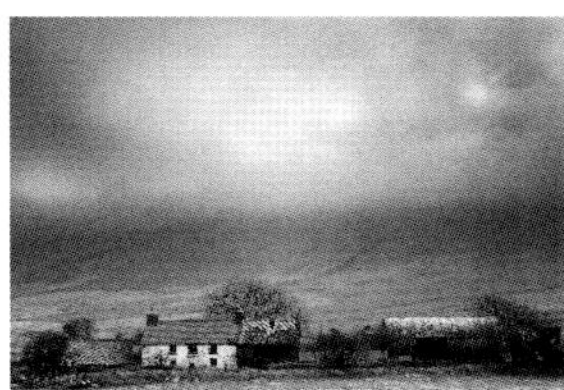

01 Abandoned Farm, the Preseli Hills
Film speed setting: ISO 100
Shutter speed: 1/10
Aperture: f16
Focal length: 70mm

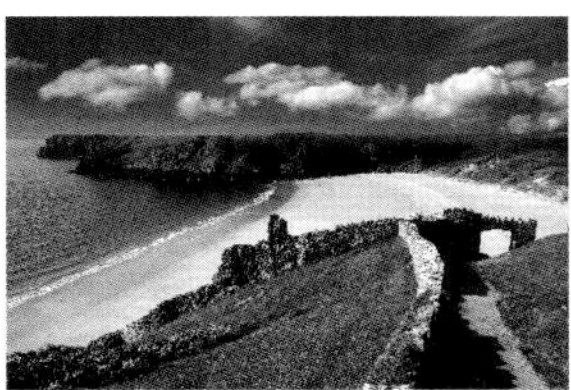

02 Barafundle
Film speed setting: ISO 100
Shutter speed: 1/25
Aperture: f16
Focal length: 28mm

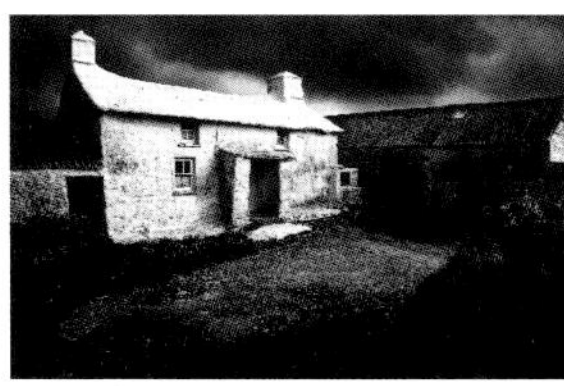

03 Treleddyd Fawr, near St Davids
Film speed setting: ISO 100
Shutter speed: 1/60
Aperture: f16
Focal length: 28mm

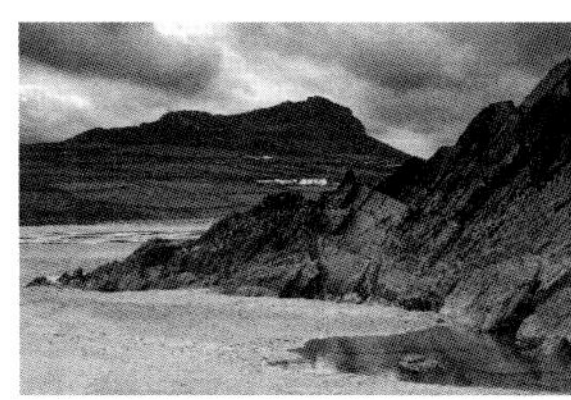

04 Whitesands
Film speed setting: ISO 100
Shutter speed: 1/6
Aperture: f16
Focal length: 70mm

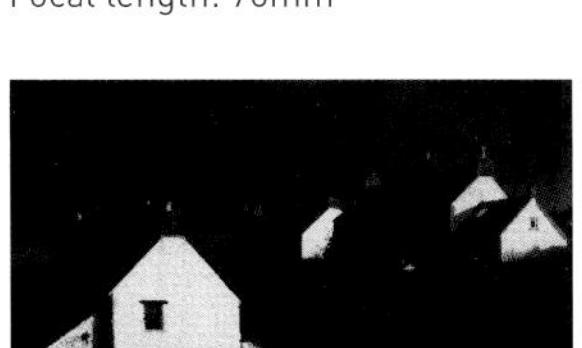

05 Abereiddi
Film speed setting: ISO 100
Shutter speed: 1/8
Aperture: f16
Focal length: 85mm

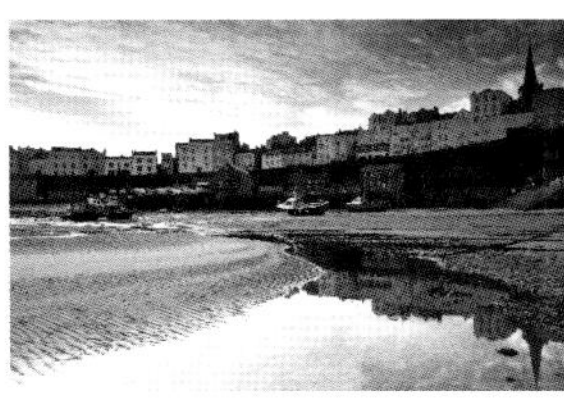

06 Tenby Harbour
Film speed setting: ISO 100
Shutter speed: 1/5
Aperture: f18
Focal length: 28mm

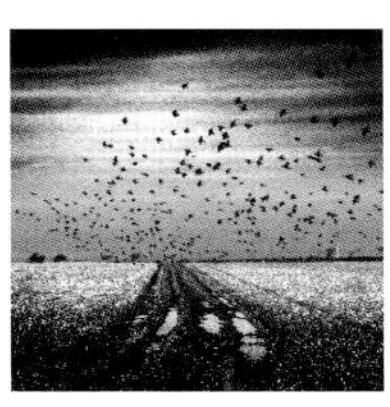

07 Starlings
Film speed setting: ISO 1250
Shutter speed: 1/640
Aperture: f16
Focal length: 50mm

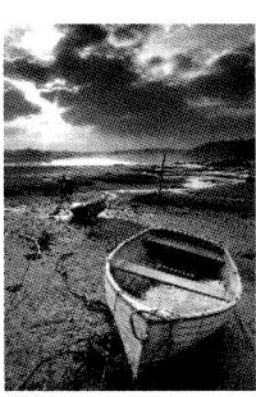

08 Port Lion
Film speed setting: ISO 100
Shutter speed: 1/50
Aperture: f18
Focal length: 35mm

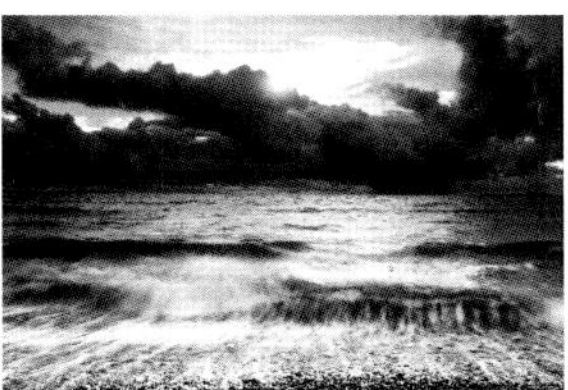

09 Newgale
Film speed setting: ISO 100
Shutter speed: 1/2
Aperture: f18
Focal length: 40mm

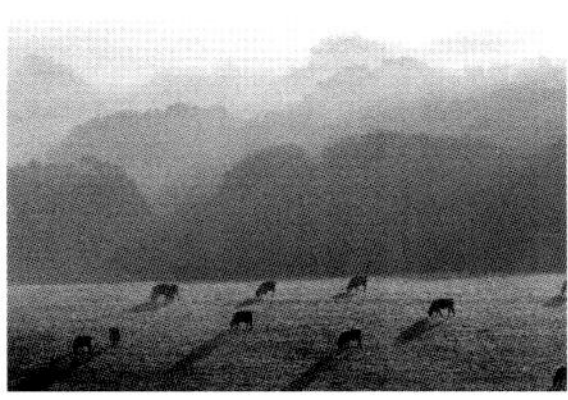

10 Llawhaden
Film speed setting: ISO 100
Shutter speed: 1/100
Aperture: f11
Focal length: 300mm

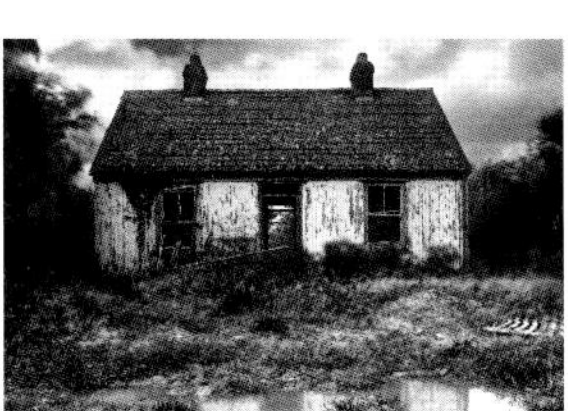

11 Camrose
Film speed setting: ISO 100
Shutter speed: 4 seconds
Aperture: f18
Focal length: 50mm

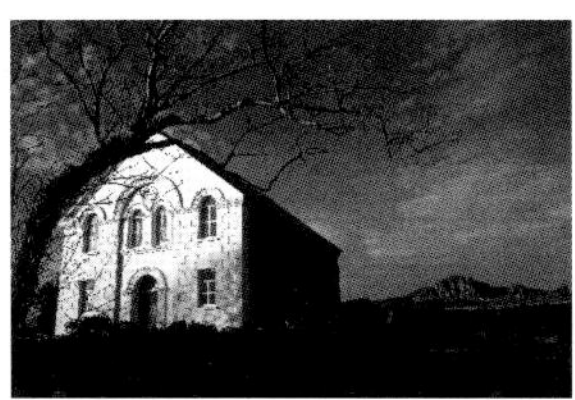

12 Capel Harmoni, near Strumble Head
Film speed setting: ISO 100
Shutter speed: 1/20
Aperture: f18
Focal length: 35mm

PLATE INDEX

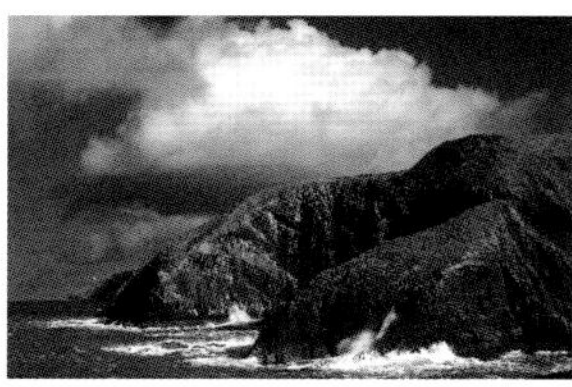

13 Ceibwr Bay
Film speed setting: ISO 100
Shutter speed: 1/50
Aperture: f16
Focal length: 50mm

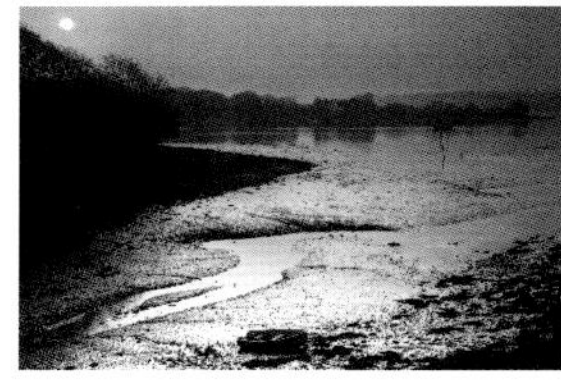

14 Edward's Pill
Film speed setting: ISO 100
Shutter speed: 1/8
Aperture: f16
Focal length: 65mm

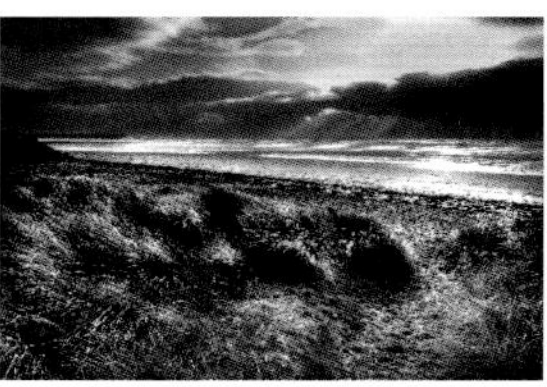

15 Freshwater West
Film speed setting: ISO 1600
Shutter speed: 1/250
Aperture: f16
Focal length: 35mm

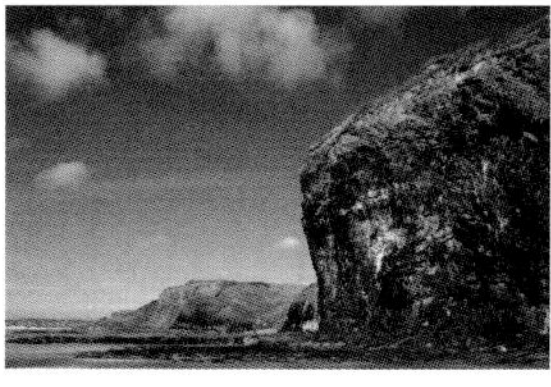

16 Druidston Haven
Film speed setting: ISO 100
Shutter speed: 1/25
Aperture: f18
Focal length: 32mm

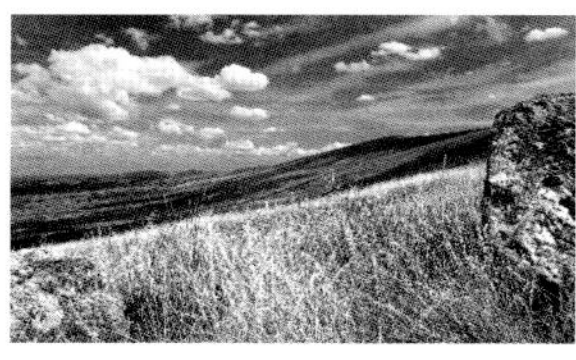

21 Towards Brynberian, the Preseli Hills
Film speed setting: ISO 800
Shutter speed: 1/250
Aperture: f18
Focal length: 35mm

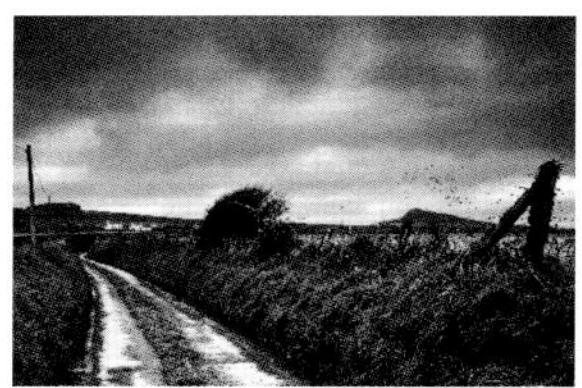

22 Towards Treleddyd Fawr, near St Davids
Film speed setting: ISO 3200
Shutter speed: 1/80
Aperture: f14
Focal length: 40mm

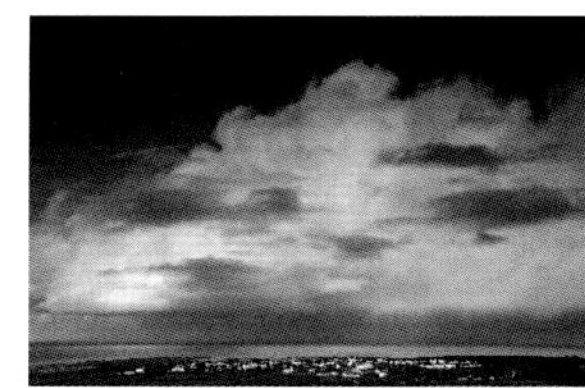

23 Trefin
Film speed setting: ISO 100
Shutter speed: 1/50
Aperture: f16
Focal length: 50mm

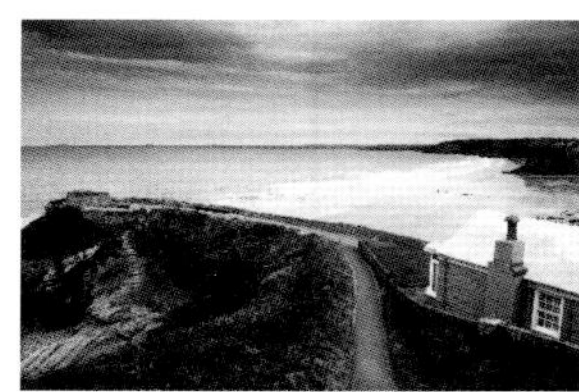

24 The Point, Little Haven
Film speed setting: ISO 1600
Shutter speed: 1/125
Aperture: f18
Focal length: 28mm

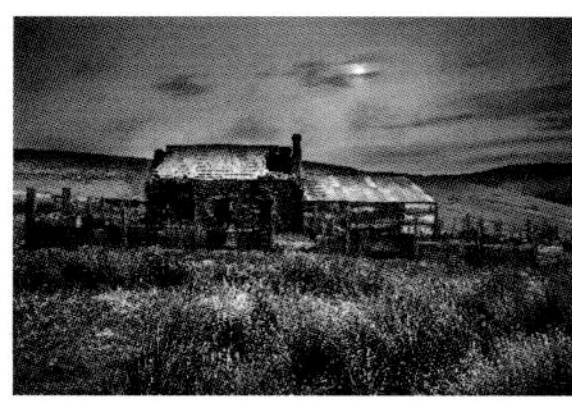

29 Trinant II, the Preseli Hills
Film speed setting: ISO 100
Shutter speed: 1/8
Aperture: f16
Focal length: 32mm

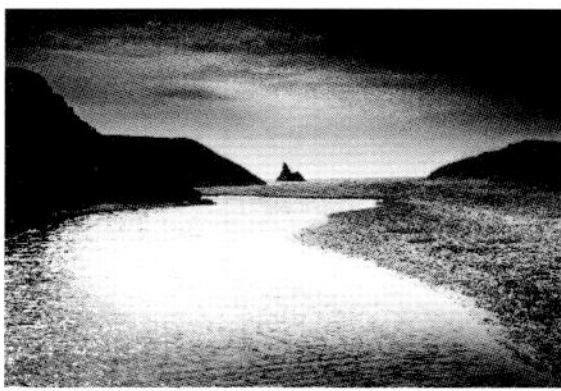

30 Broad Haven South
Film speed setting: ISO 3200
Shutter speed: 1/1600
Aperture: f16
Focal length: 55mm

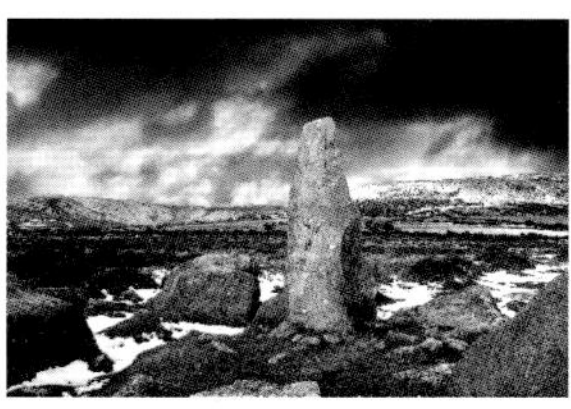

31 Carreg Waldo, the Preseli Hills
Film speed setting: ISO 100
Shutter speed: 1/10
Aperture: f20
Focal length: 28mm

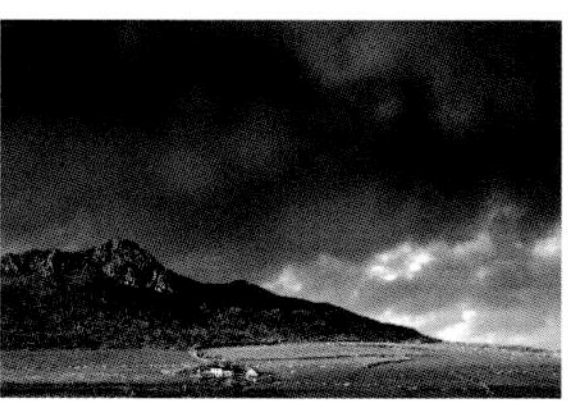

32 Carn Llidi, near St Davids
Film speed setting: ISO 1600
Shutter speed: 1/100
Aperture: f16
Focal length: 95mm

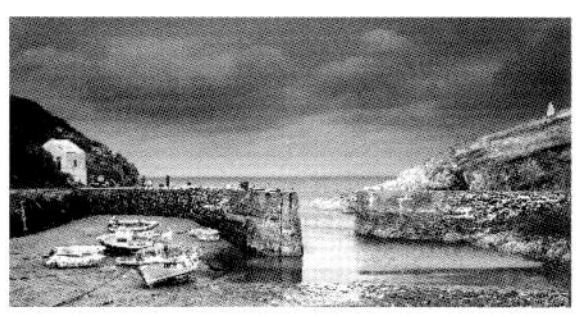

17 Porthgain
Film speed setting: ISO 100
Shutter speed: 1/15
Aperture: f16
Focal length: 45mm

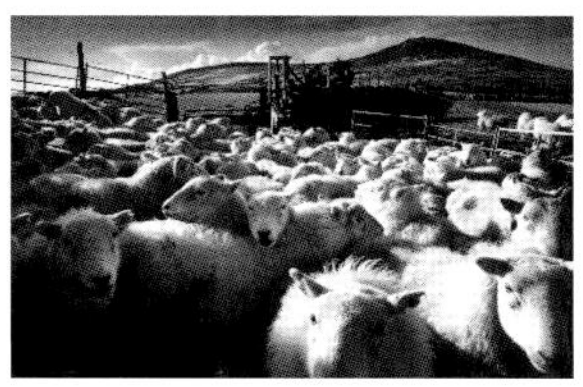

18 Sheep at the foot of Foel Drygarn
Film speed setting: ISO 3200
Shutter speed: 1/250
Aperture: f18
Focal length: 24mm

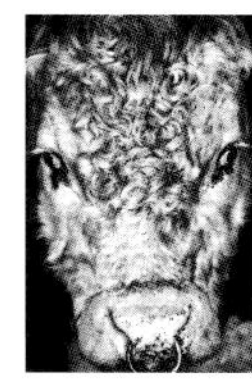

19 The Bull
Film speed setting: ISO 800
Shutter speed: 1/100
Aperture: f8
Focal length: 250mm

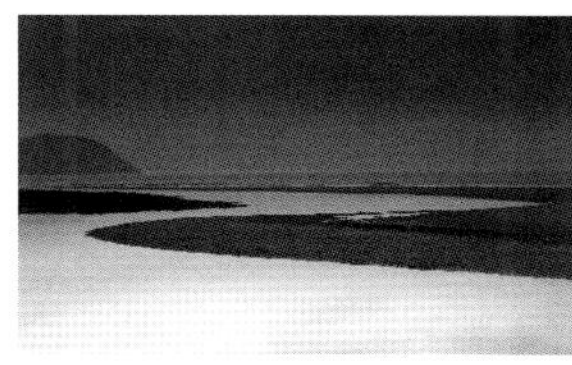

20 The Parrog, Newport
Film speed setting: ISO 100
Shutter speed: 1 second
Aperture: f16
Focal length: 85mm

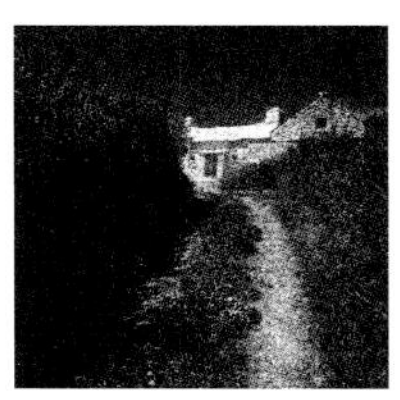

25 Treleddyd Fawr II, near St Davids
Film speed setting: ISO 3200
Shutter speed: 1/500
Aperture: f18
Focal length: 24mm

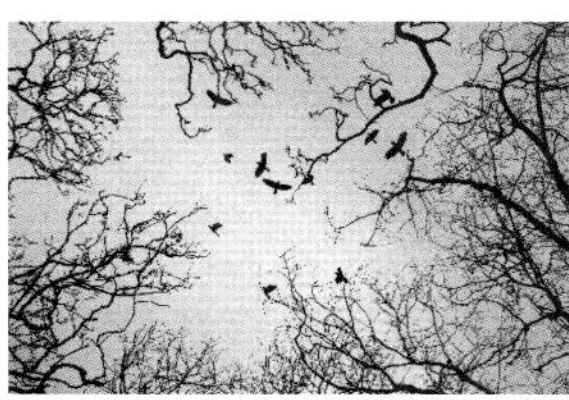

26 The Crows
Film speed setting: ISO 3200
Shutter speed: 1/800
Aperture: f14
Focal length: 50mm

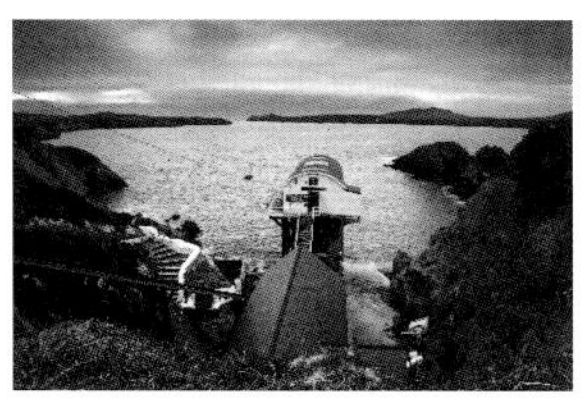

27 Porthstinian, near St Davids
Film speed setting: ISO 3200
Shutter speed: 1/100
Aperture: f16
Focal length: 24mm

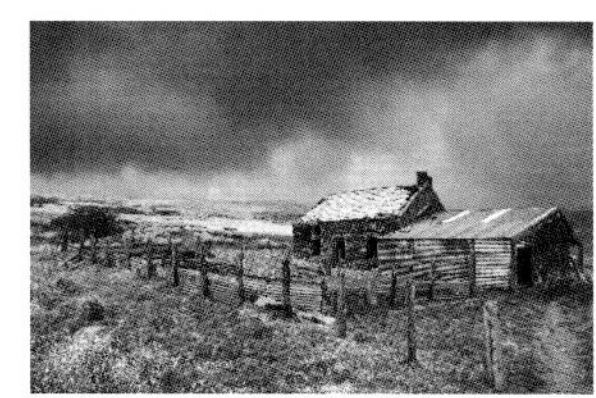

28 Trinant, the Preseli Hills
Film speed setting: ISO 100
Shutter speed: 1/5
Aperture: f20
Focal length: 24mm

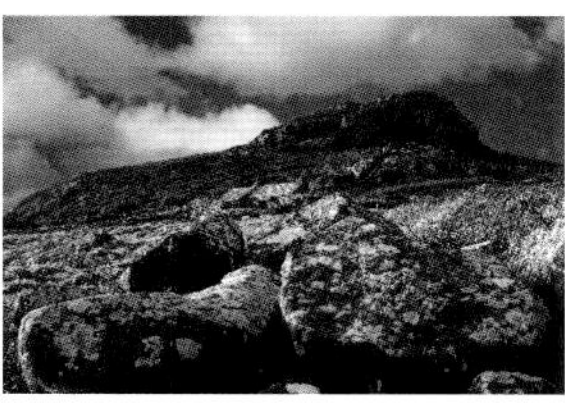

33 Garn Fawr, Strumble Head
Film speed setting: ISO 100
Shutter speed: 1/4
Aperture: f20
Focal length: 40mm

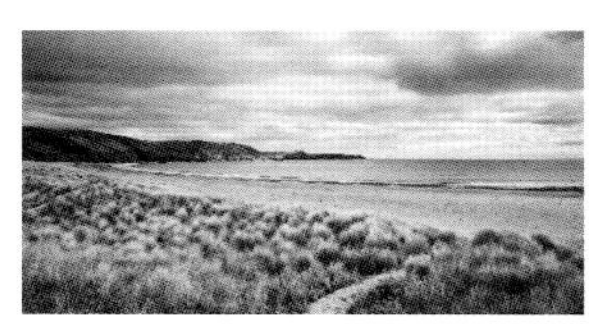

34 Freshwater East
Film speed setting: ISO 100
Shutter speed: 1/15
Aperture: f18
Focal length: 24mm

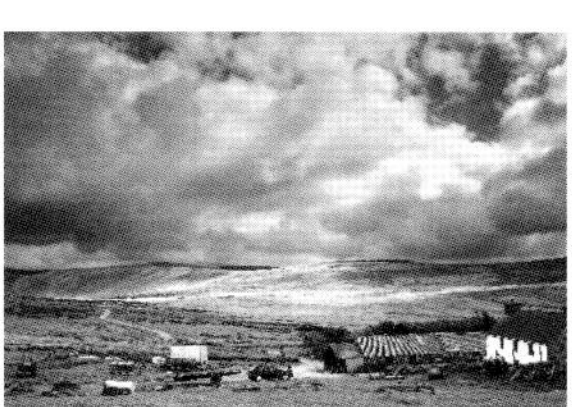

35 Gernos Fach, the Preseli Hills
Film speed setting: ISO 100
Shutter speed: 1/15
Aperture: f18
Focal length: 50mm

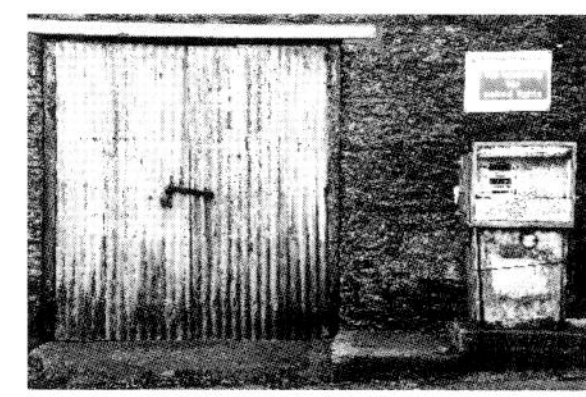

36 Petrol Pump, Mathry
Film speed setting: ISO 100
Shutter speed: 1/50
Aperture: f11
Focal length: 50mm

PLATE INDEX

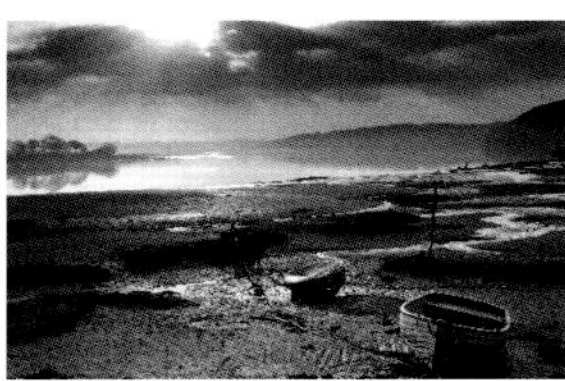

37 Port Lion II
Film speed setting: ISO 100
Shutter speed: 1/40
Aperture: f16
Focal length: 50mm

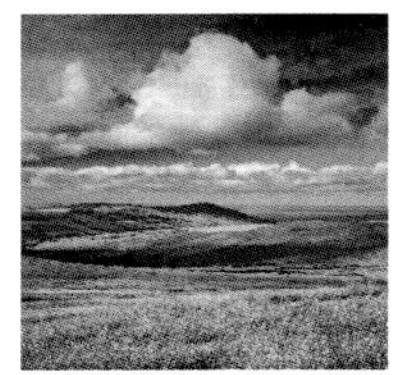

38 Towards Carningli
Film speed setting: ISO 100
Shutter speed: 1/20
Aperture: f18
Focal length: 85mm

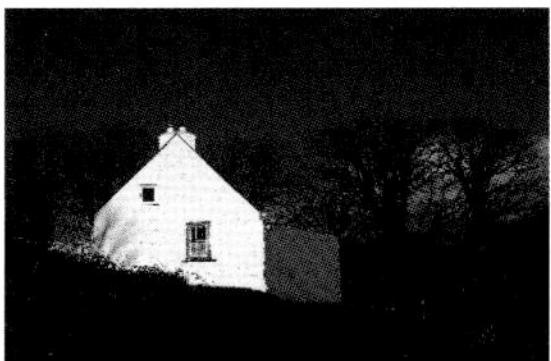

39 Tretio, near St Davids
Film speed setting: ISO 100
Shutter speed: 1/100
Aperture: f16
Focal length: 60mm

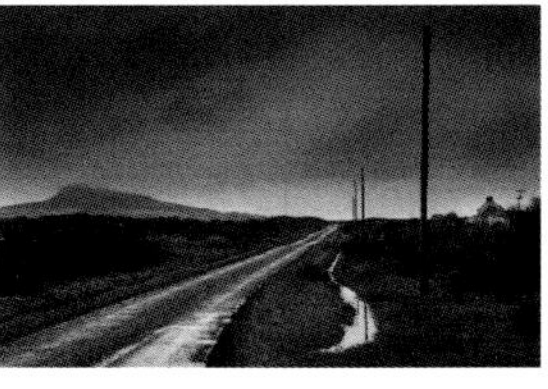

40 Treleddyd Fawr Common, near St Davids
Film speed setting: ISO 1600
Shutter speed: 1/125
Aperture: f16
Focal length: 65mm

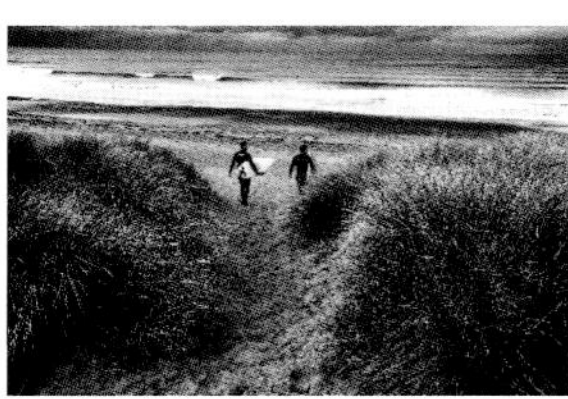

45 Freshwater West II
Film speed setting: ISO 1600
Shutter speed: 1/250
Aperture: f8
Focal length: 35mm

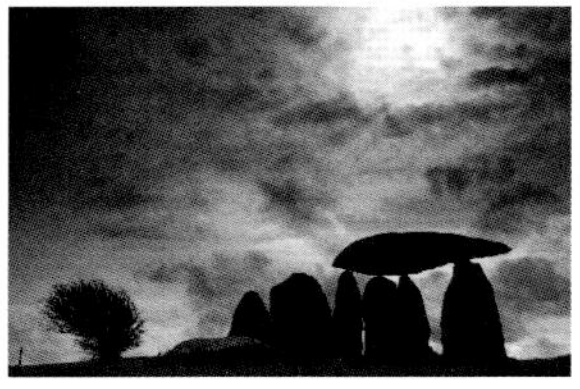

46 Pentre Ifan, the Preseli Hills
Film speed setting: ISO 100
Shutter speed: 1/15
Aperture: f16
Focal length: 28mm

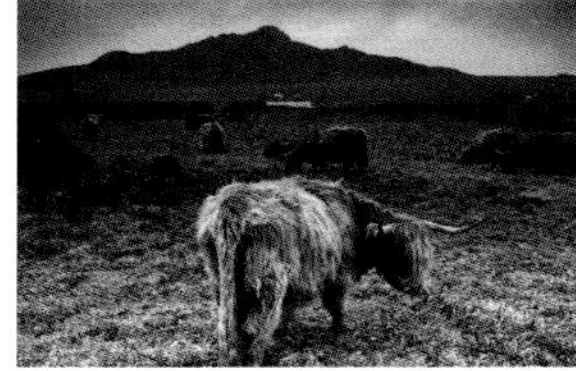

47 Cattle, Carn Llidi, near St Davids
Film speed setting: ISO 3200
Shutter speed: 1/60
Aperture: f14
Focal length: 40mm

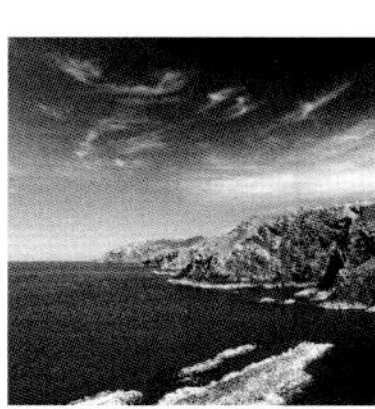

48 Ceibwr Bay II
Film speed setting: ISO 100
Shutter speed: 1/125
Aperture: f16
Focal length: 75mm

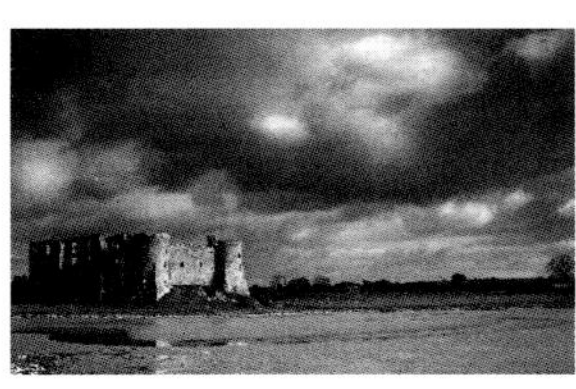

53 Carew Castle
Film Speed Setting: ISO 1600
Shutter Speed: 1/500
Aperture: f16
Focal Length: 35mm

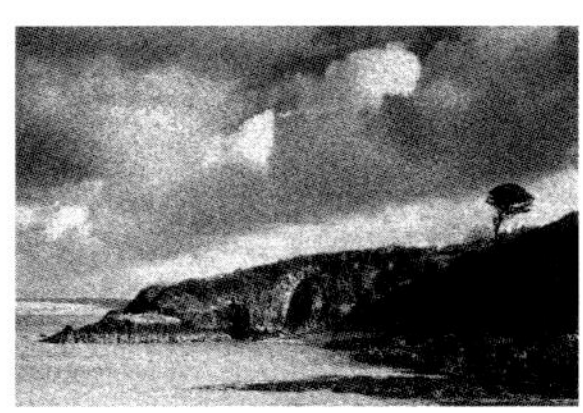

54 Cwm yr Eglwys
Film Speed Setting: ISO 3200
Shutter Speed: 1/160
Aperture: f16
Focal Length: 35mm

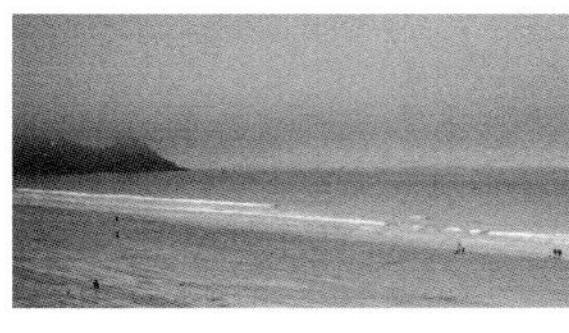

55 Newgale II
Film Speed Setting: ISO 400
Shutter Speed: 1/125
Aperture: f16
Focal Length: 105mm

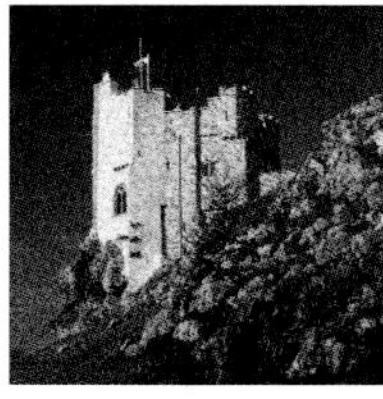

56 Roch Castle
Film Speed Setting: ISO 1600
Shutter Speed: 1/1000
Aperture: f16
Focal Length: 55mm

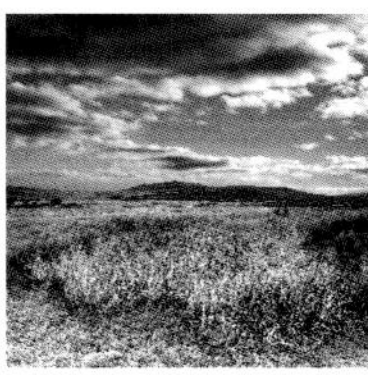

41 Towards Carn Menyn, the Preseli Hills
Film speed setting: ISO 100
Shutter speed: 1/4
Aperture: f18
Focal length: 35mm

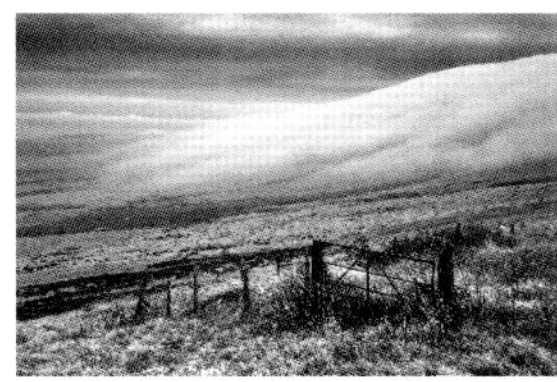

42 Towards Pontyglasier, the Preseli Hills
Film speed setting: ISO 100
Shutter speed: 1/20
Aperture: f18
Focal length: 85mm

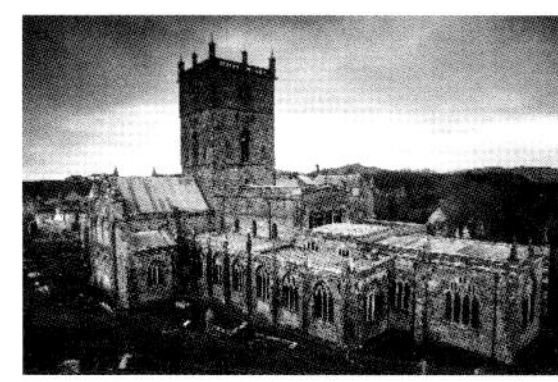

43 St Davids Cathedral
Film speed setting: ISO 3200
Shutter speed: 1/320
Aperture: f16
Focal length: 24mm

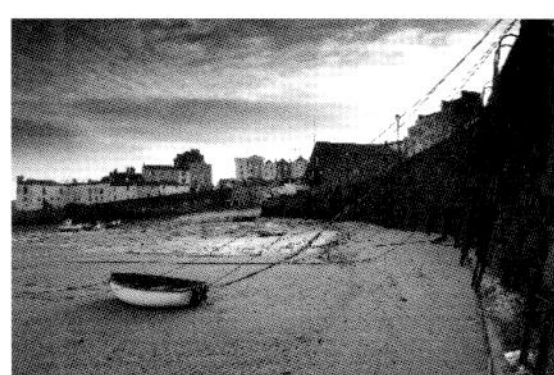

44 Tenby Harbour II
Film speed setting: ISO 100
Shutter speed:1/4
Aperture: f18
Focal length: 24mm

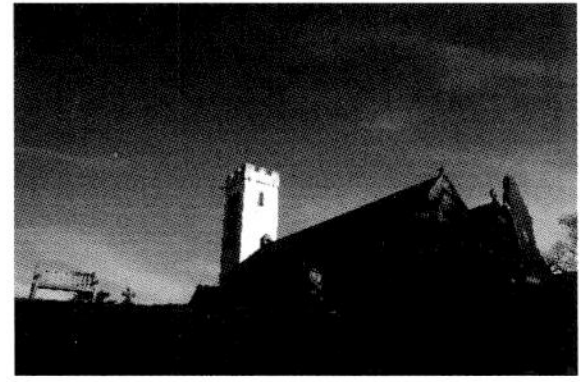

49 Manorbier Church
Film speed setting: ISO 400
Shutter speed: 1/100
Aperture: f16
Focal length: 24mm

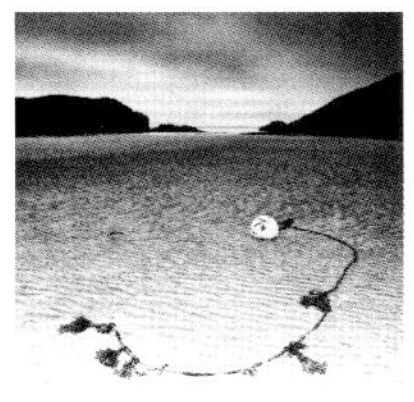

50 Entrance to Solva Harbour
Film speed setting: ISO 3200
Shutter speed: 1/40
Aperture: f16
Focal length: 24mm

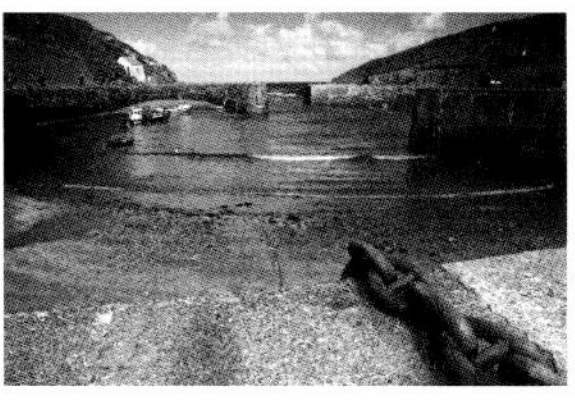

51 Porthgain II
Film Speed Setting: ISO 800
Shutter Speed: 1/250
Aperture: f16
Focal Length: 24mm

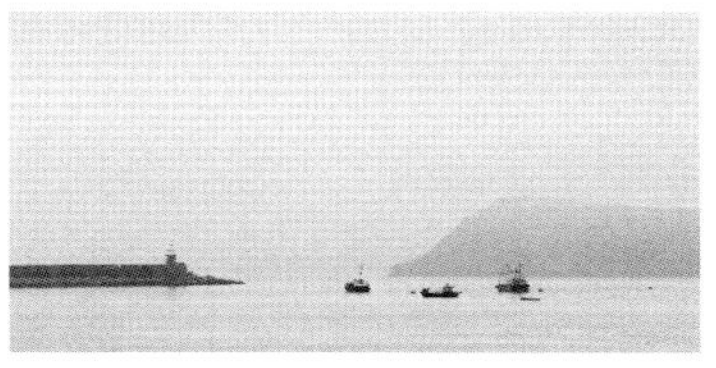

52 Goodwick Harbour
Film Speed Setting: ISO 250
Shutter Speed: 1/160
Aperture: f14
Focal Length: 200mm

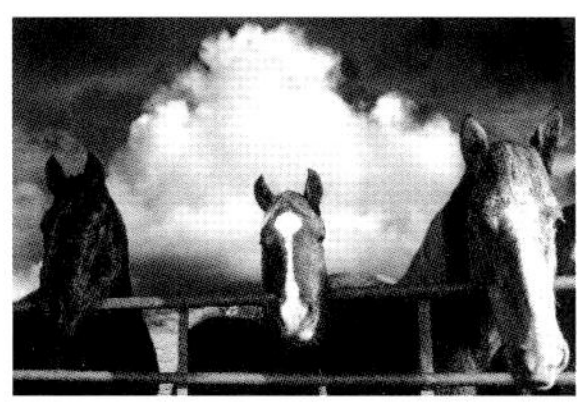

57 Strumble Head
Film Speed Setting: ISO 1600
Shutter Speed: 1/1000
Aperture: f8
Focal Length: 40mm

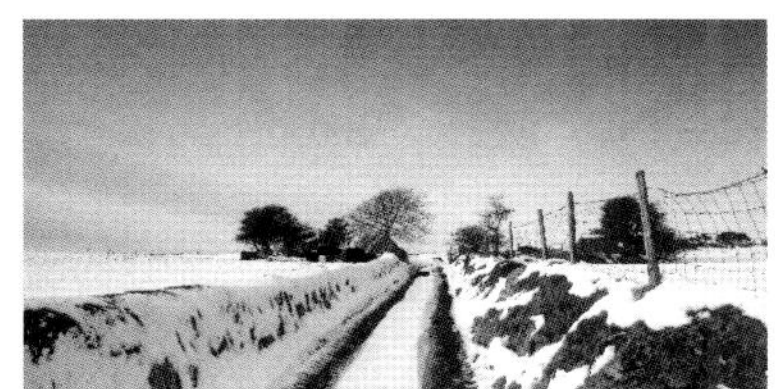

58 Preseli Hill Farm
Film Speed Setting: ISO 640
Shutter Speed: 1/100
Aperture: f16
Focal Length: 105mm

OTHER BOOKS BY DAVID WILSON

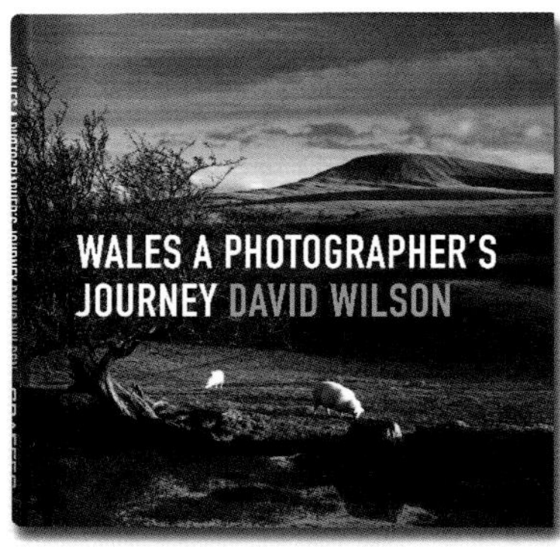 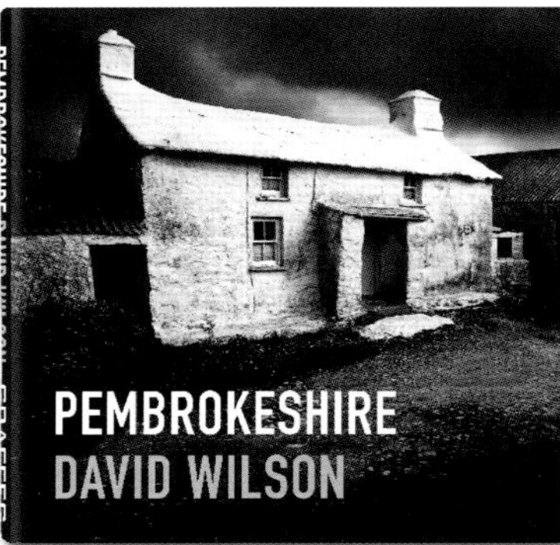 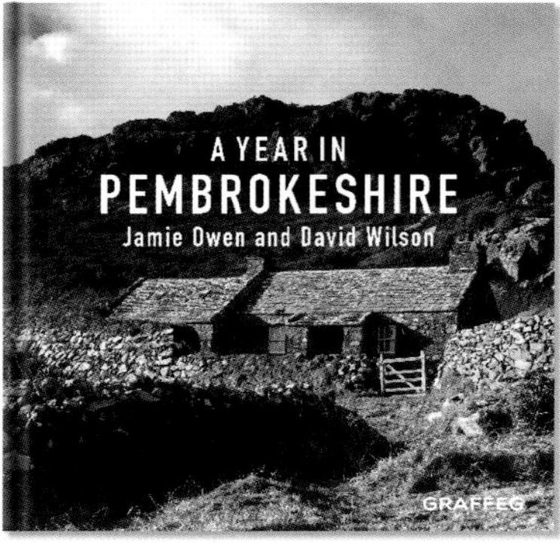 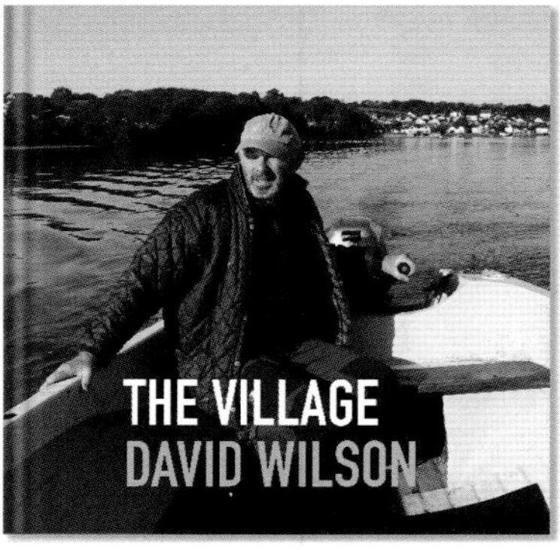

Wales – A Photographer's Journey
Large format
- Author David Wilson
- Size 250 x 250mm
- ISBN 9781802580068
- Hardback, 160 pages
- **Price £25.00**
- Publication January 2022

Wales – A Photographer's Journey is a collection of over 150 black and white landscape images by Welsh photographer David Wilson. More than just a travelogue, *Wales A Photographer's Journey* is a unique visual exploration of Wales; from Snowdonia in the north to Gower in the south, Pembrokeshire in the west to Hay-on-Wye in the east. With a foreword by Griff Rhys Jones, it includes images of 36 locations across Wales as well as notes on composition and a plate index.

'These are powerful images. They remind us that rural Wales has a stark and demanding beauty.'
Griff Rhys Jones

Pembrokeshire
Compact Edition
- Author David Wilson
- Size 150 x 150mm
- ISBN 9781905582938
- Hardback, 128 pages
- **Price £9.99**
- Publication August 2013

From the rolling Preseli Hills to its dramatic cliff-top coastline, Pembrokeshire both excites and enthrals with a sense of timeless beauty. And yet there is also a story to be told, one of meaning and of ancestry, which acclaimed landscape photographer David Wilson brings to life through his remarkable black and white images.

Join David as he explores his native county through 58 stunning images and discover for yourself what the landscape really looks like.

A Year in Pembrokeshire
- Author Jamie Owen
- Photographer David Wilson
- Size 200 x 200mm
- ISBN 9781912213658
- Hardback, 192 pages
- **Price £20**
- Publication June 2018

Broadcaster Jamie Owen and photographer David Wilson capture Pembrokeshire through the seasons in words and pictures. This is a journey to mountains and coast, farms and fishing boats to capture life over the course of a year in an engaging and immersive portrait of one of Britain's most treasured places.

'Owen writes engagingly, weaving personal observations and childhood memories in amongst the plentiful factual information … Wilson's images are a fine illustrative accompaniment to Owen's prose.' **Buzz Magazine**

The Village
- Author David Wilson
- Size 200 x 200mm
- ISBN 9781802580488
- Hardback, 160 pages
- **Price £20**
- Publication November 2021

David Wilson lives and works in Llangwm and since 2019 has been photographing people at home, at work and at play, capturing their stories and contributions, as well as the landscape and environment in the immediate area. Through David's intimate photography and conversations with local people, *The Village* offers a snapshot not just of its subject but of a community whose feel is universal.

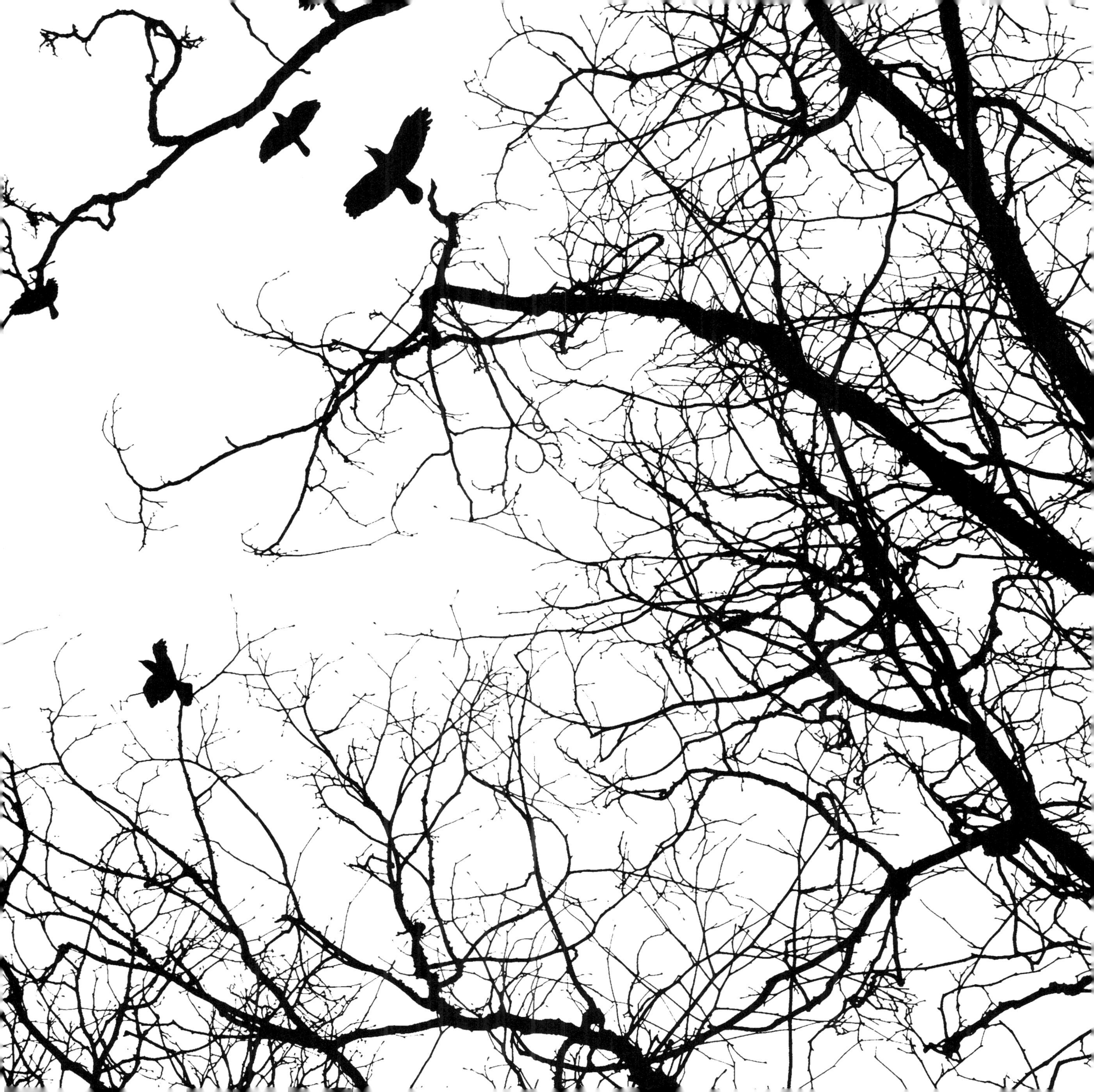

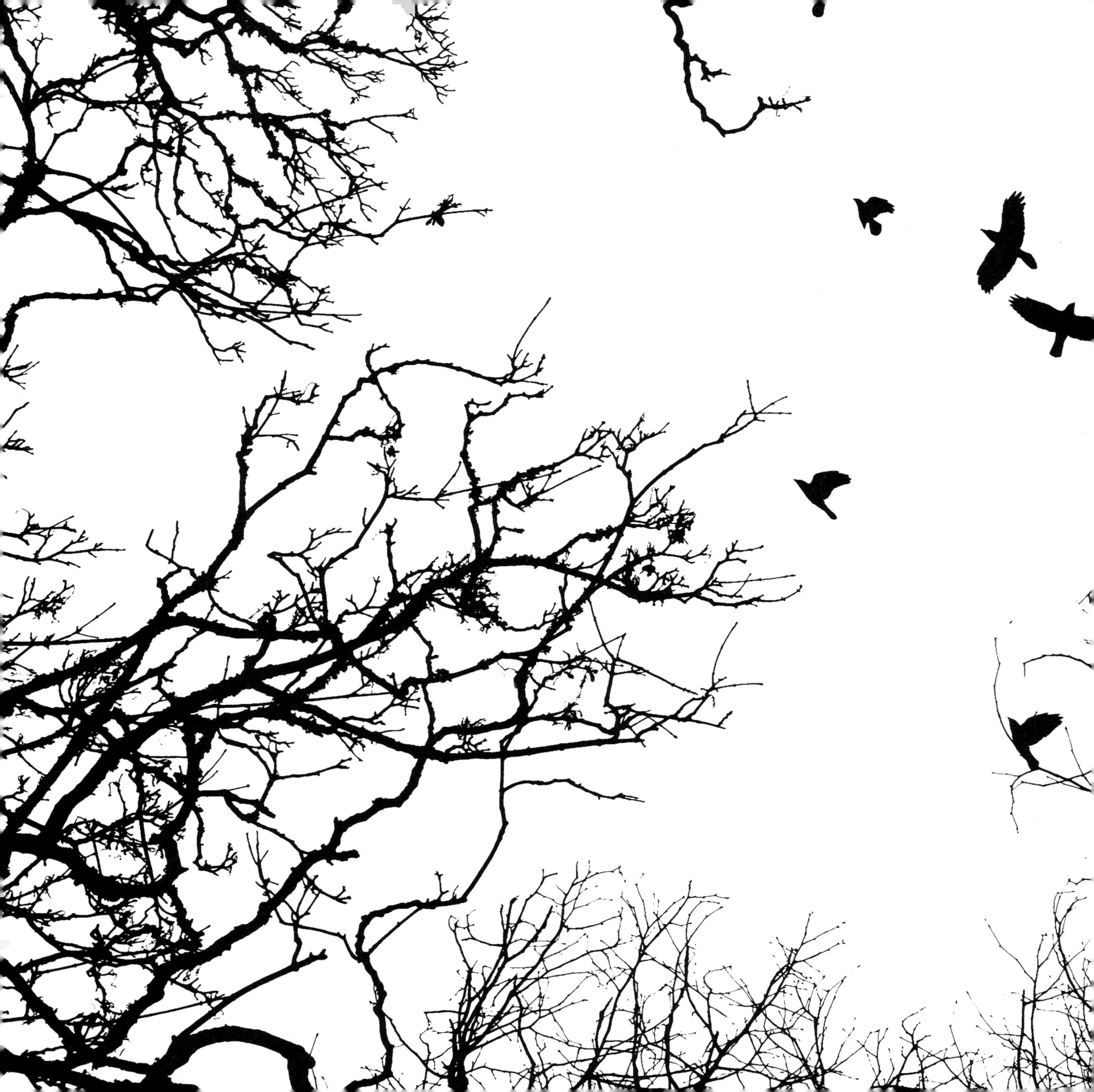